EXPEDITION
WHYDAH

THE *WHYDAH*

The *Whydah* (pronounced *Whi-da)* was an English slave ship named after a noted slave-trading domain in western Africa.

Built in 1716, she was returning to England after her second voyage from Africa to Jamaica when she was captured east of Cuba by pirate Black Sam Bellamy.

EXPEDITION
WHYDAH

The Story of the World's
First Excavation of a
Pirate Treasure Ship
and the
Man Who Found Her

Barry Clifford

with Paul Perry

Cliff Street Books
An Imprint of HarperCollinsPublishers

Photograph and illustration credits appear on page 312.

HarperCollins books may be purchased for educational, business, or sales promotional use. For information please write: Special Markets Department, HarperCollins Publishers, Inc., 10 East 53rd Street, New York, NY 10022.

FIRST EDITION

Designed by Pagesetters, Inc.

Library of Congress Cataloging-in-Publication Data

Clifford, Barry.
Expedition Whydah : the story of the world's first excavation
of a pirate treasure ship and the man who
found her / Barry Clifford with Paul Perry. — 1st ed.
p.   cm.
ISBN 0-06-092971-5 (pbk.)
1. Whydah (Ship)   2. Shipwrecks—Massachusetts—Cape Cod.
3. Clifford, Barry.   I. Perry, Paul.   II. Title.
G530.W5787C56   1999   99-13849
974.4'92—dc21

07 08 09 ❖/RRD 10 9 8 7 6 5 4 3

In memory of my mother,
Shirley Ann Clifford, who believed my dream.
And to all the other dreamers who worked with me
in bringing "THE WHYDAH GALLY 1716" to light.

—Barry Clifford

To my children, Paul Jr., Paige, and Ben,
the real treasures in my life.

—Paul Perry

Contents

Contents

BOOK III
BACK TO BASICS

BOOK I

---❖---

A MYTH AND A DREAM

Pirogue Espagnole

1
The Stuff of Daydreams

Uncle Bill as a young man.

❋ I spent much of my childhood following my uncle Bill around Cape Cod. He was a child at heart and didn't mind having me as a constant companion. My mother said that he had money and smarts, but I liked him because he never acted as though he had too much of either. Bill was a Cape native who made a living doing a bit of everything, from fishing to carpentry, and I learned a lot just by being with him. The times I enjoyed most, though, were spent talking in the fishing shack.

Uncle Bill's fishing shack was an escape from reality. It was a weathered wood structure that leaned from the weight of the honeysuckle vines that had been growing over it for nearly twenty years. Inside were boxes of tools, a couple of chairs, and a pile of ancient fishing net that gave off heat as it rotted away to nothing in the hot sun.

It was there, as I lay on the rotting net and listened in awe to the stories he told, that I first heard the tale of Black Sam Bellamy and Maria Hallett.

I was maybe nine years old when he first told me the story. Bill was standing at the wooden bench working on an engine part when he asked if I had ever heard of Sam Bellamy, the pirate.

"No," I said, turning my full attention to Bill.

"Did you know that Cape Cod was teeming with pirates in the 1700s?" he asked.

Visions of treasure chests being hauled ashore by swarthy and dangerous men flashed through my mind. I wanted to hear more.

"It's true," he said, looking at me matter-of-factly. "In the 1700s there was hardly anybody living on the Cape, just a few hearty souls who, for one reason or another, didn't want to live in Boston or any of the other big cities. It was a perfect place for pirates and all other types of misfits and outcasts to live."

Uncle Bill lit up an unfiltered Camel cigarette and filled the room with a white cloud of smoke that looked like salt haze. He thought a moment and then sat down in one of the creaky chairs. He said nothing until I was leaning forward with anticipation.

"The legend of Black Sam Bellamy and his lover Maria Hallett is a dark version of the Romeo and Juliet story," he said. "It is a story that has captivated people for hundreds of years because it is about love, pirates, a shipwreck, and buried treasure. Best of all, it's true."

Bill took another drag and eyed me through the cigarette smoke that poured from his mouth. The veil of smoke was creepy to me because I could see human shapes in it the way some people see faces in cumulus clouds. I conjured images of pirates in the smoke and held my breath as Uncle Bill took me back in time.

There were always more pirates on the Cape than anywhere else in America. None of them was more respected and feared than Black Sam Bellamy. He was called Black Sam only after he became a pirate and began to sail under the black flag. Before that, he was just Sam Bellamy, an unemployed seaman from Plymouth, England, who moved to Cape Cod looking for work in the New World.

Bellamy was from the bottom rungs of English society, the abused class, and was forced to work hard just to survive. His mother had died when he was born, and he had probably been out of the house and working hard from the age of ten. I guess Bellamy finally had enough of the English class system and left for America to get a fresh start.

Bellamy arrived in Cape Cod in 1714, when he was twenty-four years old. He had relatives here and moved in with them long enough to get on his feet. During this period he met the two people who would change his life. One of these was Paulsgrave Williams, the jeweler who would lend him the money necessary to buy a ship. The second was Maria Hallett, the woman he would love until the day he died.

Maria was a beautiful woman, with long hair the color of straw and eyes as deep and blue as a freshwater pond. Sam met her one perfect June day as he was walking past the cemetery in the town of Wellfleet. She was sitting underneath an apple tree covered by a white mist of apple blossoms. He slowed and then stopped. Wherever he was going was no longer important. He had to meet this girl.

Bellamy introduced himself and soon the two were talking like old friends. Maria was only sixteen and excited by the worldly stories that this young Englishman told her. He told her of his difficult childhood in Plymouth, and how hard it was to be raised only by his father. He talked of going to sea in his teenage years to work in the queen's merchant fleet, and how thousands of seamen had been laid off because the war with the Spanish had ended and the size of the navy was cut back.

He told her of his hopes and dreams in the colonies, where a man could work his way to success instead of just work himself to death. Then he told her of another plan, a plan to get rich.

As many as a dozen Spanish ships loaded with chests of gold and silver had sunk in a storm near Florida. The wrecks were supposedly in shallow water, and rumor had it that the gold was available to anyone who could beat the Spanish to the spot. The news was causing a minor gold rush in the colonies, with ships leaving Atlantic ports daily and heading south to the wreck site. There was a good chance that a man could get rich if he got there quickly. It was a chance Bellamy wanted to take.

Maria liked what she saw in Bellamy. He was cocky and not ashamed of being poor. Though her clothing made it obvious that she was from a family with money, Bellamy talked proudly of his lower-class upbringing in England. He was confident and seemed to be driven to succeed, and Maria liked those qualities. From this first meeting Maria could tell that she wanted to see more of this forthcoming young man.

Maria's parents were not happy with their daughter's new friend. They were successful farmers with high hopes for their beautiful daughter. They thought her interest in this sailor—someone who would be gone at sea most of his life—meant she was deciding on a life of solitude.

Still, against her parents' wishes, Maria continued to see Sam Bellamy. He spent a lot of time at the Great Island Tavern, an establishment that was more than a tavern. Located on an island about two miles from Wellfleet, the Great Island Tavern was difficult for many customers to reach. In reality, it was a temporary warehouse for stolen or smuggled merchandise.

Bellamy frequented the tavern with his uncle, Israel Cole. Eventually Maria became a visitor to the remote outpost, too. Bellamy and Maria spent their days helping the tavern's owner conduct the bustling business of buying and selling black-market goods.

When they weren't busy in the tavern, Bellamy and Maria shared their thoughts and feelings in the deep green of the forest that covered Great Island. This was a place of solitude, one where a couple could be alone among the trees and tall grass and indulge in romance on a mattress of soft and mossy ground.

It wasn't long before Maria was pregnant with Sam Bellamy's child.

Suddenly, Bellamy had a more urgent need for money. Through his uncle, Bellamy approached Paulsgrave Williams for money to buy a ship and head for the sunken Spanish treasure fleet in Florida. Williams was a jeweler, and jewelers played the role of bankers in these early days of colonial America. Williams purchased a sloop that could make the lengthy trip to Florida and even decided to become Bellamy's quartermaster. It would be Williams's job to take charge of any Spanish treasure that they found and make sure that it was divided properly. With a crew of about thirty men, Bellamy sailed south to search for the sunken treasure. Before leaving, he promised Maria that he would return with a ship filled with gold.

That was not to be. By the time Bellamy reached Florida, the gold was gone. The highly efficient Spaniards had hired local Indian divers to recover the treasure. The only thing left for Bellamy and his crew was to retrieve what they could by dragging the area with grapnel hooks.

This was frustrating work for Bellamy's crew, as it was for the crews of many other ships in the area, including one captained by Henry Jennings, an out-of-work English privateer. He was not given to grapneling for treasure. When he found that the coins that had been recovered by the divers were being stored in a Spanish fort on shore, he decided to go get the money.

When Jennings and his motley troops demanded access to the fort, the Spanish commander tried to bribe him with twenty-five thousand pieces of silver. Rather than accept, Jennings threatened to shoot the commander if the guards did not open the gate. The Spaniards immediately surrendered, and Jennings ransacked the fort, making off with a quarter million silver coins.

With opportunities like that, who could resist becoming a pirate? Not Bellamy. He was now desperate to succeed. With great care, he explained the options to his crew. On one hand, they could return to New England with nothing to show for their efforts. That would subject them to a life of hard work and poverty, since all on board had now gone into debt to make this run for the gold. On the other hand, they could "go on the account," as becoming a pirate was called, and become looters of nations. To do that, they needed only to hoist the black flag that a crew member had sewn and that Bellamy now held in his hands.

"This flag represents not death, but resurrection," Bellamy told his crew. "Never again will you be slaves of the wealthy. From this day, we are new men. Free men."

The vote in favor of becoming pirates was almost unanimous.

Bellamy and Williams decided to join Benjamin Hornigold, a great teacher of the pirate arts who had just one flaw as far as Bellamy was concerned: he would not attack British ships. Whether out of patriotism or fear, Hornigold drew the line at taking a ship that was flying the British flag.

This was not a sentiment shared by most of the men who sailed with Hornigold. They were an international crew that included British men as well as French, Spanish, Dutch, and others. Most pirates felt no loyalty to merchant ships that flew the flags of their nationality. For the men who served under the black flag, all the ships on the sea were fair game.

As was the custom among pirates, they discussed their feelings openly and then held a democratic election for a new captain. Ninety of the crew members, a majority, voted to make Bellamy the new captain. Hornigold

SERVING KING DEATH

When stalking a vessel, pirates often flew the flag of a European government as they assessed their target's strength, a process taking hours, or even days. Once they decided to attack, they maneuvered into range and raised the Jolly Roger.

Unfurling Jolly Roger was *not* a death threat; it was how pirates defiantly identified themselves as men who were dead in the eyes of the law—men to whom the law no longer applied—and who now served under the banner of "King Death."

An estimated 80 percent of the pirate captains of the period 1715–1726 flew some version of Jolly Roger.

While there were variations of Jolly Roger—possibly as identification among the brethren—Bellamy's was a "large black Flag with a Death's head and Bones across." The skull symbolized death while the crossed leg-bones meant resurrection.

was stung by the loss but left peacefully, taking with him the men who wanted to stay under his command, including an outrageous young recruit named Edward Teach, who drank heavily and lit his hair and beard on fire during fights so people would think he was the devil. He would later become known as Blackbeard.

Bellamy's pirates scoured the seas. They stopped every ship they could find, stealing choice booty. Sometimes, if they liked the look of the ship that they were robbing, they took it too, offering the displaced captain and his crew an opportunity to become pirates or to leave safely on the ship the pirates were abandoning.

Eventually Bellamy had choice booty from more than fifty ships, more than two hundred men under his command, and a flotilla of five ships to carry it all, including the *Whydah*. The *Whydah* was a slave ship captained by Lawrence Prince, a veteran slaver, who had recently sold his human cargo in Jamaica and was headed for England with holds full of gold and silver and perhaps even one perfect ruby the size of a hen's egg.

The ship had everything that would appeal to a buccaneer. She was new and had enough cargo space to carry six hundred Africans to the slave market. She was also packing plenty of armament, eighteen large cannons and about a dozen swivel cannons—weapons that could be filled with shot and fired at close range, a sort of high-powered shotgun. In addition to her capacity and armament, the *Whydah* was fast. Bellamy had to chase her for three days across a good portion of the Caribbean to catch her.

When Bellamy finally caught the *Whydah,* his crew was overjoyed to find that the ship was full of gold and silver. After eighteen months of plundering vessels on the high seas, Bellamy and his crew could retire as rich men.

They didn't retire, though, at least not right away. It was now spring of 1717 and time to head north for the summer, where they could divide their spoils, repair their boats, and decide on the future of their band of pirates.

They plundered boats all the way up the coast on their way to Maine, where they planned to put in at Damaries Cove near Richmond Island. As they came even with Cape Cod, Bellamy ordered the helmsman to steer a north-by-northwest course toward the tip of the Cape. He was heading for Wellfleet. He was going home to see Maria.

Although Bellamy didn't know it, life had not gone well for Maria. Her pregnancy had made her an outcast in her family. Her parents could not accept the disgrace of their daughter having a child out of wedlock and they asked her to leave.

Maria moved out of the house and into a tiny hut on the beach near Eastham. From there, she could watch the ships sail toward the Cape and wait for Bellamy's return. She hid in the hut, coming out only at night to conceal her pregnancy from the unforgiving Puritans.

Seven months after Bellamy left to find his fortune, Maria Hallett gave birth to a black-haired boy. She delivered the child herself in the barn of John Knowles and kept the baby hidden in a bed of hay in the barn. Several times a day she would sneak back to the Knowles barn to feed the baby, then she would carefully conceal him under a pile of hay and return to her hut.

One day she opened the barn door to find John Knowles holding the child in his arms, a look of fright in his eyes. The baby was dead, having choked to death on a piece of straw.

The sheriff of Eastham took the frightened young woman into custody. She was jailed for the crime of pregnancy out of wedlock and neglect of her child, but a sympathetic jailer left her cell door unlocked and she walked out, returning to her hut in Eastham. The sheriff returned her to jail, but again the jailer did not secure the door and she went back home again. This time she stayed free and was never put on trial.

People accused her of being a witch, and said that the young woman could at times be heard conversing loudly with the devil. Most people avoided Maria's cabin lest they be cast under a spell that might bring them the kind of tragedy she had suffered. But there was more tragedy ahead for Maria. Her cabin was within eyesight of the spot where the *Whydah* wrecked.

As the *Whydah* changed course that night and came closer to the Cape, winds from a frigid nor'easter collided with the warm and moist southern wind that had been propelling Bellamy's flotilla up from the Caribbean. The result was the greatest storm on record to hit Cape Cod. It couldn't have hit at a worse time for Bellamy and his men. Even a ship with an engine would have had difficulty staying off the beach that night. Winds were as high as eighty miles per hour and visibility was zero. The seas were probably fifty feet or higher in that kind of wind. Even with all the sails down and the anchors dragging, the ship was pushed toward the shore, where the roar of the surf foreshadowed their doom.

The pirates had no chance. The *Whydah* hit a sandbar about two hundred yards from shore and was buried by tons of water that poured over her wooden decks. Sailors were swept into the sea. The ones who managed to hang on were killed when the ship rolled. Only nine pirates survived the wreck of the *Whydah* and two of the other ships they had taken. Bellamy was not one of them. He had become the most successful pirate of his day. At the height of his success, he drowned in a freak storm, his body swept overboard practically at the doorstep of his lover.

Bill was quiet for a moment, in an almost reverent sort of way. In this moment of silence, I imagined the howling wind and the crashing waves and the screams of men who knew that this horrible instant was their last on earth. Then he continued,

> Legend says that Maria walked up and down the beach looking for the body of Sam Bellamy. The bodies of more than a hundred pirates washed ashore in the days after the wreck and Maria examined every one. She never found her Sam and she never found peace. To this day, locals say that they can still hear her wailing for Sam Bellamy from the cliffs of Eastham.

Once again Uncle Bill fell thoughtfully silent, and then chuckled as though he had just remembered something.

> There may even be a surprise ending to this story. Some people claimed that after the wreck, a stranger showed up at Higgins's Tavern near the cemetery where Bellamy first met Maria. He had long black hair and a deep scar across his head as though he had been struck by the blade of a cutlass. He was secretive about his purpose. When asked, he would simply say he was waiting for someone. He never took a job and never needed money.
> One spring day in 1720, the stranger went to the cemetery and sat underneath the apple tree, which was covered with a mist of blossoms. The stranger lay down and went to sleep. It was there, a few days later, that he, this man some thought was Black Sam Bellamy, was found dead.

I could imagine the entire story, scene by scene. Pirates and buried treasure were the stuff of daydreams for kids on the Cape, and my mind was spinning wildly from the images in my head. I imagined myself in the holds of the *Whydah,* running my hands through a huge pile of coins with other pirates, when Bill interrupted my fantasy.

"Of course, some people on the Cape don't think the story is true," he said.

"What do you think?" I asked, hoping for confirmation.

"I know it's true," said Bill. "I know who has part of the treasure."

"Who?"

"Jack Poole. He dove on the wreck with that writer, Edward Snow. Poole said they got some coins and found a cannon before a storm came up and almost killed them."

I went back to dreaming about pirates and sunken treasure. For days I could think of nothing but the legend of Black Sam Bellamy. Not a day went by that I didn't think of the *Whydah,* Bellamy, or Maria Hallett. They would be my obsession for the next thirty years.

2

Dreaming the Dream

✳ I've told this story myself hundreds of times over the years and heard it told by others in thousands of different ways. In one of the most popular versions Bellamy survived and lived secretly with Maria. Another version has Maria living off the *Whydah* treasure, which was mysteriously delivered to her after the shipwreck. Still another variation was written by Henry David Thoreau in his 1857 book *Cape Cod:*

> For many years after this shipwreck, a man of very singular and frightful aspect used every spring and autumn to be seen traveling on the Cape, who was sup-posed to have been one of Bellamy's crew. The presumption is that he went to some place where money had been secreted by the pirates, to get such a supply as his exigencies required. When he died, many pieces of gold were found in a girdle which he constantly wore.

Then, of course, there were those who did not believe the story at all. They thought the legend of Sam Bellamy and Maria Hallett was a myth and the *Whydah* herself was picked clean of anything valuable within a day of running aground. My parents were among this group, and it actually led to some surprisingly heated discussions, especially when Bill was around to defend his point of view.

I remember talking to him about the *Whydah* one day at our home in Martha's Vineyard. We were sitting at the kitchen table trying to figure out exactly where the shipwreck had taken place when my father came in. See-ing that we had a map spread out on the table and were talking about the *Whydah,* he let his opinion be known.

"What's the point, boys?" he asked sarcastically. "Even if you find the wreck, there won't be anything left but some nails and cannonballs. That ship was cleaned out by the locals as soon as the sun came up."

"Oh really?" said Bill. "Have you ever seen any of the cannons from the wreck? Have you ever heard of anyone finding thousands of pounds worth of gold and silver coins?"

"Maybe it wasn't any*one,*" my father said. "Maybe the cargo washed up on the shore over the years and hundreds of people have found it and just kept their mouths shut."

"Not possible," said Bill. "People on the Cape can't keep their mouths shut about anything, let alone things like that."

My father shrugged because he knew that was true. There were hundreds of stories about people finding coins and other objects from shipwrecks. There was probably no way that a Cape Codder could keep a find like that to himself.

"Well, you can keep wasting your time about this treasure," said Dad. "At least you're giving Barry a lesson in map reading."

"Yeah, right," said Bill, pointing his finger to the table. "I hope the person who 'wastes his time' looking for this treasure comes and pours a pile of it right here on this spot."

"Sounds good to me," said Dad, laughing. "And I hope he leaves it, too."

Sports replaced hunting and fishing when I entered high school. I still saw Bill as often as I could, but virtually all my time was consumed on the athletic fields of Whitman-Hanson Regional High School. My life had a new purpose—football. Subsequently, my grades went to hell.

I soon fell under the tutelage of the late Massachusetts high school Hall of Fame coach Robert Teahan. He needed a linebacker and drafted me from the freshman squad. I was proud to join the varsity team and naive enough to believe that the rest of the team would welcome me. I soon discovered that they resented me. The specter of a freshman occupying a position on the varsity team was a fate worse than death to any respectable upperclassman and I was treated like a leper. To make matters worse, a sophomore cheerleader and girlfriend of the star fullback had a crush on me.

Led by the fullback, a group of upperclassmen conspired to eliminate me from the squad. I was more humiliated than frightened. I decided that the best defense was a good offense.

It was the Wednesday scrimmage before the first game. Coach Teahan knew I was having a rough time. He took me aside: "Clifford I think you can become good football player; but you need to believe in your abilities more than I do." He also told me that he would understand if I wanted to go back to the freshman squad.

Football at Whitman-Hanson High School toughened me (top row, second from right) for the years ahead.

That day I had taken a couple of cheap shots in the back but didn't react, choosing instead to ignore the shots. Coach Teahan wanted more aggression. He pulled me aside and spoke to me in a very direct manner. "Clifford I expect a hundred ten percent from you, nothing less. If you're going to pussyfoot around, turn in your jockstrap and go back to the cranberry bog with your uncle Bill Carr."

My adversaries needed little encouragement and saw my public admonishment as an opportunity to finish me off. They began to chant, "Kill Clifford! Kill Clifford!"

I felt like the loneliest man on earth as I looked at the offensive line setting up in front of me. I knew that the fullback would be the lead backer (the first person to come at me).

Something took hold inside of me as I remembered the "forearm shiver," a defensive technique that the coach had showed me a few days earlier. The shiver is a karate-like move where you thrust your forearm into the face mask of an offensive player. If done correctly it is a devastating tool, which was just what I needed right then.

I charged the hole recklessly and met the fullback with a devastating forearm shiver. My enemy hit the ground, writhing in teeth-grinding seizures. He was carried from the field and taken to the hospital and never allowed to play football again.

That day I learned a lesson that I have often employed in the salvage business: meet aggression with even greater aggression.

I continued to play with the same attitude throughout high school and was approached my senior year by several college scouts.

Subsequently, I entered Trinidad Junior College in 1965. Known as an outlaw school, Trinidad was a place where guys like me went who needed to improve their grades while honing their athletic skills for the big leagues. Trinidad spawned the likes of football running back Joe Don Loony and basketball player Spencer Hayward.

I was fortunate to have met another great influence in my life, Coach Marvin Wetzel, who was fond of telling us that he first played football wearing his "pappies wing tips" with roofing nails driven through the soles for spikes. Playing for Coach Wetzel was an experience not soon forgotten.

During a bus ride home after loosing a game, for example, Ed Kelly, a huge African-American tackle with a gold front tooth, had been fouling the air as a result of a gaseous meal at a Mexican restaurant. In order to exorcise the toxic gas from our bodies, Coach Wetzel stopped the bus and kicked us out, forcing the entire team to walk over a mile to "clear our intestines."

On other bus trips, Wetzel would divide the bus into sections, depending on the quality of our voices, and we would sing songs like "Fifteen Miles on the Erie Canal," and "Old Man River."

After being elected to the all-conference team my sophmore year, I had numerous colleges offering me scholarships. I had fallen in love with the beautiful surroundings at Western State College in Gunnison, Colorado, when we stopped to practice there on our way to a game in Nebraska. I decided that rather than go to a big school I would play at Western State where they had just won the Division III National Conference. There I would be free to explore the mountains and old ghost towns of the Rockies. It was there, amid the jagged mountains, tall trees, and high altitude, that I fell in love with Patsy. She was a champion skier, and we spent most of our free time on the slopes in Crested Butte. After knowing each other for more than a year, Patsy and I married, and I continued to plod through school.

Soon she was pregnant, and I felt the responsibility of impending father-hood now and fell away from the football crowd and into more individual sports.

Powerlifting and javelin throwing became my focus. I liked powerlifting because it presented an almost unachievable constant personal challenge. If I reached the point that I could bench-press 400 pounds, I had only to add five pounds for a whole new personal challenge to present itself. Eventually I became the New England powerlifting champion in the 198-pound class and joked that I liked it because I loved to move nearly immovable objects.

Javelin throwing presented a challenge of a different stripe, calling for the elements of strength, grace, and speed to work in concert with each other. If everything happened like clockwork, the javelin went the distance. But if just one movement was a little bit off, no amount of muscling could make the spear fly. I later realized how much javelin throwing is like finding a sunken ship, which also involves a number of calculated moves that have to be made correctly to ensure success.

Barry Junior was born when I was twenty-four. My first daughter, Jenny, followed when I was twenty-five. At the age of twenty-five I graduated with a double major in history and sociology and a minor in physical education. I felt that the birth of my children and graduation from college were three steps forward in my life, because they represented phases in the maturing process.

What happened next was a giant step backward. Our marriage broke up. Although we tried to reconcile our differences, I soon found myself a di-vorced father with custody of the children.

After the breakup of my marriage, I wasn't sure what to do. If I hadn't had children, I would have left the United States myself, but I had custody of Barry and Jenny and needed to do what was right. I decided our new residence would be Kalispell, Montana, or Martha's Vineyard, Massachusetts. Montana and the vast expanses and freedom of the American West appealed strongly to me, but I was drawn back to the Vineyard, where I could be close to the sea.

I started the process of rebuilding my life. I worked as an administrator for the Boy Scouts of America, saving enough money to make a down pay-ment on a house. I left that position to teach physical education at Bourne High School on the Cape. Then, in search of the independence I still ad-mired in my uncle Bill, I left teaching to start a construction firm. The Vine-yard was changing now, "upscaling," as Bill said. Monied outsiders were buying up old houses in need of remodeling, and I wanted to get my share of the business. I hired a crew and started working very hard.

The divorce had left me unsure about marriage or any long-term relationship. I had come to accept not having a partner and was really quite happy as a single father. Jenny and Barry went with me everywhere when they weren't in school. They were great companions and thoroughly enjoyed the various construction sites.

Still, relationships happen, as another one did in my life. I was looking for someone to paint murals on my children's walls and one of my clients recommended a Swedish woman named Birgitta. She came and did the job and never left. We were married in 1979 after having a son, Brandon.

Still, I was restless.

In the seventies, I started a small salvage and diving company as a sideline. Most of the time, I did easy jobs like inspecting ships' hulls for insurance companies, underwater surveying, and raising small anchors. I was after excitement, and excitement is what I got. I became known as a salvor who would do almost anything, or at least try.

One time I received a call from the harbormaster at Martha's Vineyard, who told me that a Portuguese fishing vessel had just made an emergency call from about twenty miles out to sea. The crew members had lost their net and wanted to know if there were any divers capable of searching for it. A couple of divers had turned the job down. Too risky, they thought. A loose net that might entangle a diver is something most salvors won't tackle, no matter how much the pay. Was I interested in giving it a try?

I went out to the fishing boat and was greeted warmly by the Portuguese fishermen, none of whom could speak English. Through sign language, I realized that the net had snagged on something and the lines that held it to the boat had snapped. The captain was wringing his hands as he asked me if I thought I could find it. I didn't know and shrugged my shoulders to indicate my uncertainty. I offered to try, since replacing a net would cost the fishermen thousands of dollars.

I suited up and dove into the water. The boat's sonar told us that the net was in about one hundred feet of water, but I was not prepared for the darkness. I began descending very fast. Then I realized I was being foolhardy. Fishing nets are designed to snag and hold fish or anything else with which they come into contact. I didn't want to find the net by running into it, because I would certainly be ensnared.

Despite the coldness of the water, I could feel my skin tingle as I perspired from nervousness. I slowed my descent and widened my eyes to take in more light. Ahead, I saw the net. Although it looked like a field of seaweed, I knew it was not that benign. I floated above it, holding a rope I had pulled down from the fishing boat. Gingerly, I strung the rope through a

Salvage was hard work, but it taught me most of my diving skills. Above, I am salvaging the Martha's Vineyard *Islander,* a frightening job because the boat threatened to sink on top of us. Below, I have just retrieved a ship's propeller.

large portion of the netting and tied it firmly. Then I swam up the rope to the boat and told them to haul the net in.

For this dangerous salvage, I made four hundred dollars and received the cheers of a grateful crew.

My diving skills improved greatly through this kind of salvage work. I learned how to locate objects in deep water and how to raise them safely and without damage. I also began to look at diving as a form of recreation. My idea of fun was looking for shipwrecks. Undersea exploration was a relatively new endeavor in the seventies. Until the perfection of practical scuba equipment by Jacques Cousteau in 1942, diving had required the diver to wear a bronze helmet that would receive a constant stream of air fed to him through a hose manned by a highly skilled crew. Now, with the freedom of movement afforded by the Aqua-Lung, more divers were looking for wrecks, and doing so with greater ease and safety.

I began to research local wrecks and to dive on them. Sometimes I found nothing but the rusted hull of a ship. Other times I found bottles, pieces of china, and even a ship's bell. I became interested in finding older ships with interesting histories and began to look for the *General Arnold,* a Revolutionary War ship that sank in Plymouth Harbor.

The suggestion that I might want to search for that ship came from Larry Geller, the curator of the Pilgrim Museum. I was in the museum studying early-seventeenth-century Pilgrim houses when he told me about the *General Arnold.* The first American privateer, it had been driven ashore in a storm in 1780. The ship didn't sink immediately, but icy water poured over her decks and the frigid weather froze the poor seamen and soldiers together in a tangled mass.

These frozen servicemen were brought to shore and the townspeople tried to thaw them apart by soaking them in a creek. When that failed, it was obvious that they could not be buried separately, and they were buried together in a mass grave north of Plymouth.

After reading this sad story, I hired an ex–navy pilot to fly over Plymouth Harbor in an area identified as the wreck site. Below us was an unusual sight. The undersea plants were brown from absorbing the iron from the ship's fittings and were visible from the air. By connecting the dots, we could easily make out the outline of the *General Arnold.*

After that, I hired a boat called the *Pluto* to go out to the site and take a closer look. The captain was the first of many one-eyed villains I was to clash with in my career as an undersea explorer and looked like an inhabitant of his boat's namesake.

He was short and extremely stout, with curly red hair that nearly covered the Indian-head pennies that dangled from his ears. He spoke with an accent I had never heard before and could barely understand. His good eye shone with a dangerous glint, and his missing eye was disfigured by a terrible white scar that ran jaggedly down his cheek like a lightning bolt, a sad reminder of the cod-fishing hook that had gouged the socket.

I took my son Barry along the first day we went on the boat. It was late in the year and extremely foggy when we stepped on the deck. Water was dripping from the ends of the captain's hair and nose where the fog had condensed. With rough, gnarled fingers, he shook my frightened son's hand, and we were off.

We anchored over the site, and I went down. Even with visibility limited by the overcast sky, I could see pieces of the *General Arnold* everywhere. Even after two hundred years, there was wood and so many nails and other iron artifacts that I knew this was it.

My next step was to go before the Plymouth Board of Selectmen to tell them what I had found. As confirmation, I invited the captain of the *Pluto,* a move that proved to be a mistake. Just the sight of him and his entourage stole the show, and the smell of liquor that they brought with them into the room nearly ended the meeting entirely.

He was wearing a mismatched plaid outfit that looked like seat-cover material from a 1970 Ford Pinto. His pants were too short to reach the tops of his shoes and left exposed his dirty white athletic socks. With him was his half-sister (who looked just like him, *sans* scar and vacant eye socket) and her husband, a massive man wearing motorcycle leathers with a Harley-Davidson patch stitched to the back.

They sat sleepily in the front row while Captain Pluto told the board of finding the *General Arnold.* I told them of my initial research into the location of the ship and what I had seen when we flew over the site and later when I dove on it. Since the board would issue a search permit for only a very specific area, I was careful to indicate exactly where it was that I wanted to search.

The meeting went well, but a few days later I received a puzzling telephone call from a board member. Captain Pluto had come back a few days later and filed an identical application to lay claim to the wreck site. As it turned out, he had told an acquaintance of our find and they decided to see if they could steal the site.

At the time I was shocked, but I have come to expect duplicity like this. There is nothing like finding any kind of artifact—even ones that aren't gold or silver—to bring out the worst in some people. Greed, theft, and ego inflation are just some of the symptoms of gold fever.

Despite this attempt at claim jumping, I received a permit to excavate the ship, the first to be granted by the Massachusetts Board of Underwater Archaeological Resources (MBUAR). I later returned the permit to the board when I had doubts that what I had found was the entire *Arnold*. Some people claimed that the ship had been refloated shortly after it sank. Others maintain that I found the ship and that no record existed of it having been refloated at all.

Despite returning the permit, I was not disappointed. I began to realize what a fertile area of study this could be. The whole world used to move by ship. All merchants had to do was point their ships out to sea and raise sail and they could move cargo thousands of miles, which was far easier and cheaper than moving it by wagon over the hilly and rutted roads. For that reason, all of history's great civilizations were started on rivers or estuaries. Without water connections, most ancient cities could not have survived.

There was clearly a lot to be found in the ocean, including many interesting and important artifacts, not just treasure. The way people lived, the way they thought, and where they had been headed as a society could all be deduced by artifacts brought up from the ocean floor. A dive to a shipwreck could be like a trip in a time machine, bringing you in contact with objects that were last touched hundreds of years before, putting you closer to the past than you ever thought was possible. "There is more wealth at the bottom of the sea than there ever was or will be on land," said Jules Verne in his classic novel *20,000 Leagues Under the Sea*. It was clear to me that he wasn't just talking about treasure you can cash in, but about intellectual and historical treasure as well.

The notion of finding history intrigued me. I began to dream of becoming an underwater explorer because I could think of nothing more exciting.

3

Full Speed Ahead

Uncle Bill, me, and my dad after a successful deer hunting trip.

❈ When I look back now, I can see that 1981 was a pivotal year. I had imitated my uncle Bill in many aspects of my life. I owned land and houses and had a successful business that left me free some of the time to pursue diving. I had begun to think more and more about the *Whydah*, and wanted to become the first person to excavate a pirate ship. I was then thirty-six years old, and I knew that if I was going to accomplish something unique I had to do it before I became hopelessly stuck in the rut that success had dug for me.

And then there was my uncle Bill. He had been diagnosed with lung cancer and was fading fast. It was painful to look at him. Gone were his ruddy skin and lively eyes. They were replaced by gray flesh and eyes that were wide and fearful of the future.

When I looked at Bill struggling for breath, I hurt. In him, I could see every phase of my life pass in review. I could not remember Bill not being around. From my early childhood to those difficult adolescent years when he was the only adult I would talk to, Bill was always there.

Bill had helped me grow up. It was he, more than anyone in my life, who opened my eyes to the opportunities of life. It wasn't that I didn't love my parents. I did. But I wanted to become a free spirit like my uncle Bill.

I could hardly imagine life without him, and I decided to let him know just how much he meant to me. I canceled much of my work and devoted the summer to seeing as much of Bill as I could.

In a few short months, we tried to relive our experiences together. We spent time talking in the fishing shack while working on fishing equipment. We went into the woods and tracked wildlife, and even spent time tracking the wildlife in the basement of my parents' home, which was infested with snapping turtles with beaks like wire cutters. I even accompanied Bill as he visited old friends who knew that this might be the last time they saw him alive.

By the end of summer, I was emotionally drained. At the same time, I knew that life was for living and that I had to do something more meaningful and exciting than the dull moneymaking ventures in which I was involved. If I was going to change my life, I realized that I had to do it right then. The question was, what was I going to do to change it?

Late that summer we drove up the rocky coast of Maine. This was one of Bill's favorite drives, and its rugged beauty helped ease the pain of his illness. At times we stopped to look at the cobalt blue ocean, but we didn't get out of the car, since Bill was too weak to walk.

It was during one of these stops that we again started talking about the *Whydah*.

"Maybe I'll try to find the *Whydah*," I said, half joking.

"I don't know, boy," he said, smiling through his pain. "I think that ship might never be found."

"Still, I might give it a try," I insisted. "No one ever found the treasure, we know that. If it's still there I could find it."

Bill looked out at the ocean and was silent. For a moment I didn't think he heard me, then I could tell that he was just lost in his thoughts. He nodded for a moment and then looked at me with a wry grin.

"You'll never know unless you try, boy."

One month later, Bill died.

I was still unsure about searching for the *Whydah*. Since no one had found her treasure, I reasoned, maybe there was none to be found. Should I leave my comfortable life on Martha's Vineyard to search for an unknown quantity? It wasn't until Thanksgiving Day that I could finally say, "Yes." That was the day that I left the real world and became an explorer.

I was at the home of William Styron, the Pulitzer Prize–winning author of *Sophie's Choice*. I was a longtime friend of the family and was there as the guest of Styron's children, Tom and Polly.

Although I had arrived after dinner for cocktails, it was clear that their Thanksgiving feast had been special. On the dining room table I could see the carved remains of one of Bill's massive, oven-browned Virginia baked hams surrounded by bowls of mashed potatoes, candied yams, and cranberry sauce and a half-emptied bottle of champagne.

The living room was packed with Styron's good friends, including Jules Feiffer, the cartoonist, and Walter Cronkite, the former CBS newsman who had been recently recognized in a national poll as "the most trusted man in America."

Dinner and wine had made everyone mellow, and the room was filled with the pleasant chatter of afternoon conversation. It wasn't long before the talk turned to life in the early American colonies, a perfectly good subject, since the Mayflower Pilgrims had landed at Provincetown and scouted the Cape before making their final crossing to Plymouth.

Suddenly I heard my name mentioned.

"Tell them about the famous pirate, Black Sam Bellamy," said Tom.

By now, I had told the story so many times that it was almost second nature. The room fell silent as I described the meeting of Bellamy and Maria and the way that her life unraveled. By the time I related the details of the shipwreck and painted the picture of Maria looking for Bellamy among the bodies that had washed ashore, the room was almost uncomfortably quiet.

When I ended the story, champagne gurgled freely as glasses were being refilled. "What a marvelous story," said one of the women. "But what happened to Maria Hallett?"

"No one really knows," I said. "Some think that she went mad from being forced out of society. Whatever the case, there wasn't much heard from her after that."

As the conversation continued, I suddenly realized that Walter Cronkite was speaking to me from across the room.

"You said that you are interested in looking for the *Whydah;* why don't you do it?" asked the veteran newscaster.

Why not? I asked myself. I had dreamed of doing this for years, since I had first heard the story of Bellamy and his ill-fated ship. In what seemed to be a split second, I assessed my life. I saw a man who was successful, but living a life of quiet desperation. Why shouldn't I try to dig up a piece of the past and make an impact on history? How better to gain satisfaction? And besides, I thought, it shouldn't take very long . . .

"That's exactly what I am going to do," I said to Cronkite. "I have really been researching this ship for most of my life now. This spring I am going to search for the *Whydah*."

I was surprised by my own words. As the conversation picked up around me, I realized there was no turning back. I had committed myself to the search for the *Whydah*. Starting the next day, I would search for a pirate ship that had been lost for 265 years.

4

The Riches with the Guns

The beach where the *Whydah* shipwreck took place.

✳ I knew the *Whydah* story well and knew she would not be easy to find. I considered blindly looking for the ship, but realized that my chances of finding her without some kind of a map were very slim. In fact, few people have ever found much sunken treasure without targeting an exact location. Some who have been successful, like William Phips of Boston, must have had God on their side.

Phips, in fact, made one of the greatest recoveries of sunken treasure ever, and he did it without a map.

In 1641, a Spanish treasure fleet of more than thirty ships was struck by a hurricane off the coast of Florida. Nine of the ships were driven onto the shore and broken into pieces. The most heavily laden of the ships, the *Nuestra Señora de la Concepción*, lost all three of her masts, filled partway with water, and floundered in the sea for more than a week, floating at the mercy of the winds and currents.

Only a few of the seamen aboard survived the storm. Afterward, they watched as the ship staggered to her final destination, a reef now known as Silver Shoals lying ninety miles north of Hispaniola. The reef's sharp coral tore holes in the ship's hull, sinking her in less than one hundred feet of clear, tropical water.

The survivors could not remember the exact location of the ship and the Spanish government searched for years in vain for her valuable cargo.

Enter Phips. As a child in Maine, he listened to tales of treasure told by seafaring men. Later he became a carpenter in Boston, where he heard more tales at the Boston docks. His fascination with these stories grew until he launched a treasure expedition of his own to the Caribbean in 1681. Although he found little treasure, he did find several sunken ships. That was no small feat, given the primitive state of deep-sea diving. His success at finding these wrecks gave the young colonist courage to travel to England to ask Charles II for funds to carry out further expeditions.

After waiting in London eighteen months, Phips was finally granted a royal audience. When he left Whitehall, Phips had the full financial backing of the king in exchange for a large percentage of whatever he found.

For a while, Phips seemed unable to find any more sunken ships. He searched the Caribbean in vain for a wreck and finally thought he had found one in Nassau. After working the site for a month with the physically powerful Lucayan Indian divers, he came up with nothing. Desperate for gold and angry at not finding it, Phips's crew plotted mutiny. That wasn't surprising, since his crew was a disreputable lot of rapists, murderers, and thieves. Phips was able to quell the mutiny and sail to Port Royal, where he signed on a new crew. It was here, in the bars of this seafaring town, that he first heard the story of the *Concepción*.

The stories revived his enthusiasm. Phips searched the waters north of Hispaniola for several months before giving up on the wreck and returning to England. Charles II had died in his absence. Phips was jailed by James II for nonpayment of debt. But the adventurer was not in jail for long. A number of London businessmen heard of Phips's exploits and convinced the king to release him. By 1686 he was fully funded and sailing for the Caribbean again, with two ships under his command.

Phips was now driven even more strongly to succeed. He pushed his crew mercilessly and the Lucayan Indians even harder. The Indians were considered the best divers in the New World. Phips tested that reputation by working them seven days a week, sunup to sundown. They descended on the reefs of Silver Shoals by holding stone weights that allowed them to drop effortlessly to the bottom. Many of these Indians could stay down for as long as five minutes, crawling naked along the sharp coral, struggling with no goggles to see the outline of a ship. After examining a few hundred square feet, they rose to the surface and caught their breath in preparation for the next dive.

The slow search continued this way for many days and dozens of miles. Since no record existed of where the *Concepción* sank, no map could help. Phips was searching blindly, like a sightless man looking for house keys on a dance floor.

After several frustrating weeks, Phips began to doubt his information and once again feared a mutiny by his crew. Then an Indian popped to the surface and announced a strange sighting. He had been looking at a piece of fan coral when he noticed the angular lines and thick timber of a Spanish galleon. He would go down and look again, he said, but he was certain they had found the ship.

Phips began to weep upon hearing the news. Over the next several weeks, the Indian divers brought up more than thirty tons of silver, gold, chests of pearls, and leather bags containing precious gems. Despite the rich find, things did not always go smoothly. Pirates and bad weather plagued the salvage operation. Dwindling provisions left the crew worried about starvation. Phips finally called an end to the operation and returned to England with treasure that would equal $50 million in today's currency.

The recovery of treasure from the *Concepción* was widely regarded as the most successful commercial venture of the seventeenth century. Phips was knighted by the king, who was grateful for such an impressive return on investment. The treasure hunter returned to Boston as one of the richest men in America and was later made governor of the Massachusetts colony. Phips had found this incredible bounty relying only on word of mouth and hunches, using no treasure map.

Unfortunately, finding the *Whydah* did not prove to be so easy. Over the years, I had spent much of my time reading about the pirate ship and her crew, but none of my research revealed the actual spot where she had gone down. Unlike the *Concepción,* the *Whydah* did not sink in clear water where her remains could easily be seen. Rather, she wrecked on a rough North Atlantic beach with coarse sand that swallows objects with the finality of quicksand. One thing I knew for sure was that the *Whydah* would be found underneath about twenty feet of sand. Where that sand was, I did not know.

I did know that I would not be the first person to look for the ship. In 1947, an author named Edward Rowe Snow made a heroic effort to find the *Whydah.* Snow wrote uncounted books on New England lore and legend, and wasn't afraid to take risks in researching some of these stories. He would spend nights in haunted hotel rooms, hoping to see the legendary ghosts that supposedly lived in them. In the days before scuba equipment was invented, Snow dove in the ocean with rubber hoses connected to gasoline cans in hope that his contraptions would provide enough air to stay underwater for several minutes.

Snow, a publicity hound and sometime radio talk-show host, was also an aviation buff known as the Flying Santa. At Christmastime, he flew gifts to lighthouse keepers on the coast. During one of his flights down the Cape, Snow looked down into the water about one thousand feet off Eastham Beach and saw what he thought was the wreck of the *Whydah*. Making a U-turn, he swooped low and dropped a buoy to mark the spot.

At great personal expense, he constructed a fifteen-foot platform and towed it to a spot over the wreck. From the rickety diving platform, Snow and several divers scoured the bottom, digging into the sand to search for objects.

He later claimed that the wreck was virtually intact under twenty feet of sand, but I doubted that he had really determined that, since in several days of diving he found little. A handful of coins were found along with a few cannonballs, but it wasn't the chest of treasure for which Snow hoped. The search seemed to intensify when an excited diver came up to report that a cannon had been found. The explorers tied a rope to the cannon, which now resembled a misshapen rock from all the minerals the sea had deposited on its iron surface, and tried to winch it onto the platform. When it proved too heavy, they attached the rope to a truck on shore and tried to pull the cannon out of the water. When the tow line broke, they abandoned the cannon and kept searching the bottom for more manageable objects.

Some small objects were found cemented together by sea minerals, but such minor finds were not worth the danger that the divers were now facing. At the end of an exhausting day, one of the divers developed a leak in his diving suit and nearly froze to death. Rough water made staying on the platform too risky and the divers moved off. Finally, a storm rolled in, destroying the platform and putting an end to the Snow expedition just a few days after it started.

After this failed expedition, Snow recorded his sentiments about searching for the pirate ship:

> It will be a very lucky treasure hunter who ever does more than pay expenses while attempting to find the elusive gold and silver still aboard the Whydah.

As it turned out, Snow's group was over the site of the *Castagna,* a 1914 wreck, not the *Whydah,* a fact we discovered later through our own research.

On a coast with three thousand shipwrecks, it is easy to find the wrong one and, of course, hard to find the right one.

Snow was not the first undersea explorer to claim he had found traces of the *Whydah*. In about 1900, Captain Webster Eldridge asserted he had recovered two cannons from the *Whydah* revealed by the ever-shifting sands of the Cape. Such an event takes great luck, since the churning sands rarely show what is in them, and then only briefly. These cannons were subsequently dated to the Revolutionary War era and were not from the *Whydah*.

Henry David Thoreau wrote in 1793 about a similar sighting of an object believed to be from the *Whydah* by the citizens of Wellfleet. "At times to this day," he was told by a local historian, "the violence of the seas moves the sands on the outer bar, so that at times the iron caboose of the ship at low tide has been seen."

Although this written record confirmed the existence of the *Whydah,* it did little to pinpoint her remains. In an effort to do that, I sought out the work of Captain Cyprian Southack, who had charted the waters around the Cape in the late seventeenth and early eighteenth centuries. His diary, which I found at the Massachusetts State Archives, is a tale of frustration and anger aimed at man and nature alike. If he had not recorded the location of the *Whydah* accurately, I knew I was in trouble.

Southack was a careful cartographer whose maps were the savior of many seamen on the New England coast. The son of a British naval lieutenant, he came to Boston in 1685 at the age of twenty-three and for nineteen years commanded the *Province* guardship, a vessel used against the French and Indians in skirmishes in Maine and Nova Scotia. Later, he commanded ships that guarded the coast against privateers and pirates.

Southack's true love was the making of accurate maps. For him, an ocean chart provided safe passage through a world of unseen dangers, which are rife on the New England coast. Sailors able to note undersea obstacles like shoals and sandbars on their maps were in control of their destiny. For Southack, mapmaking was a mission, and he performed it with great diligence. His charts were so good that they were used to navigate much of the New England coast for nearly forty years after his death, until more accurate means of cartography came into use.

Southack's attention to accuracy led him to the most frustrating duty in his life, the attempted salvage of the *Whydah*. Southack was appointed the task of recovering the valuables from the *Whydah* by Samuel Shute, the new governor of the province of Massachusetts Bay. Less than forty-eight hours after the shipwreck, Shute had received a handwritten message from Colonel William Basset of Sandwich telling him that the "pyrate" ship

"Whido" was stranded on the shore at Eastham, "Man'd with about 130 men, 28 Guns, who had not any commission from any Prince or Potentate." There was no danger from the pirates themselves, because, as Basset wrote, "about 130 men were drowned and none saved except two."

With no physical threat to worry about, Shute concentrated on salvaging what remained of the ship. Since British law laid claim to pirate property, it was Shute's aim to gather as many goods as he could for the Crown, and himself, for that matter. He issued a proclamation urging all of His Majesty's officers and subjects to seize any pirates that remained as well as "money, bullion, treasure, goods and merchandize" from the scene of the wreck. He also appointed Captain Southack as his official representative on the scene. That is when the cartographer's nightmare began. From the moment he arrived at the wreck site, there was nothing but trouble for Southack.

Arriving at Provincetown by sloop on May 2, 1717, Southack ordered two of his deputies to travel quickly to the *Whydah* to establish a watch over the wreck site. It had been a week since the ship had gone down and Southack felt it best to secure the site as quickly as possible. The people of the Cape had a reputation for looting wrecks with professional efficiency. Southack wanted to get there before the ship was stripped clean. Although

The canal used by Southack to row through the Cape to the wreck site looked much like this one near Orleans.

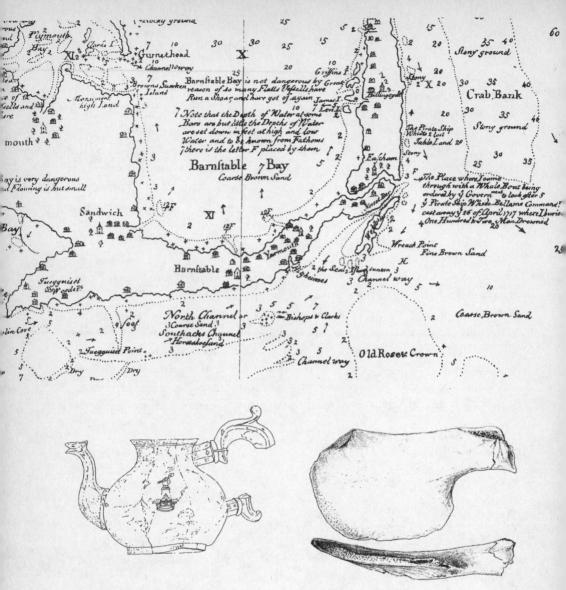

VICTIMS OF VIOLENT NATURE

The wreck of the galley *Whydah* still ranks as the worst to ever occur on the shores of Cape Cod. There were 146 men on board at the time of the wreck: sixteen prisoners and 130 pirates. Although the beach was just five hundred feet away, only two men are known to have made it ashore alive. Aside from the raging surf, the crushing weight of falling cannon, and toppling rigging that pinned men to the sea bottom, ocean temperatures at that time of year were enough to kill the strongest swimmer in a matter of minutes. On this chart of Cape Cod, Cyprian Southack noted that a total of 101 bodies had come ashore during the time he was at Cape Cod.

Graphically attesting to the violence of the wreck, this bone was found jammed in the ebony-wood handle of this Queen Anne–style pewter teapot. Both were recovered from the encrustation surrounding a cannon. The family crest depicts an arm with a fist clenching three wheat stalks rising from a crown.

he was authorized by the governor to take salvage from people by force if necessary, he knew it would be easier to take it from the wrecked ship where most of the booty was still stored.

Southack began to snoop around Provincetown to see what the locals knew about the wreck. To his chagrin, the *Whydah* was the talk of the town. It seemed as though everyone had heard about it, and much of the town had been to the site or was planning to go.

Afraid that the locals might beat him to the loot, Southack left the next day for the site. He immediately encountered trouble. In his rush to get to the *Whydah*, Southack, the mapmaker, relied on information from an old map that showed passageway by canal through the Cape to the Atlantic Ocean. This canal was supposed to be at Billingsgate, about eight miles south of Provincetown and almost directly across the Cape from the wreck. Thinking that navigating the canal would be faster than traveling by horseback, Southack ordered his eight remaining deputies into a whaleboat for the trip to the canal.

The canal was still there, but barely. One hundred years of tidal action and heavy winds had all but erased it. Still, Southack insisted on trying this approach. Since it was May 3, and time for the spring high tides, he reckoned that they would have enough water in which to manuever.

The nine men rowed until they hit muddy bottom. Then they stood and began to pole their way through the waterway. When that failed, they tied a rope to the bow and pulled the boat through the frigid and muddy water. Finally, when that approach failed, they lifted the boat on poles made of ash trees and portaged until they reached water deep enough to row again.

At Nauset Harbor there were more problems. The ocean was still treacherous from the same weather system that had driven the *Whydah* to her destruction. Seas were high and the waves made it difficult to launch a boat. Now the nine exhausted salvors had to row into the high seas and up the Cape to the wreck site, an open ocean trip of several miles. Finally, after fourteen hours of hard travel, the representatives of the governor saw what was left of the *Whydah*. The sight was disappointing. Waves had already beaten the pirate ship to pieces, which, he wrote, were strewn "north and south distance from each other 4 miles." Pieces of the once-proud *Whydah* were drifting onto the shore, mixing with the lifeless bodies of "54 white men and five negroes."

Despite the horrific scene before him, Southack had time to record a number of physical facts about the *Whydah*. She was capsized, or "turned bottom up" as he wrote, but still he ascertained that she was about three hundred tons and "a very fine ship."

On May 4, his first full day at the wreck site, Southack sent six of his men out to work on the wreck. Gale-force wind and driving rain forced them to retreat. When the weather did not abate, Southack directed his men to pick up pieces of cable "and other things" for transport back to the town of Billingsgate.

I would guess that much of this first day was spent chasing locals away from the wreck site. Cape Codders had been salvaging what they could in the week before Southack arrived and thought they had as much claim to the shipwreck as the Crown did. The two men Southack sent ahead to secure the wreck had chased away hundreds of salvagers, all bent on getting what they could from the ship. Undoubtedly, the scavengers who had returned on this day were very unhappy about being told to leave.

Using his official status to hold the looters at bay, Southack surveyed the wreck site from atop the white sand cliffs of Eastham. When the tide was low, he could see one of the ship's anchors. The cartographer was especially interested in the anchor because, as he wrote to Governor Shute, "where the anchors are the money is, I fancy."

Still, they could get to none of it. Unlike Phips, Southack had no divers. The weather was literally beating the remains of the *Whydah* into the sand, heavy objects first. No cannons washed ashore, nor did any cannonballs, pistols, or sheets of lead that were used for repairs. Some coins may have made it to shore, but if they did, they were picked up by the scavengers who had gotten to the wreck site before Southack.

The only salvage at this point that Southack and his men could cart off to Billingsgate was rigging from the masts, cable used on the deck, and iron fittings they retrieved by burning the wooden parts of the ship that they had been able to recover. They were not able to retrieve anything from the main part of the wreck.

5

Southack's Fruitless Search

In my spare time, I would search the beach in front of the wreck site for coins and other metal objects from the *Whydah*.

✸ Southack took a different tack with his search. If he couldn't get any salvage from the ship, he would get what he could from the Cape Codders who had beaten him to the site. He placed an ad in the newspaper establishing his authority to conduct a search-and-seizure operation. This was the first writ of assistance ever issued in the colonies and amounted to the equivalent of today's "no knock" drug raid:

> Whereas . . . His Excellency the Governor hath Authorized and impower'd me the Subscriber, to discover & take care of S. Wreck & to Impress men & whatsoever Else necessary to discover & Secure what may be part of her . . .

with Orders to go into any house, Shop, Cellar, Warehouse, room or other place, & in case of resistance to break open any doors, Chests, trunks & other packages there to Seize & from thence to bring away any of the goods, Merchandize, Effects belonging to S. Wreck, as also to Seize any of her men.

Forewarned, the citizenry of Eastham and the surrounding area were subject to a door-to-door search by the driven cartographer. He searched houses within a thirty-mile radius of the shipwreck. Although most of the residents freely allowed Southack and his deputies to examine their property, none admitted taking anything from the wreck site. After searching the countryside for anything from the *Whydah,* Southack came away empty-handed. He wrote of his frustration with the locals in a letter to the governor: "All these people are very stiff and will not own [up to] nothing of what they got." This frustration was well warranted. In Cape Codders, he was dealing with skilled smugglers who had plenty of hiding places for contraband.

One of the locals, Samuel Harding, was more forthcoming than his fellows. He readily admitted having scavenged the beach in the early morning hours of April 26 and having hidden the purloined cargo on his Wellfleet farm. Although he refused to return any of the booty he felt was rightfully his, he willingly told the cartographer the story of how he discovered the wreck.

Fast asleep during one of the worst storms ever to hit Cape Cod, Harding was awakened after midnight by a frantic pounding on his door. Opening his door to the gale-force winds, Harding found a man who was soaking wet, exhausted, and nearly dead on his feet. He was weeping and begging for warmth, which Harding did his best to provide by stoking the fire in the fireplace and boiling water for tea.

Gradually the castaway's story emerged. Thomas Davis had been a carpenter on the *St. Michael,* a cargo ship sailing from Cork, Ireland, to Jamaica. Just east of their goal, the ship was overtaken by pirates captained by Black Sam Bellamy. Bellamy's crew had been decent, for pirates, Davis told his savior. In a businesslike fashion, they looted the ship and then offered everyone on the *St. Michael* a chance to "go on the account" and become a pirate.

Before leaving the *St. Michael* and her frightened crew, one of the pirates asked if there was a carpenter on board. Unwittingly, Davis identified himself. In the next moment, he was conscripted into the ranks of the pirates.

This was not something Davis wanted. He had no interest in a life of robbery. He knew that wealth was one possible result of piracy, but being hanged as a criminal was another. He appealed directly to Bellamy to let him go, but since he was not married and seemed to have no deep attachments at home, his appeal for freedom was denied.

Though Davis's pleas were at first rebuffed, later Bellamy promised the unhappy carpenter he would be set free with the next vessel captured. That promise was not kept. When Bellamy's crew took their next ship, the *Whydah,* the crew members learned of the agreement between their captain and the carpenter and put it to a vote. The crew voted to reverse Bellamy's decision and forced Davis to continue service as the carpenter of their new ship, the *Whydah.* Some of the men became so angry with Davis that they even threatened his life. "Damn you," one shouted after the voting, "we would shoot you or whip you to death at the mast before we'd let you go!"

After that, Davis kept his mouth shut and attended to the upkeep and repair of the *Whydah,* duties he carried out until the ship was wrecked.

Harding and his wife listened with wide eyes to the carpenter's tale. It was fast approaching dawn, and the farmer decided to take his horse-drawn wagon to the beach. Salvaging shipwrecks was a way of life on the Cape. The locals even had a prayer for the occasion:

> We pray thee, O Lord, not that wrecks should happen, but that if any shall happen, Thou wilt guide them onto our shores for the benefit of the inhabitants.

This solemn prayer was certainly descriptive of Harding's motives that morning. After listening to Davis he must have felt sorry for the crew of the *Whydah* and their horrifying last moments on the frigid and angry sea. But he was also a practical man, and there was certainly a lot of merchandise on the beach that Harding and his family could put to good use. After all, colonial America was by no means a land of plenty. Most Cape Codders like Samuel Harding were barely getting by.

Harding walked the beach, loading the best of the items that washed ashore into his wagon. He may have ignored the bodies that were being swept onto land, but more likely he stripped the dead of clothing, pistols, and other objects. Many wreck combers did strip the dead of valuables in those days.

If Harding did not strip them, the next wave of citizens to descend on the wreck site certainly did. It is likely that the locals took everything they could find of value, attached to a dead man or not. That would include shoes, pistols, and even rings and earrings, which were likely removed by cutting off fingers and ears. What is certain is that at least two hundred men, women, and children braved the foul weather to get whatever it was that washed up on shore these first days.

Being a Cape Codder myself, I can imagine Harding's response when Southack asked him to return the goods he had found. Southack had confronted at least eight men who had been among the first at the wreck site, and none would surrender his booty to the Crown. Their refusal to give the king his due infuriated Southack. In a letter to the governor, he called for their arrest:

> [My deputies and I] have rid at least thirty miles among the inhabitants, whom I have had information of their being at the Pirate wreck, and have got considerable riches out of her, the first men that went down to the wreck with the English man [Thomas Davis] that was saved out of the wreck, I shall mention their names to you Excellency in order for a warrant [to be issued] to me for bringing them to Boston before your Excellency.

If his anger with the so-called thieves was clear in the letter, so was his frustration with weather and sea conditions. As Southack wrote,

> Sir, the weather has been very bad, and Great Sea, so we can do nothing as yet on the wreck with my whale boat and men, but see the anchor every low water. . . . Sir, 72 dead men are come ashore out of the pirate ship at this time.

With the letter written and some of his frustrations vented, Southack continued to recover what he could from the *Whydah*. On May 8 he wrote in his journal of "fog, strong gale, and great sea," saying that there was "nothing to be done on the wreck. The gentlemen [deputies] have been cruising but can find nothing, nor [do] the people bring in nothing."

On May 9, the weather broke enough so that Southack and his crew were able to row out to the wreck. It was wasted effort.

> Small gale and fog at three afternoon I sent my whale boat off but the sea being so great could see nothing for the sand making the water thick and muddy.

The rest of his report was even more grim.

> Several cart loads of wreck goods came in today but of little value. Seventy-six men came onshore out of the pirate ship dead.

On May 11,

Strong gale and rain, a very great sea nothing to be done. I am getting of carts to load his majesty hired sloop Swan.

On May 12,

This morning wind at Northeast, frisking gale and clear weather—but a great sea at ye wreck.

And so it went. Southack's dogged pursuit of salvage from the *Whydah* came almost to naught. He searched the shore for items that were worth something, but everything of true value seemed to be trapped in the *Whydah,* which he described as being upside down in water too deep, too rough, and too cold to be reached. It is doubtful that the hull was even intact by the time Southack arrived. It was probably splintering and disintegrating with each wave that pounded against it.

As he continued to search, his bills mounted. He had to rent the whale-boat he used in his failed attempts to reach the ship and the booty trapped inside of her. He had to pay the men who searched the houses and beaches of the Cape for what was left of the *Whydah*. He had been billed eighty-three pounds by the coroner for the burial of sixty-two of the pirates. Southack refused to pay that bill, telling the governor in a letter that "I am of the mind that the coroner . . . should have nothing for burying any of those men after they knew them to be pirates." The coroner put a lien on Southack and it is likely that he eventually had to pay.

Southack finally gave up on May 13. He was £260 in debt and had collected very little of value from the *Whydah*. What had been collected was carted to Billingsgate, where it was loaded onto the *Swan,* a sloop sent by the governor to haul the salvage back to Boston.

Southack stood on the cliffs overlooking the wreck and surveyed the situation one last time, his face stung by sharp grains of sand blown by the fierce wind. From his perch, he could see some timbers from the ship and maybe even a waterlogged body or two, since dead pirates continued to wash onto the shore for several weeks after the wreck. Rough water had worked the ship deeper into the porous sand so that little could be seen above the surface of the ocean. The anchor was still stuck on the sandbar and looked like a rock that was holding its own against the water's swirl and tug.

In his last official dispatch from the scene, Southack wrote to Governor

Shute of his hopes that he could return to find the treasure. "I find most of the wreck is come ashore in pieces," the letter reads in part. "I am afears that when weather permits to go off [search], the riches with the guns would be buried in the sand."

There is one final irony to Southack's nightmare. As the *Swan* was making her voyage from Boston to Billingsgate, she was intercepted by pirates and robbed of £80 worth of supplies. Had the pirates robbed her on the return trip to Boston, they would have had the opportunity to take £263 worth of salvage from the *Whydah,* which was all Southack's salvage garnered at public auction. One bidder at the auction, which was held at the Treasurer's Warehouse in July, described the items from the *Whydah* as "two anchors, two great guns, and some junk."

Southack, unlike Phips, had lost his shirt treasure hunting. His expenses were covered by the proceeds of the auction, but barely. Although there was nothing in the public record indicating Southack was supposed to get more than his expenses for salvaging the *Whydah,* it is my guess that he would have been in line for a little booty himself had he found any of the substantial riches that were on the lost ship.

That was not to be. Instead, Southack returned to mapmaking, his first love. He never again returned to the site of the *Whydah.*

6

Pushpins and Hunches

My den at Martha's Vineyard, where I studied about the *Whydah*. The bell on the table is the fruit of other salvage work.

❋ There were many questions about the treasure and why no one had found it, or why no one had *admitted* to finding it.

Some believed that Southack had found the gold and silver and kept it to himself. Stories of secret wealth dogged the dour cartographer for years. He had only pretended to be frustrated in his search for pirate gold, claimed angry Cape Codders. They declared that sometime during the salvage operation, perhaps even alone and late at night, Southack had recovered bags of money and buried them in a secret spot. Later, when all the excitement died down, Southack recovered the booty and returned to England a rich man. Some insisted that he even took a beautiful Creole lover with him.

The truth about Southack bore no resemblance to the legend.

In fact, he stayed in America, making a living at mundane pursuits. After his vain attempt to salvage the *Whydah,* Southack made extra money by selling gravel through advertisements in the Boston newspapers. Although frustrated by his effort to recover the pirate treasure, Southack was only temporarily fazed. He returned to cartography and continued to turn out some of the most accurate maps in colonial America. In 1720 he published *New England Coasting Pilot,* the collection of charts for which he is remembered.

Although he encouraged the governor to "order a memo" from a surviving *Whydah* crewman revealing the location of the money on the ship, it does not appear that any such memo was ever forthcoming. The surviving pirates testified about the presence of gold and silver worth twenty to thirty thousand pounds sterling that had been equally divided and put into 180 bags. As to the treasure's exact location on the ship, they remained mum. One of the pirates said that the riches were laid together in one heap, "kept in chests between decks without any guard."

Southack claimed that the locals stole everything that floated ashore, but it is doubtful that they found anything of real value, either, beyond cable, canvas, and items they could scavenge from the dead. There is no indication in the property records of the day that Harding or any of the other early salvors enjoyed sudden wealth. Had their salvage efforts been a windfall, rumors would certainly have swept the Cape, since the entire population in those days amounted to just a few thousand hardy souls.

Although Southack declared that Harding was "as guilty as the pirates" and called for the eight "plunderers" to be summoned to Boston and tried, no one was ever prosecuted or even questioned for unauthorized salvage. The governor, after all, did not want to waste his time pressing charges over petty items. For several years coins and other objects were found by beachcombers, but it was almost as though they appeared magically out of the sand. The *Whydah* had completely disappeared.

How long did it take for the ship to vanish? Not more than a few weeks and possibly not more than a few days. The sands of the Cape change so dramatically that a strong storm can raise their levels by as much as ten feet, burying heavy objects before your very eyes. Henry David Thoreau wrote of one such incident in his book *Cape Cod.* In describing the effects of a minor storm on a beach near the wreck of the *Whydah,* he wrote:

It moved the sand on the beach opposite the lighthouse to the depth of six feet, and three rods in width as far as we could see north and south, and carried it bodily off no one knows exactly where, laying bare in one place a large rock five feet high which was invisible before, and narrowing the beach to that extent.

It is not uncommon for a sunken ship to be rapidly devoured by sand, especially sand that is so porous that you can push your arm into it with little effort. The most striking example of this is the HMS *Lutien,* a ship that sank in a heavy gale in the mouth of the Zuider Zee, in the Netherlands, in October 1799. She was heavily laden with bullion and coins. When she reached the bottom she barely stopped, plunging into the porous sand like a rock being dropped into silt.

The ship was insured by Lloyd's of London, which funded a salvage operation that proved ultimately to be unsuccessful. Only a small amount of gold was recovered despite numerous attempts to find the *Lutien's* treasure. One item salvaged was the ship's bell, which hangs in Lloyd's and is rung whenever there is an important announcement to be made.

The *Whydah's* booty was guarded by something more than the Cape's quicksand. The *Whydah,* like many other ships to wreck on the Cape, never reached the shore. Rather, she struck a sandbar and capsized in deep water, too deep and cold to be reached by even the most driven of beachcombers. As Southack made clear in one of his letters, there were no divers on the Cape because the water was so cold and the sandbars so dangerous, a fact that was officially put into writing by—of all organizations—the Humane Society of Cape Cod in the 1850s:

> Large, heavy ships strike on the [sandbars] even at high water; and their fragments only reach the shore. . . . Seamen shipwrecked at full sea, ought to remain on board till near low water; for the vessel does not then break to pieces; and by attempting to reach the land before the tide ebbs away, they are in great danger of being drowned. On this subject there is one opinion only among judicious mariners. It may be necessary however to remind them of a truth, of which they have full conviction, but which, amidst the agitation and terrour of a storm, they too frequently forget.

This sort of advice was not pertinent to Bellamy's pirates, whose ship capsized on the sandbar hours before low water and gave none of them the option of remaining on board. But the warning about the risk of drowning between ship and shore was the kind heeded by the salvage-hungry Cape

Codders. They knew the danger of the savage sea and they opted not to go to the *Whydah*.

I was convinced that the bulk of the treasure and everything else heavier than water was still out there at the wreck site. As Southack put it so succinctly in 1717, "the riches with the guns would be buried in the sand." Although I knew that this was true, I didn't know what patch of sand they were under.

I began to study Southack's writings as if they were holy scriptures. I analyzed every word, considered every nuance. I was convinced that the clue to the *Whydah*'s exact location was somewhere in his work and that I just hadn't figured it out yet. I knew I would be relying only on hints. No map existed with an actual *X* to mark the spot. Southack never wanted to return to the *Whydah,* so he wasn't precise about the site's whereabouts.

Still, Southack was a mapmaker, and a meticulous one at that. By force of habit, he must have noted something that would provide a clue to the ship's exact location. Even on a subconscious level, I reasoned, a man who makes maps is always noting his location.

The need to find the exact spot where the ship lay was both a blessing and a curse. If the *Whydah* were in clear water or even in the type of location where it could be snagged with a net, then finding it would have been no trick. The ship would also have been found already by someone else. In that sense, the curse of rough seas and a sandy grave was a blessing to me. A blessing, that is, if I could find clues to her location.

Since Southack was the only person to have written about the site of the wreck in 1717, the study of his work became my life. Copies of his maps were taped to the walls of my home office. One of the maps, from a zoology book in the Harvard University library, referred to Billingsgate as "the place where I came through with a Whale Boat being ordered by the Governor to look after the Pirate Ship Whido Bellame Command cast away 26 of April 1717 where I buried one Hundred and Two men Drowned." On the shoreline above Billingsgate is written, "The treasure ship Whido lost." There is no *X* to mark the spot, only Southack's crabbed writing over an area of the map that covers about ten miles of ocean.

On either side of Southack's charts I posted newer maps and aerial photos of the coast. They revealed little, other than the obvious fact that the Cape had bent substantially to the northwest in 250 years. Southack's work showed a Cape that protruded like the arm of a muscleman flexing his biceps, east from Buzzard's Bay at the bottom of Massachusetts and then directly north at a right angle, its end curling inward like a fist. Contemporary satellite photos show that wind and water erosion have tilted the Cape to the northwest. Wherever the *Whydah* was when she hit the shore, she was now at least two hundred feet farther out to sea.

Day after day, and usually night after night, I pored over Southack's letters and diary. At first, the old mapmaker's handwriting was extremely difficult to read. Flourishes from capital letters collided with other letters on other lines, his spelling was bad, and his syntax was all off. Reading him was at first painfully difficult, but gradually it became second nature.

As I read his work over and over, I began to pick up on certain geographical reference points. I would then mark these points on the maps with colored pins.

For example, on May 4 Southack wrote of pieces of cable that he had transported from the site of the *Whydah* to a boat moored in a bayside town. Taking the cable to a vessel on the seaboard side would have been too dangerous because there was "no harbor in 25 miles of the wreck." By examining his map I could see that Cape Cod Harbor, now known as Provincetown Harbor, was twenty-five miles away from Eastham Beach (in an area now known as Marconi Beach). I drew a line from Provincetown to Eastham that represented twenty-five miles and pushed in a pin. I did the same on a number of the wall maps.

Another entry referred to the wreck being three and one-half miles from Billingsgate. I was able to locate Billingsgate on Southack's map, but it was missing from all of the others. A victim of the Cape's shifting shape, Billingsgate had sunk more than a hundred years ago. The last reference I saw to this submerged town was in Thoreau's book *Cape Cod,* in a passage where Eastham locals were telling him how the Cape had changed shape over the years.

> The old oysterman had told us that many years ago he lost a "crittur" by her being mired in a swamp near the Atlantic side east of his house, and twenty years ago he lost the swamp itself entirely, but has since seen signs of it appearing on the beach. He also said that he had seen cedar stumps "as big as cartwheels" on the bottom of the Bay three miles off Billingsgate Point, when leaning over the side of his boat in pleasant weather, and that that was dry land not long ago.

To make an accurate measurement on my maps I had to visit the public library and consult a number of local histories. Within a few days I learned that only part of Billingsgate was underwater. The rest of the town was still part of Wellfleet.

I set out to find the Billingsgate church that was used in 1717, assuming that Southack set his distance from the town center. The church itself was gone, but the graveyard that surrounded it was still there on the fringe of modern Wellfleet. I used the site of the graveyard as my reference point. I marked the maps and felt the satisfaction of being that much closer to my goal.

Another reference point in Southack's writings was the location of Samuel Harding's farm. In his letter to the governor, Southack described the location of Harding's house, putting it at "two miles from the Rack."

In hopes of finding yet another reference point, I contacted Slade Associates, a surveyor in Wellfleet. From them I hoped to find exactly where the Harding residence had been. Admittedly, I was looking for a needle in a haystack, since Harding's house was small and probably hadn't existed in at least one hundred years. Still, I had to give it a try.

I didn't tell the surveyor why I was looking for the Harding house, only that I had an interest in local history. He didn't seem to care so much about the "why" of searching for Harding as he did about the "how."

"When did you say the house was built?" he asked.

"I don't know. I just know it was there in 1717."

"Did he own the farm?" asked the surveyor.

"I assume he did," I said. "His brother Abiah lived nearby, so maybe you should include him in the search."

"I'll do that," said the surveyor. I could hear him taking notes on the other end of the line, but I didn't feel too optimistic about finding this landmark. The information I had given him was sketchy, and the time period was so distant that I didn't know if legal records were still in existence.

But the meticulous record keeping of the British paid off. Within a week, I received a call from the surveyor, who was able to tell me exactly where the Harding house had once stood. With the information he provided, I was able to walk to the property and find the probable foundation of Harding's house, where an angry Southack had demanded that Harding return his salvage to the king.

It was another reference point that I could mark on the wall maps with colored pushpins.

7

X Marks the Spot

❋ The pushpins in the wall maps might as well have been in my brain, too. I was obsessed with the *Whydah*. I thought about her day and night, and began to wonder if anything short of having a girlfriend could possibly be as damaging to my marriage as hunting for a sunken ship. I began to understand what Joseph Conrad meant when he said, "There are few things as powerful as treasure, once it fastens itself on the mind."

There were daily signs of my overt obsession. Sometimes I would sit at the breakfast table with my wife and children and open the newspaper. After actually reading two or three lines of a story I would start thinking about the *Whydah*. Then I would "zone out," and not even see the page anymore. Instead, I would see those maps in my mind, with the treacherous Cape coastline, hoping that a picture of the ship would suddenly emerge.

A loud cough by my daughter would bring me back to the table. "Dad forgot how to read again," she would say, and I would manage a lame laugh.

One day I was sitting at a stoplight when, in my mind, the face of Cyprian Southack materialized. It was as though he were standing in front of me, a scowl of concern on his face as he scanned the terrain for landmarks. He had a map in his hand, and I knew for certain that he was looking for the *Whydah*. I was excited to have company in the search and may even have begun to talk to him had the honking horn of the car behind me not brought me back into the real world.

I wasn't sleeping well, either.

It was not uncommon for me to spring out of bed at night and race to the map room when a thought struck me just before I drifted off to sleep. Even sleep itself was no protection against obsessive thoughts. I would dream of finding the *Whydah,* or of missing an obvious clue as to her whereabouts. Sometimes I even dreamed of being a crew member in those last few moments when everyone was still alive and terrified at having hit the sandbar.

I loved and detested these early days of the search. Everything I did felt infused with purpose and drive. I have always thrown myself headlong into whatever I am doing, but for the first time in my life, I had the sense of being a man with a mission. My gradual immersion in history gave me a different awareness of my surroundings. As I walked through the colonial towns of the Cape in search of clues, I realized that Southack and Bellamy had walked these very streets at a time when the world was vastly different from the one I walked through now. The size of the buildings, especially their doorways and rooms, told me that most colonists were about as large as our average high school freshmen. This size discrepancy was a result of nutrition: ours is far better than theirs was. The lifespans carved into the gravestones of the colonial cemeteries show they died much younger than we do, largely as a result of diseases controlled so easily by modern medicine that we take the cures for granted.

Living with a constant sense of history made me feel rooted in the era of the *Whydah*. Day by day, I felt a stronger kinship with my forefathers and a deeper understanding of their thought processes.

On the other hand, I discovered that undersea exploration, at least at this phase, is a lonely profession. Finding the target area for the *Whydah* on a map was something I did largely alone, partly out of the need for deep concentration and partly out of paranoia. I had no one to share my thoughts with, nor anyone with whom I could trade ideas. At this stage of the search, I wanted it this way. My experience with the *General Arnold* had convinced me that no one could be trusted when treasure was involved. I did not want to find the *Whydah* on a map only to have someone else try to stake a claim to the area before I did. The fear of having my claim jumped kept me isolated throughout much of my early search.

The problem with this approach was that isolation had a way of limiting my vision, of keeping me from seeing the obvious clues that would help the watery X emerge on the map. If I had been working with another researcher, I am sure that the X would have been obvious much sooner than it was. I had become so close to the project that I couldn't see the X for all the pushpins.

Then one day it all came together. I was standing in the map room, looking at all the pins, when I decided to connect the dots. I drew a line from Billingsgate to the general area of the wreck site and then followed suit with lines from Provincetown and Harding's house. Where they crossed at the shoreline gave me a sort of X.

I knew this spot wasn't totally accurate, but it was as close as I could get without getting wet. And getting wet, by the way, was out of the question.

If I donned my wet suit and started gathering artifacts from the site, I would never be given a permit to excavate the spot by the Massachusetts Board of Underwater Archaeological Resources (MBUAR). This state regulatory agency, founded in 1973 as "the sole trustee of the Commonwealth's underwater heritage," puts its members in control of underwater sites, which, according to their charter, charges them with the "responsibility of encouraging the discovery and reporting, as well as the preservation and protection, of underwater archaeological resources." Among their strictest rules is one forbidding the collection of artifacts without permits. This rule has a way of hampering discovery, since the board will not issue a permit without artifacts from the wreck in question first being delivered to the board.

These rules presented a catch-22, but one that I was able to circumvent with a little effort. I had a man with a metal detector scour the sandy beach in front of the presumed wreck site. He found several nails, ship fittings, and other pieces of metal that might have belonged to the *Whydah*. I took photos of these objects and combined them with the historical and survey research.

Then I experienced a stroke of luck. I had just finished speaking about the *Whydah* to the Wellfleet Historical Society and was gathering my lecture material to leave when a beautiful elderly woman approached. She was frail and nervous yet very determined to tell me something in private. Other members of the audience were asking me questions, but she just stood there in silence, gripping her handbag with both hands and quivering like a nervous bird. It wasn't until everyone left that she came closer and spoke.

"My grandfather used to find coins on that beach all the time," she said, her Cape Cod ancestry betrayed by her accent.

"What did they look like?" I asked, excited by the fact that someone finally knew of *someone* who had gathered riches from the wreck.

"They weren't quite round, but they were gold," she said. "They were uneven circles with crosses and letters and numbers on them."

She was describing *escudos,* coins minted by the Spanish in South America and loaded onto galleons for the trip to Spain. These coins were probably made from religious artifacts of the Incan Indians that were melted down by Indian goldsmiths, who were literally destroying their own culture at the direction of their Spanish overlords. This gold was re-formed into coins that were then stamped with the mark of the mint where they were made. Some of these mint marks look like large crosses, while others resemble tic-tac-toe games. Other defining letters or numbers on them reveal such information as the date of the coin and who made it.

"Did he just find these coins on the beach?" I asked.

"Yes, he had eagle eyes," said the woman. "He loved to find things. He said that a couple of times these coins were sitting on pedestals of sand, like a jeweler had come along and placed them there for display. Could that be possible, or was he just telling a tale to a child?"

"That's the way coins on the beach are often found," I said. "The wind blows the sand out from around them and they are left perched on a column of sand. Usually no one finds them and they are washed away in the next high tide."

"Well, my grandfather saw these coins," she said, warming to the discussion. "And he brought them home for us all to see."

"It's too bad you don't have them anymore," I said. "It would really help me get a permit from the board."

"Whoever said that I didn't have them anymore!" the woman exclaimed. "I've got 'em right here."

She held up her hand and there, dangling from a bracelet on her wrist, were eight shiny *escudos*. I took her hand and examined the gold discs. Since gold doesn't deteriorate in seawater, they were as perfect as the day they were minted. Each one had a deep gash across its face, as if someone had whacked it with a sword. As it turned out, that is exactly what had happened. I later discovered that pirates cut coins in half with their knives to divide them among the crew or to make sure they were not counterfeit.

"These are stunning," I said, a grin breaking across my face.

The woman was smiling proudly and admiring her treasure bracelet as though she were seeing it for the first time.

"Mr. Clifford, do you realize what this is?" she asked. "This is just a little bit of what is out there. Somehow this washed ashore. The rest of it is still underwater, waiting to be found."

During the next several weeks, I thought many times about that woman and the coins she wore around her wrist. I knew there were more out there and I hoped that I would be allowed by the MBUAR to search the area.

I expected at least one of the members of the board to be difficult, and I prepared my case for that person, whoever he might be. I assembled all of Southack's writings on the subject of the *Whydah,* and prepared to show the board photographs of the site and samples of the artifacts that had been found with a metal detector on the beach. I was even prepared to talk about the old woman with the bracelet of gold coins if I had to. I planned to hold nothing back in my attempt to get a permit.

In the end, it was surprisingly easy to get the permit from the board members. I presented my evidence, and they were enthralled by what they saw

Gold coin.

and heard. One of the board members even offered to help me search for the *Whydah,* and all of them wished me luck.

They issued a reconnaissance permit in my name, which would allow me to locate artifacts without bringing any to the surface. The permit declared that this searching had to be done with "minimal site disturbance," which seemed illogical, since the sea had been disturbing the site for 265 years.

Still, I didn't argue. It was a start, and I was more than ready to start searching for the *Whydah.*

8

The Mel Fisher Show

The gold chain Mel Fisher let me wear shows why he was the world's best-known treasure hunter.

✵ Seeing treasure for the first time is almost a spiritual experience, one that transforms you. The story of Teddy Tucker illustrates this point. In 1955, this adventurer decided to explore a spot in the sea ten miles off Hamilton Harbor in Bermuda where he had discovered cannon and musket balls five years earlier. A storm had recently passed over the area and, on this particular day, the bottom was clear of sand.

Tucker dove down with just a face mask and found a bronze apothecary's mortar with the date "1561" stamped into its side. Excited, he returned to the boat and put on a shallow-water diving mask that connected to an air compressor and went back down for a longer search.

Using a board to fan the area where he had found the mortar, Tucker uncovered a handful of silver coins. He was breathing heavily now as a new future became visible before his very eyes. Another swipe of the board revealed a gold cube that he picked up and examined with awe.

Tucker was in such a rush to reach the surface and show his brother-in-law what he had found that he rammed his head hard into the bottom of the boat, nearly ending his treasure-hunting career right there.

When he dumped his glittering find in the bottom of their boat, Tucker and his brother-in-law became instant treasure hunters. The next day they dove on the site again. Pistols stuck in coral attracted their attention, so they chopped them out with axes. It wasn't until they brought them to the surface that they realized that the coral held more than two hundred French and Spanish coins, the most recent dated 1592. Tucker also found several muskets and three gold buttons studded with pearls.

A storm kept the treasure hunters away from the site for the next three days, but it didn't keep Tucker from dreaming about it. In his dreams, he kept seeing a bright yellow brain coral near the spot where he found the buttons. He fanned the area directly beneath the coral and discovered a gold ingot and two smaller pieces of gold. When he told the dreams to his wife, she insisted they were omens of a bigger find to come.

She was right. On his next dive, Tucker found the brain coral and, within ten minutes, two ingots of gold, one weighing two pounds.

Tucker found treasure a few days later that even he had not dreamed of. Using a high-pressure water hose to clear sand from the bottom, he uncovered a large hole. Sticking his head into the hole he saw a gold cross studded with seven emeralds, each the size of his thumb. It wasn't until a year later that the British Museum examined the find and declared the emeralds to be real. Museum officials estimated the cross's value at $200,000.

Months of detective work by Tucker showed the wreck was the *San Pedro,* a Spanish merchant ship lost in 1596 on a voyage from Mexico to Spain.

Tucker became a wreck hunter and found dozens of them in the waters of Bermuda. But he kept revisiting the site of the *San Pedro,* and he never left the site disappointed. For years he found gold and other artifacts there, enhancing his reputation as the finder of the ship with the emerald cross.

I wish I could say that my first dive on the *Whydah* was as fruitful as Tucker's discovery of the *San Pedro.* It wasn't. Rather, it was a sobering affair that left me to realize how much work there was ahead of me.

I began to prepare for the dive shortly after I received the permit from the archaeology board. It was already November 1982, and a tough time to be mounting an undersea adventure in the North Atlantic. The water can be fickle at that time of year, with the ocean calm one day and roiling like a beast the next three. Worried that my operation might be shut down by bad weather, I nevertheless decided to put together a group of experts to see what was down there. Who knows, I thought, maybe I'll be as lucky as Teddy Tucker.

The first person I invited was Mel Fisher, perhaps the world's best-known treasure hunter. It was Fisher, along with Kip Wagner, who discovered hundreds of gold and silver coins and other artifacts from the same fleet of Spanish ships that had attracted Black Sam Bellamy to the coast of Florida in 1715. A 1965 *National Geographic* article pictured their treasures and reveled in their exploits. Fisher's discovery of the *Nuestra Señora de Atocha* in 1973 caught everyone's attention. This Spanish galleon contained as much as $400 million worth of treasure, according to some experts. For better and for worse, Fisher became the focal point of treasure hunting. Many people were put off by him. He was a braggart who sometimes annoyingly flaunted the gold he had found.

He was also someone who had suffered immensely to pursue his dream. His son and daughter-in-law had both drowned in a tug accident during the search for the galleon, a search that had driven Fisher to the brink of bankruptcy several times. He had been sued by investors, taken to court by the United States government, and accused by outraged archaeologists of destroying shipwrecks.

Still, Fisher was an optimist, and a reckless one at that. He had stopped at nothing to keep the legal rights to the *Atocha,* battling the state of Florida for the rights to the ship. In the end, Fisher won his fight with the state.

I had spent time on the telephone with Fisher. One of the first pieces of advice that he gave me was to "find a good lawyer and pay him on time." It turned out to be the most sound advice I received from anyone for years to come. On matters of wreck hunting, he was patient and knowledgeable. Now that I had my reconnaissance permit, I wanted to include him in the first dive.

When I finally got him on the telephone, he was clearly preoccupied with his own legal problems in Miami. He was being sued by another treasure hunter for possession of the *Santa Margarita,* another of his shipwrecks, and the court proceedings were all that he could talk about. Between that and mechanical problems with his boat, Fisher said he only had time for his own work.

One week later, everything changed. The courts awarded Fisher the rights to the *Santa Margarita,* and he was feeling like a free man. He called me at eleven o'clock on a weeknight to tell me the good news about his court case. Then he said he would fly up to the Cape.

"Great," I said. "When will you be here?"

There was a rustle on his end of the line as he shuffled through papers.

"I'll be there at nine in the morning," he declared. "I'll bring a magnetometer and Fay Feild with me to operate the thing. You do have a boat, don't you?"

I didn't. I was between boats at the moment, and the challenge of finding one on such short notice was daunting. I called a friend, John Beyer, and asked him if he knew anyone who had what I needed.

"I can only think of one person," said Beyer. "There is a giant named Stretch Grey who owns a boat that is the right size for this operation. He's a lobsterman though, so he has to get up early to do his job. I don't think he would appreciate being called at this time of night."

"I have to call him," I insisted. "I need a boat and I'm desperate."

"Well, watch this one," said Beyer. "When I say he's a giant, I mean it, he's a real Goliath. And he doesn't have the best disposition sometimes. He moved to the Cape because he got pissed off at some guy in Nantucket and punched him. The guy didn't wake up for several days, and Stretch was hiding out because he thought the fellow was dead."

I got Grey's telephone number anyway and made the call. As the ringing started, I noticed that the time on my clock read midnight. I gulped and let it ring. Ten rings later he picked up the phone.

"What is it?" he growled.

I introduced myself and told him that I wanted to charter his boat to tow a magnetometer over the site of the *Whydah*. By now, several newspaper articles had appeared about my search, and I thought that Stretch might be impressed at receiving an emergency telephone call from a major local figure in the news. He wasn't. When I finished explaining what I wanted, he simply snorted and hung up.

He was friendlier when I called him at seven the next morning. He listened again to what I wanted and then offered to charter his boat for one day.

"I want to know what's down there, too," he declared.

We agreed to meet at the dock that afternoon.

We never made it out that day. Fisher's airplane was late, and by the time he arrived on the Cape, it was late afternoon and rapidly approaching sundown.

Fisher was wearing a summer jacket and lightweight khaki pants, unsuitable dress for the cool weather of New England. Feild, tall and thin with a mustache and a tweed overcoat and golf hat, could have been dressed for an appointment with a New England banker. The only article of clothing that would have set him apart at a conference table of bankers was a large gold coin glistening from a gold chain that hung outside of his tie. Each of them wore one of these coins, which Fisher described as a "royal strike worth a hundred thousand dollars."

In the backseat of the car was a puzzled-looking man who introduced himself as John. He had been listening to their stories of treasure hunting on the airplane from Florida, he explained, and in his excitement said that he might want to become an investor. They invited him along.

The rest of the day was the Mel Fisher show. He talked about his search for sunken treasure and the endless travails involved in fighting the government. His battles with state and federal authorities had been legion. On this particular day, Fisher seemed to have no interest in searching for another sunken ship.

We talked until evening, then went to eat at Provincetown's Red Inn. At first, Fisher was much too loud for the evening dinner crowd. We received some angry stares as Fisher brayed on about his activities in Florida. John, the would-be investor they had brought from the airplane, became embarrassed by the loud talk and excused himself from the table, not to return until much later. It was too bad for him, because he missed the main attraction. Shortly after he left, the angry stares turned to curious ones as the diners picked up on our conversation. In minutes, about the time Fisher began telling about a mound of gold he had uncovered by accident, most of the people in the restaurant had stopped talking so they could hear the tales of treasure.

A woman at a neighboring table began to take notes, I assume to recount the overheard conversation later to her children. Another patron repositioned his chair to face us, brazenly listening as Fisher talked. It was as though he were listening to a lecture at some explorers' club. With very little effort, Mel Fisher had gone from gauche nuisance to center of attention.

Suddenly, he got up from the table and walked out of the restaurant, only to return lugging a bar of gold. There was an audible gasp as he took a couple of labored steps and theatrically dropped the gold on the floor.

"It's too heavy to carry it all," he said to no one in particular. "Can I get some help with that one?"

Chairs shuffled as patrons scrambled to their feet. Before any of them could reach the gold bar, a waitress picked it up with both hands and carried it to our table following Fisher, who still seemed to be laboring under a significant weight.

"Take a look at this," he said, pulling gold artifacts from his pockets and dropping them onto the table. A small pile of chains, coins, jewelry, and bars grew in front of us, worth perhaps $500,000. The dining room was dead silent.

"That's what you'll find if you look hard enough," he said. "I had to look damned hard to find this. But it's out there if you keep your eyes open."

And sure enough, as I looked around the restaurant all the patrons had their eyes wide open in stunned disbelief. As we left, I could tell from the wishful thinking on the faces of most of the customers that their lives would not be the same for several days.

9
—
A Sahara of Sand

✳ The next morning we boarded Stretch Grey's boat and headed around the tip of Cape Cod for the Atlantic Ocean. In addition to the four of us, I brought John F. Kennedy, Jr. The son of the late president had worked for me the summer on my salvage boat in Martha's Vineyard. After hearing so many stories about the search for the *Whydah,* young Kennedy wanted to be a part of the "magging" operation (locating wreckage with a magnetometer). He would spend the next three days with us, and eventually make the first official dive on the assumed wreck site itself.

The plan was to map the site using the magnetometer that Fay Feild had brought with him. A magnetometer, extremely heavy and shaped like a small torpedo, is the best instrument to use to locate artifacts. It would respond to metal by registering a "hit" on a strip chart that Feild had set up in the boat's cabin.

A hit means that the mag has detected some kind of ferrous metal, something made of iron or steel. As the mag was towed over the ocean's bottom, a strip of paper would reel out as a stylus drew a line on it. Regular ocean bottom registered as a relatively straight line, while metal made the pen jump. The larger the metal object, the sharper the jump. Each jump of the stylus would be noted on a map by Feild.

As we rounded Race Point and headed down the Atlantic side of the Cape, Mel Fisher told me about one of his greatest "mag moments," the discovery of the *Santa Margarita* off the Florida coast.

"We didn't know where that ship was," he said, shouting over the drone of the boat's diesel engine. "We had historical information that put the wreck either east or west of the *Atocha,* and as far as three miles away. That's a lot of ocean. Unfortunately, we didn't have much time to find the *Margarita.* Other salvage companies were moving in, and we were afraid that they would find it before us. We had to move quickly."

To expedite matters, Fisher called a meeting of his search crews. Over a large map, they shared information about the search area, including archival letters dating to the 1600s, random mag hits, and depth charts. At the end of the session, Fisher and four of his most experienced hunters all drew circles around the areas they thought might contain the *Margarita*. Then the search began.

"Feild here had just developed his new magnetometer, and we wanted to test it out," said Fisher. "It was damned expensive—I wanted to make sure it was worth the money."

The mag was installed on Captain Robert Jordan's boat and towed through the water west of the *Atocha* site. Back and forth, like a tractor plowing, the boat plied the ocean. The pen barely moved on the strip chart. After conferring with Fisher, Jordan took his boat, the *Castillian,* to one of the eastern sites and started the search all over again. This time, at the edge of a wide sandbar, the pen jumped sharply. A diver was sent down and found a six-foot copper cooking cauldron, a grapnel hook, and three small anchors.

"A little ways away, we found a bunch of pottery and four Spanish coins," said Fisher. "We cleaned those coins and found that they were minted in 1621, the same period as the *Atocha*. We knew we had her then."

The rest of Fisher's story was a treasure hunter's dream. Gold and silver were found exposed on the ocean bottom; no digging was even required to bring it up. One gold bar, weighing more than four pounds, was just sitting next to a bed of coral. Clumps of coins were found, dozens of them. Amid broken pottery and human bones were silver plates, a sword, the ship's bell, and a navigator's broken astrolabe.

The most visually spectacular portion of the wreck did not register on the magnetometer. Fisher's son Kane dove on the site and found six silver bars, evenly spaced and sitting on bedrock. Towing the ingots to the surface, he looked down and could see the wooden ribs of the ship sticking up, delicate survivors of more than 350 years of the ocean's erosive power.

"Hell, I didn't know wood could last that long underwater," said Fisher. "It really should have just turned into sawdust and floated away."

The *Santa Margarita* site was a bonanza of gold, silver, and artifacts, including a cannonball fashioned from stone quartz. So plentiful was the treasure that it gave rise to a severe case of gold fever in Captain Jordan. He weighed anchor and left for Key West with a boat full of treasure. There, in a fit of poor judgment, he filed claim to the wreck site and all of its artifacts. It took several court rulings to convince Jordan that it was his employer, Treasure Salvors, who owned the *Margarita*. Since the last of those rulings would not come for several months, Fisher was still slightly nervous at the thought that his claim might be jumped by an employee. He hadn't lost his sense of humor, though.

"See the kind of trouble your super-mag got me into?" he shouted at Feild.

I was hoping for some of that same trouble. As Stretch steered careful parallel passes back and forth over the presumed wreck site, I dreamed about the search I would soon undertake. In my mind's eye I imagined the wreck of the *Whydah* looking just like the *Margarita*. For a moment I was floating above her, gazing down through my face mask at a broken, three-masted galley. The deck was still in place and a hatch lay invitingly open. I took a breath and headed for the hatch. Beyond it lay the booty of fifty ships, including gold doubloons and pieces of eight. It would be the easiest find in the history of treasure hunting. Why hadn't anybody else found it before me?

"That's a big something down there," said Fisher, bringing me back to reality.

The needle that measured hits was jumping sporadically and Feild was carefully marking the position of those hits on the map, using our Loran coordinates to provide the greatest accuracy. Mel was looking over Feild's shoulder, jumping and nodding in rhythm with the meter. At times it looked like Fisher was listening to a jazz band, the meter was so active.

The treasure-hunting team of Fisher and Feild was an impressive sight. Once the mag's needle started to jump, they left the storytelling behind and began concentrating on the hits measured on the strip chart. There were plenty of them. At one point Fisher looked up and said, "Christ, Barry, it looks like every shipwreck in the world is down there."

That was no great overstatement. By some estimates there might be as many as six thousand ships nestled in the shifting sands of Cape Cod. That amounts to about a hundred ships per mile, an astounding amount of carnage for what seems to be such a benign finger of land.

The concentration of shipwrecks along the Atlantic seaboard was made even greater by a nefarious group of criminals known as "moon cussers." These wreckers, rumored to have operated even into the twentieth century, would cause ships to crash into shore by sending them false signals. Once the ship wrecked, they would rob it of its goods. Sometimes they stood on the beach with a lantern and waved it at a ship, other times they would fasten a lantern to a horse and tie it to a stake so the animal would walk in circles, which is how Nag's Head, North Carolina, got its name. If things worked as planned, the ship would be misled by the light and turn too soon, thinking the light marked a safe passage. When the vessel ran aground, the wreckers would run out to it and help themselves to anything of value and murder any survivor who happened to be around. The criminals were called moon cussers because their method only worked on moonless nights when the shoreline wasn't visible. The remnants of their work littered the ocean floor off Cape Cod.

Some historians say that there were no such things as moon cussers, that it was just a myth started by old-time Cape Codders with a wicked sense of humor. In some cases, the myth may have been more powerful than reality.

Take the Italian bark *Monte Tabor,* for example. She wrecked on the night of September 14, 1896, on Peaked Hill Bar, several miles north of the *Whydah* site. Six of the crew managed to float to shore by desperately clinging to the wreckage of the cabin while another made it through the surf on his own. Five men died. The bodies of Captain Luigi Genero and seaman Ippolito Biago were found with their throats cut. The steward was found with a bullet in his head.

Murder was initially suspected, but at the inquest the testimony of the cabin boy, together with a message in a bottle hurled overboard by Captain Genero, indicated possible suicide—out of fear that they would be murdered by moon cussers!

Whether caused by moon cussers or the tumult of the elements, it was not uncommon in years past for the seashore to be littered with human remains from a ship that had struck the outer bar and had its crew disgorged by the sweeping surf.

Thoreau once found himself on a windswept beach near Eastham after a ship had wrecked there. He found a dead sailor whose body had been badly mangled by a shark. The sight stunned him, and the raw splendor of the ocean that he was enjoying took on a dark and terrible beauty. Suddenly, he said, the hollow roar of the ocean became overwhelmingly loud, as if "that dead body had taken possession of the shore, and reigned over it as no living one could."

For weeks after his sighting, beachcombers reported finding cloth and tow ropes washing ashore from that wreck. They found nothing made of heavy metal, because it had sunk through the slushy sand and rested on the clay bedrock of the Cape, where we were now reading it or metal from some other wreck with the magnetometer.

We mapped the site for a couple of days, charting virtually every piece of metal that could be found. When Feild announced that he was finished, we gathered in the pilot house and looked at the map. It was a shotgun blast of pencil marks, circles of varying size with Loran coordinates written next to them. Hovering over the map, I felt a tingle of excitement in the pit of my stomach. As Fisher and Feild pondered the hits and guessed at which might be cannons, I could hear the voice of my uncle Bill as he told me his stories about the *Whydah.*

The legend of Black Sam Bellamy and the captured slave ship suddenly became real. I no longer questioned "if" I was going to find the *Whydah;* that seemed to be a sure thing. The question now was "How?" I remembered the words of a frustrated Cyprian Southack, who wrote, "the riches with the guns shall be buried in the sand." Now, modern technology had placed me over those guns, the spot that Southack had longed to find. Would I face a mountain of problems that would cause me to end up frustrated like the wily mapmaker? At this point, there was no way of knowing, but had I been able to look ahead there is a good chance I would have ended my search right then and there, with an *X* to mark the spot and enough stories to get free meals up and down the Cape for years to come.

"Why don't you go down and take a look?" said Fisher. "We are right over some of the strongest hits. You might find something right now."

I had brought a wet suit and scuba tank for just that purpose, and now I had Kennedy suit up. This would be the first dive on the site, and I hoped for the same luck that Fisher had with the *Margarita,* an immediate sighting of gold bars, followed by a cannon or two and then the spiny ribs of the ship. Instant treasure!

Kennedy lowered himself into the icy ocean and slipped beneath the waves. The November light, so clear and sharp on the surface, sent soft beams streaming into the water. He followed them down. The wave action whipped up grains of sand and soon the visibility was as limited as in a desert sandstorm. Kennedy dropped headfirst, farther and farther, until his face mask was almost against the sand bottom. Then he righted himself and looked around.

The ribs of the *Whydah's* hull were not visible, nor was any other part of her, for that matter. All he could see was sand.

He followed his bubbles up and surfaced next to the boat. Three faces peered over the side at Kennedy as he tipped his face mask back and removed the regulator from his mouth.

"It looks like an underwater version of the Sahara Desert," he said. "There's nothing down there but sand."

Great, I thought. Wherever the *Whydah* is located, it will be under feet and tons of sand.

I sighed, thinking about all the time this excavation would take, and all the money. The money worried me the most. There is no hole more expensive than one that has to be dug on the bottom of the ocean.

Fisher looked toward the shore at the mountain of sand that made up the cliffs of Marconi Beach. They were at least sixty feet high and dropped to a sandy beach that was being pounded by surf clouded with large granules of sand. There wasn't a rock in sight, just sand.

"I guess that makes sense," he said, helping Kennedy up the ladder and into the boat. "There's nothing around here but sand, anyway."

10

Sage Advice

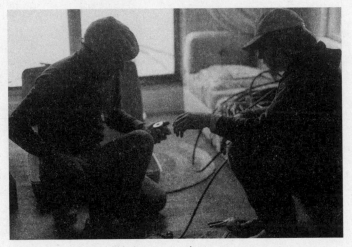

Fay Feild, left, repairs the magnetometer.

❋ Fisher and Feild stayed on Cape Cod for several days after that initial dive. I rented a small house for them in Truro and moved in with them to hear what they had to say about wreck diving. In many ways, it was like a kung fu student moving into the master's cave. Just being in their presence and listening to their stories was a form of education as well as motivation.

Fisher and Feild were hard-core treasure hunters who researched lost ships like the most meticulous of archaeologists. They spent much of their time, along with Dr. Eugene Lyon, examining the shipping records of old Spain to find out the exact route the treasure ships took. Before they even started looking for their ships, they had studied the complete record of the vessel itself and the particular fleet in which it was sailing. There were many instances in which Fisher and company knew more about the Spanish gold fleets than the most well-versed historians. But because their livelihood was in selling the sunken treasure they found, they were vilified by the archaeological community, where treasure hunters are on a par with grave robbers.

At this point I didn't know if I wanted to be considered an archaeologist or treasure hunter. After all, famed underwater explorer Jacques Cousteau was a treasure hunter. At one time, he had even purchased a wreck site from Fisher to film a treasure hunt for his television program. In fact, a number of very good undersea archaeologists had learned their trade from Mel Fisher and now refused to admit it.

Although I was not sure in which camp I belonged, I did know that Fisher and Feild knew more than anybody about finding and recovering objects from sunken ships. I was glad that they had come to the Cape. By the end of their stay, I had a good idea of the formidable task of excavation that lay ahead.

The big problem, said Fisher, was the sand, which at twenty feet was deeper on this site than any he had ever worked on. To his way of thinking that was both the blessing and curse of this project. Had there been no sand to trap the *Whydah,* most of her booty would have been scattered by the Atlantic currents that brush roughly against the Cape. Anything too heavy to be swept away would have been easy prey for almost anyone else who tried to look for this wreck in the last 265 years.

"Without the sand, the *Whydah* would have broken up and floated away like a wheat field in a tornado," said Fisher.

As it was, the sand held firmly to the ship and all her booty—cannons, gold, trapped dead bodies, pistols—shuffling it down until everything was resting on the clay subsurface that forms the underpinnings of the Cape. This shuffling action of the sand engulfs objects so completely that sometimes little oxygen reaches them, which can prevent oxidizing. Sometimes even wood can be preserved by this encapsulation process and preserved for hundreds of years.

A great example of this was the *Slot ter Hooge,* a silver-laden ship that wrecked off the coast of Portugal in 1724. Treasure hunter Robert Stenuit found the ship's anchor on the first day of his search, but the rest of her was buried underneath a deep layer of sand. In 1974, he used airlifts to suck up several tons of sand and expose hundreds of artifacts. His most valuable find was a stack of more than one hundred silver bars, all held neatly in place by a well-preserved wooden timber from the *Slot's* broken hull. The sand had been so effective in its encapsulation that the wood had remained in one piece for more than two centuries.

When the mailboxes are lowered, the prop wash is directed straight down where it clears sand and leaves artifacts exposed.

Of course, objects in the grip of sand are not easily wrestled free. You must dig or blow or suck sand away before getting your hands on the object. Then you must work fast before the sand sweeps back in and covers it.

Fisher was an expert at moving sand. His first big find, the *Wedge* wreck near Vero Beach, Florida, was found after Fisher and Feild developed a device that diverts a boat's prop wash straight down, blowing sand away to create a deep, cone-shaped hole. Called "mailboxes" because they look like giant metal versions of their namesake, these contraptions stick out from the back of a boat like rocket engines until they are dropped vertically at right angles to the boat and aimed at the sea floor.

Originally the mailbox was developed for a different purpose. Plagued by murky water that obscured their view of the *Wedge* wreck, Fisher and Feild pondered ways to make the water clear. They developed the mailbox as a means of pushing clear water from the surface to the sea bottom. It sounded like a crazy idea, but it was one they had to try anyway. Fisher built a deflector out of sheet metal and attached it to the back of his boat with a huge hinge plate.

The first time he tried the device they were able to follow a column of clear water that spread out into a "bubble" of clarity once it hit the sandy bottom. From inside the bubble they could clearly see an area that had been inky black only moments before. When they revved the engine, they received a benefit that they hadn't counted on. The prop wash dug a crater about six feet deep in the sand, exposing an area that would have required substantial work to suck up with the suction hose.

Now, to hear Fisher tell it, no device was more valuable to undersea wreck exploration than the mailbox.

"The second wreck I used the mailbox on really proved its value to me," said Fisher. "We were at a site near Fort Pierce beach in Florida where people had been finding Spanish coins for years from the 1715 wreck. We searched for a long time and didn't find much. Then I had a feeling that if we moved five hundred yards out to sea, we would find something."

Following Fisher's hunch, the crew moved the boat and then dropped four anchors, two on the stern and two on the bow, to hold it stable while they dropped the mailboxes and revved the engines. Within minutes, the wash cut a hole about fifteen feet in diameter that exposed a virtual carpet of gold coins. For several days, divers stuffed coins into bags and brought them to the boat. By the end of the summer, the so-called Colored Beach Wreck had yielded almost four thousand gold coins, more than six thousand silver coins, and assorted pieces of precious gold jewelry.

"I would have had a hard time finding a third of that without my mailboxes," Fisher said.

Handheld metal detectors were also important pieces of equipment. I would need them to pinpoint the location of objects and to tell how deeply they were buried in the sand. Now we locate objects with a state-of-the-art Trimble DGPS, which has totally revolutionized wreck finding. Back then, I would also need a Loran receiver and detailed charts to plot the locations of objects on a map. A crew of about ten would also be necessary to run the operations on the boat, said Fisher, with at least six of them certified to dive. And to put this army of men and technology over the wreck site, I would need a large boat with the capacity to hold everyone comfortably.

"The boat should have a big cabin for all the electronics gear and a couple of cranes that are capable of bringing up objects as large as cannon," said

Fisher. "Oh yeah, the boat should be wooden. A metal hull sometimes interferes with the magnetometer."

Since I had been in the salvage business for some time, I knew firsthand most of the techniques Fisher was describing. He did give me one piece of advice that seemed puzzling at the time. After a long talk about equipment and technique, Fisher declared that the most important attribute I could possess would be mental stability. He told me to stay realistic and focused on the work, not on the millions of dollars I thought I would bring up. He suggested that I try to keep the crew from thinking about the treasure, too.

"For some reason, daydreaming leads to paranoia and greed," said Fisher, on his last night in town. "Those things can infect a crew like a deadly virus."

"What do you mean?" I asked.

"Do you remember that Humphrey Bogart movie about treasure?" asked Fisher.

"*The Treasure of the Sierra Madre?*" I asked.

"That's the one," said Fisher. "Boy, they got that movie right. The only difference between them and me was that those guys were going crazy from gold fever in the desert instead of on a boat."

I remembered the plot of the classic movie as being a slow march toward greed and paranoia. Bogart plays a down-and-out character who hears about a rich vein of gold hidden in the Sierra Madre mountains in Mexico. He and a group of treasure hunters with nefarious pasts go into the mountains and mine the gold, only to be forced to fight with bandits to keep it. They fight with each other as well, gradually building walls of distrust, each suspecting the others are plotting to steal the gold dust.

On the trek across the desert and back to civilization, paranoia becomes their trail boss when suspicion turns to violence and one of the treasure hunters is shot by Dobbs, Bogart's character, and left for dead. Ultimately, Dobbs alone remains to face a group of bandits.

Though he pleads for his life, he is killed by them anyway. They steal his mules and supplies, but mistake the gold dust in his saddlebags for sand. One of them drives a knife into the bags, and the gold dust pours onto the ground. As Bogart dies, a windstorm blows the gold dust across the high desert plains and back toward the mountain where it came from.

"Whatever you do, don't get paranoid and crazy like Bogart did," said Fisher. "If your movie is going to have a happy ending, keep your wits about you."

"I'm just looking for a pirate ship," I said. "Right now I just plan to get friends involved in the search, guys I went to college with."

My naïveté made Fisher laugh. "It doesn't matter who is involved. Everything starts out friendly, but after a couple of coins or gold bars are found, then funny things start happening. Everyone divides up the treasure in his mind and starts wondering if his portion is going to be enough to live on the rest of his life. Can I live on a couple million? Do I really need four or five million dollars to be happy? How can I cut someone else out of the picture and get their portion? All of a sudden, friends become a liability, an added expense that they don't want anymore."

"I don't think that will happen with the guys I have in mind," I said confidently. "We are good friends, kind of like a fraternity."

"Well, if greed doesn't happen with them, it will happen from outside the fraternity," said Fisher. "As soon as you smell gold and file a claim, ten other guys are going to show up at the claims office and say that they smelled it first."

"That hasn't happened yet, and I've already filed a claim," I said.

"Maybe you'll be lucky, but make sure you have a good attorney just in case," said Fisher. "I know what gold does to men's souls. Don't let it do it to yours or you're finished."

I grinned nervously and nodded as though I knew what Fisher was talking about. In my heart, I was skeptical. I didn't foresee for one minute that many of my battles would be above the surface of the water with people I didn't even know yet or ones I thought would always be friends.

Looking back, I can say that Fisher's advice was the best I ever received.

11

A Free Prince in the Making

✳ After about a week in Wellfleet, Fisher announced that it was too cold
and time for him to leave. He was from Florida, and the Cape can be un-
bearable for a guy accustomed to warm winters. For me, the weather that
kept us from working presented a great time to study the past. A day or two
after Fisher and Feild left, I sat down next to my woodstove and began reading everything I could about the life and times of Sam Bellamy.

Up to this point, my perception of pirates was largely formed by the
stereotypes in movies I had seen and novels I had read. In my mind, pirates
fit the opposite extremes of personality types. A good number of them were
dark and cruel brutes, ready to maim and kill to get whatever they wanted.
Gnarled and crippled by the tough life they led, their gross physical defor-
mities matched the mental ones that guided their actions.

Typical of these was Long John Silver, the one-legged, eye-patch-wear-
ing, pistol-packing pirate invented by Robert Louis Stevenson in his novel
Treasure Island. I read that book and saw many of the Hollywood movies
that sprang from it. When I thought of devious pirates, the dangerous and
conniving Long John Silver played by Wallace Beery came to mind. Silver used his sense of humor to weave tall tales that enthralled the book's
young and innocent protagonist, Jim Hawkins, with whom I identified.
Yet beneath the pirate's charisma lurked a pure lust for gold that knew no
bounds. He was ruthless in his desire for the stuff.

So chilling and thuggish were Silver and the other pirates of *Treasure
Island* that I had a difficult time reconciling the other image of pirates that
Hollywood imprinted on my mind: the handsome and brilliant swash-
bucklers who fought against the establishment. Personified by Errol Flynn,

the strapping star of *Captain Blood,* these pirates were strong enough to swing through the ship's rigging like Tarzan and perform gymnastic stunts on the yardarm. They could fight lengthy sword battles with worthy opponents, drink anyone under the table, and deliver speeches that sprang eloquent and fully formed from their lips, with no speechwriter in between.

As it turned out, Bellamy represented a little bit of everything I had ever learned about pirates. He was a hearty mix of Long John Silver, Captain Blood, and many other characters as well, some saintly, some sinners. In many ways, his philosophy can be summed up by a couple of lines from *The Pirates of Penzance,* in which the Pirate King says, "Oh better far to live and die/Under the brave black flag I fly." Bellamy excelled at being a pirate, but profit wasn't his only motive. Bellamy was democratic as well, an egalitarian respected by his crew.

Bellamy best expressed what he stood for in an impromptu speech he is reported to have made during the last few days of his life. South of Rhode Island, Bellamy and his pirates came upon a sloop commanded by Captain Simon Beer, who was ordered on board the *Whydah* while his ship was being plundered. He pleaded to Bellamy for possession of his ship and must have done so quite effectively, because the pirate captain said he could have it back when the sacking was ended. Bellamy's order to return the ship to its rightful owner was overruled by his crew. This reversal of a captain's orders by his crew appalled Beer, who was accustomed to the dictatorship of captains in the merchant marine, not the democracy of pirates.

"Have you no control over your men?" Beer asked pointedly. "Or do they control you?"

The sharply worded questions angered Bellamy and inspired what was one of the most colorful speeches recorded in colonial America, part of which is quoted here from *A General History of the Pirates,* attributed to a "Captain Charles Johnson" but thought to have been written by Daniel Defoe.

"You are a devilish conscience rascal, damn you!" Bellamy replied.

I am a free Prince, and I have as much authority to make war on the whole world as he who has a hundred sail of ships at sea, and an army of 100,000 men in the field, and this my conscience tells me.

But there is no arguing with such sniveling puppies who allow superiors to kick them about deck at pleasure, and pin their faith upon a pimp of a parson, a squab, who neither practices nor believes what he puts upon the chuckle-headed fools he preaches to.

This speech, delivered in anger from the heaving deck of a captured slave ship, was Bellamy's credo. Beneath his feet was a ship filled with booty, enough to make him the most successful pirate of the early eighteenth century; surrounding him was a pleased and wealthy crew, men who had voted him captain and were now about to reap the rewards of their good choice. And this entire scene was taking place on a captured English slave ship, the *Whydah,* a symbol of oppression captured by free men.

Bellamy's life had not been an easy one, and it must have felt good to know he could now retire a rich and free man. There is, however, no indication that Bellamy planned to retire and become a free prince.

History isn't clear about the early life of Bellamy. Records show that he was probably born March 18, 1689, in Hittisleigh, Devonshire, near Plymouth. The sixth child of Elizabeth and Stephen Bellamy, he would be their last. Shortly after his birth, Elizabeth died of causes unknown, leaving Stephen to care for his children in the crushing poverty of English rural life.

With six children to care for, Stephen moved to Plymouth to take a factory job, exposing his young son to the variety of life that made this seafaring town both famous and infamous. Although no one can say for sure what profession young Bellamy was apprenticed to, it is certain that he heard many stories about pirates.

Pirates were the Robin Hoods of Plymouth. Like the legendary outlaw who stole from the rich, pirates gained their wealth from the privileged class. They robbed merchant ships, treated captured crewmen with respect, and punished brutal captains.

Plymouth was a breeding ground for pirates. The grandfather of them all was John Hawkins, whose work as a state-sponsored pirate, a "privateer," made him one of the richest men in England. His motto was not the sort one would expect from a pirate and reveals the uniqueness of this man. "Let every man serve God daily," he told his sailors. "Love one another, preserve your victuals, beware fire, and keep good company." This noted "sea dog," as privateers were known, took his first voyage from Plymouth to the African coast in 1562. In Guinea, he loaded his three ships with three hundred black slaves and sold them to the plantation owners of Hispaniola.

The tidy profit he made for his London investors caught the eye of Queen Elizabeth, who loaned him money and the warship *Jesus of Lubeck* to make another foray to the African coast, where he gathered four hundred slaves.

Once again, he sailed for South America, but this time he had more difficulty selling his human wares. Spanish authorities did not want the English trading with their colonies and had warned their settlers against doing business with Hawkins. But he persevered and was able to sell his slaves and his cargo of linen, wine, and flour for a substantial profit.

The Spanish were outraged that the British were trying to break their monopoly of trade with the New World. England, on the other hand, was delighted to discover this moneymaking opportunity. Again with the help of the queen, Hawkins assembled a third expedition, this one consisting of six ships. Commanding one of the ships was Hawkins's cousin, Francis Drake.

Fate and Spain conspired against the privateers again on this trip. It took several months of cruising the settlements of the African coast to trade for the slaves they needed to make a profit. When they crossed the Atlantic to South America, they found that, once again, the king of Spain had ordered his governors to "suffer" no trade with them. It was only through intimidation and the black market that Hawkins was able to sell his slaves and goods.

A storm forced the Hawkins fleet to seek shelter in Vera Cruz, Mexico, where he immediately captured the fort at San Juan de Ulua and waited for the Spanish treasure fleet to arrive from South America. Since this was one of Spain's secure ports, it was Hawkins's hope that the fleet commanders would arrive with their guard down. It must have been disheartening to see two fully armed warships amidst the Spanish galleons.

Still, Hawkins thought he could barter the fort for a portion of the treasure carried by the ships. As he was negotiating with the viceroy of New Spain, the Spanish were ordered to attack the British ships, and full-scale warfare broke out.

Hawkins and Drake barely escaped with their lives, and several of their men were killed. Drake made it back to Plymouth quickly and safely, but Hawkins ran low on food and water and was forced to put one hundred men ashore in Mexico who were pleading to be dropped off so they could find sustenance. Shortly after being put ashore, they were captured by the Spanish, who forced them into slavery for eight years.

Only Hawkins and fifteen men survived the return trip to England.

Drake's ordeal in San Juan de Ulua gave him a hatred of the Spanish that led him to declare a one-man war against Spain. He was a patriot who would never rob an English ship, and he would frequently let non-Spanish ships pass unmolested. When it came to Spanish ships, Drake looted every one he could capture. He became known as the terror of the Spanish Main.

Drake underwent extraordinary hardship to relieve the Spanish of their beloved gold. He attacked the treasure storehouses in Panama in a bloody battle that left several men dead and Drake himself critically wounded by a musket ball in the thigh. Although most of his men wanted to retreat, Drake insisted that they pry the doors of the treasure-house open and take what was inside.

Working through a thunderstorm, Drake's men forced open the doors and found the storehouse empty. The treasure fleet had recently sailed for Spain.

Although the attack was a failure, Drake pressed on. He raided villages up and down the South American coast and waited for the next shipment of treasure to arrive in Panama from Peru.

That opportunity came in spring of 1573, when Drake joined forces with a French privateer named Captain Le Testu and a number of escaped black slaves to attack a Spanish mule train. The attackers were delighted to find that each mule carried three hundred pounds of silver. When all the booty was divided, Drake brought home to England about fifteen tons of silver ingots and £100,000 in gold coins.

The mule train raid made Drake rich and famous. England celebrated her pirate son, and there was not an area of the British Isles that did not revere the exploits of Francis Drake.

The best was yet to come for this extraordinary seaman. Three years later, in 1577, he set sail from Plymouth on a voyage that would take him around the world and establish his reputation as a gentleman pirate.

Sailing on the *Pelican,* which he would later rename the *Golden Hind,* Drake commanded a fleet that included four other ships. He crossed the Atlantic in two months and then started the dangerous passage through the Strait of Magellan, at the southern tip of South America. The weather became so treacherous and the water so rough that the ships gradually lost sight of one another. By the time the *Golden Hind* emerged from the strait, she was alone. Three of the other ships were lost and only one returned to England.

Sailing alone didn't seem to faze Drake. Although the *Golden Hind* was only one hundred feet long and eighteen feet at the beam, the crew had faith in her seaworthiness and in their captain's navigational abilities.

Traveling up the coast of Chile, they captured their first prize of the voyage, a Spanish ship with nearly eighteen hundred jars of wine and £8,000 in gold. Other prizes followed, the most notable being a Spanish ship that yielded four thousand ducats of silver bullion and an emerald-encrusted crucifix made of gold.

On March 1, 1579, Drake hit the mother lode. His nephew was scanning the horizon from the crow's nest when he saw the treasure ship *Nuestra*

Señora de la Concepción. A wave of excitement swept the crew. This was a legendary treasure ship that carried gold and silver from Peru to Panama. To take this ship as a prize when she was fully laden would mean astounding wealth. It would also mean danger. Guarding all that treasure was a collection of sixty-four cannons, enough weaponry to give the ship the nickname *Cacafuego,* or "Shitfire."

Drake devised a plan he had probably learned from his mentor, Hawkins. To disguise his ship as a merchant vessel, he slowed his speed by towing mattresses and a number of heavy pots by a long rope. Then he ordered his men to hide and prepare for battle.

The *Nuestra* sailed to within fifty yards of Drake and demanded to know who he was. Drake responded with a demand of his own. "Strike sail," he said. "Or we will send you to the bottom."

When the Spanish captain refused to surrender, Drake's men fired their cannons and muskets and launched arrows. The attack killed or injured many of the Spanish sailors and caused chaos on her decks. The cannon fire took down the *Nuestra's* mizzenmast and left her dead in the water. Within minutes, Drake's wildly enthusiastic boarding party was on the deck of the Spanish ship and in charge of her dazed and confused crew. Drake himself boarded the ship shortly thereafter, treating the mortified captain with the courtesy due a fellow seafarer.

What Drake found when his men inspected the holds was beyond his wildest expectations. There were eighty pounds of gold, twenty-six tons of silver, and more than a dozen chests of royal plate, silver destined for the king.

It took six days to transfer the treasure to the *Golden Hind.* While this was being done, the ever-gracious Drake allowed the Spanish captain to tour his ship and examine the charts that he and his men had drawn of the South American coast. Finally, he wrote a letter of safe passage to the captain and even distributed gifts to the Spanish sailors before allowing them to sail away in their now-empty vessel.

Drake knew to quit when he was ahead. He turned his ship west and sailed into the sunset, establishing himself as the first sea captain to survive an around-the-world voyage. Despite storms, food and water shortages, battles with Pacific island natives, long periods of drifting in a windless sea, and hull-bashing contact with a coral reef in Indonesia, Drake made it back to Plymouth on September 26, 1580. He had not seen the gray skies of England for two years and nine months.

The country was completely enamored of Drake. The queen summoned him to Richmond Palace and listened in awe for six hours as he recounted his tale of piracy and global circumnavigation. She then joined him on the deck of the *Golden Hind* and, before an angry Spanish ambassador who demanded his country's riches back, she knighted him.

The queen allowed Drake to keep £10,000 for himself and divided another £8,000 among his crew. Total value of the treasure was estimated at over £500,000, more than $90 million in today's money, an impressive return on investment for the queen and Drake's other sponsors.

What Bellamy and others in lower-class England saw in Drake was the success of one of their own. He had risen from a family of farmers and sea-men to become a pirate revered by all, even the queen. He was handsome and intelligent and went on to represent Plymouth in the House of Com-mons despite the fact that he had no formal education. Sir Francis Drake was a man of action who seemed to direct his own destiny.

Drake's success and attractive looks were the exception, not the norm. The seafaring men who swarmed the docks in Bellamy's time were a sight to behold. Short, thin, and tanned a leathery brown from the sun, they walked the filthy streets of Plymouth with a rolling gait that developed after months upon a ship's constantly moving deck.

The average height of a sailor in those days was about five feet, two inches. Despite their slight stature, they were extremely strong from a life of almost constant labor. The hard work, combined with bad food and constant ex-posure to the elements, gave them a weather-beaten and emaciated look and usually forced them to find other work before they reached the age of forty.

"Men on a ship can never stop working," said Drake of the sailor's life, "because the ocean never stops working."

The sailors that Bellamy saw in Plymouth dressed like men from another world. In fact, many of them were from worlds other than Bellamy's. Along with English sailors, there were French and East Indian men and represen-tatives of other, more exotic cultures walking the docks of Plymouth. He likely saw men dressed in clothing coated with tar to make it weatherproof, leaving its wearer to move like someone wearing overstarched pants. Tri-cornered hats were popular in good weather; pinned on two sides to pro-vide that "tricorn" shape, these were usually covered with lace, ribbons, tassels, or feathers.

As Bellamy strolled the active and noisy Plymouth docks, he likely caught sight of former pirates. These men stood out from the run of average sea-men because of the clothing they wore. White shirts were popular, as were brightly embroidered vests covered in brass buttons and jewelry they had taken as part of their cut of the booty.

To stand out in a crowd in England was a dangerous thing. "Sumptuary laws" allowed for the arrest and questioning of members of the lower class who might be dressed more lavishly than an honest income would allow. Still, to be as showy as they could would certainly be the pirates' way. Pirates existed in a world that was very different from the cruel and demeaning one of their peers. They governed their own fates as much as any seafaring man could. Theirs was a democratic world in which they selected their captain by vote and helped make the decisions that ran the ship. They were not overworked or conscripted to a cruel captain, as were merchant and military sailors. In short, a pirate was a free man, and he acted the part, right down to dressing like the upper-class toffs from whom he robbed his finery.

12

The Sharks Circle

✳ I doubt that young Bellamy seriously entertained thoughts of becoming a pirate. Although he heard tales of riches and adventure from the pirates and seamen at the Plymouth docks, he was probably fascinated by their lifestyle in the same way that young kids today might be intrigued by the lifestyle of arms smugglers or bank robbers. Still, I wonder what went on in young Sam's mind when he heard the story of Henry Avery, a local boy who became one of the most notorious pirates in the world.

Avery, born in Plymouth in 1653, shipped out as a youth with the Royal Navy, where he climbed through the ranks. He eventually became second mate of the privateer *Charles*.

The ship was hired to make raids in the Spanish colonies of Africa, but saw little if any action. Instead, the captain chose to spend several months in Corunna, Africa, where the crew became restless and mutinous.

After a night of heavy drinking, Avery and a number of seamen seized the ship. As the captain was awakened from his drunken stupor, Avery stood over him and declared, "I am captain of this ship now. I am bound to Madagascar, with the design of making my own fortune, and that of all the brave fellows joined with me."

Now a declared pirate, Avery renamed his ship the *Fancy* and began to take "prizes." He captured three British ships near the Cape Verde Islands of West Africa and two Danish ships off the west coast of Africa, which gave him enough provisions and motivation to continue the search for more.

Avery's plan in Madagascar was to prey on the spice merchants who traded with the Arabs and perhaps to capture one of the ships from the Great Mogul of India's fleet as it sailed to Mecca for the annual Muslim pilgrimage.

By now the crew of the *Fancy* had grown to 150 men and the vessel had been joined by at least three other pirate ships from Rhode Island and New

York. Heavily armed and fully motivated, the pirate fleet brazenly cruised the shipping lanes, waiting for prey.

Their appetite for treasure was whetted in September 1695 when they easily captured the *Fath Mahmamadi*. In addition to stores of food and water, Avery and his men found more than £50,000 worth of gold and silver, which they took on board the *Fancy*.

A few days later, Avery watched his fortune loom as the *Ganj-i-Sawai,* the greatest ship of the Great Mogul, came into view. Avery knew that he was facing a dangerous situation if he decided to attack. The *Ganj-i-Sawai* was the Great Mogul's most dangerous ship, with forty cannons, four hundred muskets, and a well-trained crew.

Against all odds, Avery decided to attack. It was a good decision. The first salvo from the *Fancy* collapsed the Great Mogul's ship's mainmast. Confusion led to chaos as one of the *Ganj-i-Sawai's* cannons exploded, killing and maiming much of the crew. Within two hours, the battle was over and Avery's pirates were standing on the deck of the prize that would allow them to retire.

As they searched the ship, they found that one of the Great Mogul's daughters was on board, along with her attendants and several slave girls. Although Avery claimed that the women were not violated, other members of his crew testified to the contrary. Several who were caught told a tale of rape and torture that lasted three agonizing days on a windless Arabian Sea.

No one knows how much gold and silver was taken from the Mogul's ship, but it was enough for each and every pirate under Avery to retire a rich man.

Exactly what happened to Avery after that voyage is not known, though the various accounts certainly intrigued the young Sam Bellamy. Some thought that he retired to an African island and was living with a native princess. Others said that he was residing in the West Indies, where he bribed the governor of New Providence with £1,000 worth of ivory tusks. Still others said that he had returned to Devonshire, near Plymouth, where he was living in poverty, having blown much of his money.

Everyone had an opinion about Avery and pirates like him. To some, he was a sinner who should die on the gallows like the six of his sailors who were captured and hanged. Others thought he was a smart man who had made a big score and deserved to live out his life in island luxury. Ultimately, a play was based on Avery's life called *The Successful Pirate,* in which the lead character expresses a desire to "quit Imperial sway and die a private man, as I was born." The play was quite successful, despite bad reviews from Alexander Pope and others, and launched a series of pirate plays that continually found favor right through 1879, when *The Pirates of Penzance* was produced.

My research had shown me that the truth about pirates was complicated. Some thought they were murderers, rapists, and scoundrels, while others thought they were right-thinking individuals who were to be admired. I'd found each view had its points. Actually, most pirates were part scoundrel and part saint.

As I emerged from my research on Cape Cod, the sharks had begun to circle.

Although the MBUAR had given me a reconnaissance permit, I found it to be extremely restrictive. For one thing, I could not remove any artifacts I might find without an excavation permit. In fact, read a certain way, the recon permit would not even allow me to uncover artifacts, which meant I would not be allowed to blow sand away to see what their permit would not allow me to pick up.

Most disturbing to me was that part of the law that said all the artifacts had to be sold within one year at fair market value once the final report was accepted by the board. The money would then be divided, with 25 percent going to the Commonwealth of Massachusetts.

I didn't find this aspect of the law fair, nor did I find it particularly Amer-

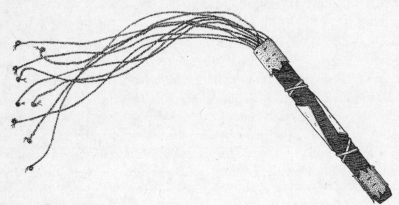

BRUTAL DISCIPLINE

During the first half of the eighteenth century the merchant captain was a virtual dictator, and there was little to restrain him from serving his crewmen with the worst of cruelties. Brutality and calculated violence were systematically and methodically applied in order to enforce discipline.

Perhaps the most common, and feared, means of disciplining at sea was the notorious "cat-o'-nine-tails," a whip with nine knotted lashes. A sentence of six or seven hundred lashes was not unheard-of in the British navy. Some men were whipped to death for offenses as minor as losing an oar, or laughing at an officer.

It was this kind of cruel discipline that drove many merchant sailors to become pirates.

ican. Although British admiralty law requires a split between explorer and state, United States admiralty law reads, or, at least did in those days, that the first person to find an abandoned ship is the owner and has to give nothing to the state.

Rather than accept the rules the state of Massachusetts and the board of underwater archaeology set down, I decided to fight the state from the beginning. I talked to my lawyer, Allan Tufankjian, a friend from high school, about my decision and he agreed. He said the state's claim to the artifacts could not withstand a challenge in court. And if it did? Well, he was pragmatic. "The worst thing that can happen is that you will end up owning seventy-five percent of the treasure," he reasoned.

In order to lay claim to the wreck and its treasures, admiralty law said that I had to "arrest the wreck." To do this, said Tufankjian, I would have to bring an artifact from the *Whydah* into court. This object would represent the ship and would allow the court to assume jurisdiction over the wreck and award it to me.

"I think we can pull this off," said Tufankjian. "Personally, I don't think the state has any claim to this or any other wreck that has been abandoned."

On November 22, 1982, we filed an admiralty action in the United States District Court in Boston seeking title to the "fruits of the wreck." After hearing Tufankjian's argument, the Court issued a warrant for the arrest of the wreck and appointed my company, Maritime Underwater Surveys, as the custodian of the vessel.

The state, of course, did not agree with this decision. Reporter Gayle Fee of the *Cape Cod Times* called me on December 2 to say the state of Massachusetts was going to lay claim to their "rightful portion" of whatever I found.

Talk about pirates, I thought, as Fee asked me for a reaction to the announcement. I was far more upset than I let on. I told her I didn't believe that the state had any jurisdiction over this wreck and that federal law should apply. "Under federal law, sunken treasure is finders keepers," I said.

The next day, I picked up my copy of the *Cape Cod Times* and read a headline and story that hit me like a bucket of cold seawater.

STATE SAYS WHIDAH BELONGS TO IT, TOO

SOUTH WELLFLEET—A team of Cape and Islands treasure hunters, who believe they have found the fortune-laden pirate vessel, Whidah, 700 yards off Marconi Beach, will ultimately seek their riches not on the ocean's floor, but in a courtroom.

A state archaeology official said yesterday the commonwealth will file the first claim to a portion of the $80 to $200 million in gold, silver, ivory and jewels that legend says was aboard the 300-ton, London built galley ship when it sank in a storm April 26, 1717.

Under provisions of the 1973 state Underwater Archaeological Act, state officials claim the commonwealth is entitled to 25 percent of what is discovered from the wreck. The act also empowers the state to oversee the salvage operation and says the state, along with private museums in Massachusetts, have the first option to buy, at market value, any historical articles recovered.

"The state will very definitely file a claim," said Joseph Sinnott, chairman of the Underwater Marine Archaeology Board, the agency that oversees the state's underwater wrecks. "We believe the wreck was found in state-owned and state-controlled waters and we will be in court when the hearings are held."

The article went on, but I was stunned. Not only was the state jumping my claim, they were even doubting that I had the *Whydah* to begin with. State archaeologist Brona Simon went so far as to say that our find "could be another ship."

When pressed by the reporter, Simon expressed her doubts about the whole venture. "I'm not ready to make a conclusive statement at this time," she said in the article. "It could be the *Whydah*. I'm not ruling that out. I'll be anxious to hear."

I read the article a couple of times and slowly put the newspaper down. Suddenly, I had a knot in my stomach and doubt in my mind. Unlike the state's expert, who had never been to the wreck site, I had a gut feeling that what I had found was the *Whydah*. I understood what Mel Fisher was referring to when he warned me about claim jumpers. I knew it would happen, but I didn't expect the first of the jumpers to be the state where I paid my taxes.

On December 10, the state's response to our claim was made official. The state attorney general filed papers suggesting that the federal courts lacked jurisdiction to rule on our claim because the Commonwealth of Massachusetts claimed to own the *Whydah*. The state also declared that Maritime's suit in federal court claiming title to the *Whydah* amounted to a suit against the state by the federal government, an act barred by the eleventh amendment of the constitution.

On the same day that the attorney general filed his papers in federal court, the Commonwealth filed an instant declaratory relief action to establish title to the *Whydah*.

When I read all these papers, I didn't know what they meant. I did know that politicians, like pirates, can smell money. And when they do, they chase it as hard as they can.

I understood what it would feel like to be chased by pirates.

THEY DIDN'T LOOK LIKE THIS

Contrary to this mythical portrait of Sam Bellamy, most pirates did *not* have the virile good looks of, say, Errol Flynn. Pockmarked by smallpox and ringworms, a sailor's skin was heavily tanned and wrinkled from prolonged exposure to the sun.

13

The Rich and Adventurous

Bob Lazier, developer and pilot, got the *Whydah* search off the ground.

❋ When it was announced that I had found the *Whydah,* I suddenly had more friends than I could handle. Old girlfriends called to rekindle the flame. Guys I had gone to college with and barely remembered called to tell me about their failed marriages and dreadful jobs and wondered if in some way they could join me in my search for pirate treasure.

I didn't need friends, I needed money. My search for investors began at the Aspen, Colorado, police department. In retrospect, that may seem strange, but who might know more rich and adventurous people than the man in charge of law and order in the West's wealthiest town? That person was Rob McClung.

When it came to ingratiating himself with well-heeled people, Rob McClung was a master. He had become friends with the likes of actors George Hamilton and Britt Eklund, and would go to almost any extreme to let the rich and powerful know that he was on their side.

We had been best friends ten years earlier at Trinidad Junior College in Colorado. I was there on a football scholarship and had turned him on to weightlifting when he was a slight, angry, 145-pound karate student who wore his black belt to class. Now he was a 230-pound plug of muscle, thanks to a regimen of constant weightlifting. Eventually I would find that ten years had changed more than just his body. If I had not been so focused on rais- ing money for the *Whydah* expedition, I might have noticed the change back then and avoided him. However, I was focused so tightly on my money-raising efforts that I would probably have asked the devil himself for a buck if the opportunity had presented itself.

If I have any questions about the motives of someone offering help, I remember the words of *Whydah* historian Ken Kinkor, who said, "If you are going to sup with the devil, make sure you have a long spoon."

My relationship with McClung rekindled on Christmas Day when the phone rang. "Hey, it's Rob," came the familiar voice over the receiver. "Don't leave me out of this."

I had heard this at least twenty times from other callers, and I was no longer delicate in stating my needs. "Right now I don't need manpower, Rob, I need money. I have found the shipwreck, but I don't have the money it takes to search the area."

I had already invested more than $100,000 of my personal money. In addi- tion, my construction business was foundering badly from neglect, as was my marriage: both were suffering from the fact that all of my time, not just spare time, was being devoted to finding the *Whydah*.

"I know a few rich people," said Rob with his usual self-confidence. "If I put together a group to talk to, will you come out and tell them what you need?"

"Sure," I said. Then I told him the amount of money I thought it would take to find the ship. "I need $250,000 to dive for an entire season. I think that is all it's going to take to find her."

"That's a lot of money," said Rob, taken aback. "But I'll see what I can do."

A few days short of New Year's, I was on an airplane flying to Colorado. Rob had called to announce that he had put together an audience of "people with money" who were interested in hearing about the *Whydah* project. Included in the group were John Levin, a long-haired judge who sat on the board of a Telluride bank; Mickey Salloway, a local real estate developer; and Bob Lazier, who owned the Tivoli Lodge in Vail, a beauti- ful, sprawling hotel at the base of that town's popular ski slopes.

I thought about my presentation during my trip and the next day as I nervously shook hands with everyone before sitting down in Lazier's pent-house, a six-thousand-square-foot apartment overlooking the mountains from atop the Tivoli Lodge.

This was the first time I had made a pitch to raise money, but I didn't think it would be something that would be particularly difficult. All I had to do was tell them the story of Black Sam Bellamy the way it had been told to me by Uncle Bill. Then I would describe my own obsession with finding the ship, right down to the investment of my personal capital to map and mag the suspected area. I wanted to make it clear to the prospective investors that I was fully invested in finding the *Whydah,* even if it meant snorkel diving on the site with a shovel and pail.

The group gave me its undivided attention as I talked on for nearly an hour. I remember few details of my pitch, other than the line I ended with: "It's a risk. But you have a chance to be the first ever to discover an authentic pirate ship."

The room was quiet for a moment. Then, like children given a chance to question Long John Silver himself, they began enthusiastically to ask questions.

"How do you know Bellamy really existed?"

"Is it possible that all of the treasure floated away?"

"Is the North Atlantic really so rough that people couldn't swim to the wreck site?"

The most interested person in the room was Bob Lazier. He said later that he wanted to invest as soon as he heard that I had invested $100,000 of my own money and didn't expect to get it back until the salvage operation was finished.

"You had obviously made the commitment," he remembered. "You were going to do it now or never."

Lazier was one of the most interesting people I'd ever met. Raised in an orphanage in Minnesota, Lazier had developed a strong independence at an age when most kids do not know the meaning of the word. When he decided to see the world, Lazier climbed out the upstairs window of the converted mansion that housed the orphanage and hopped a freight train to Chicago. He was only ten years old.

Traveling without money, he managed to feed himself by going into restaurants, selecting the most friendly waitress, and telling her that he was hungry. "I never missed a meal," said Lazier. "Waitresses care about kids."

In the summer, Lazier hopped a westbound freight to Montana and fol-lowed the same food-gathering strategy. He made these trips alone or with friends, running next to a moving train and grabbing the rungs of the ladder before the speed lifted his feet off the ground and he swung into the boxcar.

On one of these jaunts the train accelerated too quickly and Bob's foot swung under the train, in line with the wheels. Unable to pull himself up and away from the steel wheel, he imagined slipping from the rung and losing a foot. Hanging on beyond his strength for an extra mile put luck on his side. His foot hit an object on the tracks that pushed it outside the path of the wheels. In that instant he let go and was spared amputation, sustaining only cuts and bruises after falling from the fast-moving train. That event eventually earned him the name "Lucky Lazier."

Being so independent did not put Lazier high on the list of desirable orphans. He was returned to the orphanage after a few weeks of freedom, and many families took him home for a day or two, but found him to be incompatible with their families and their needs. That was fine with Bob. As far as he could tell, they were mostly looking for farmhands, anyway, and had nothing to give an adopted child but a job operating farm equipment.

Finally, a pleasant couple who had been childless for twenty-two years appealed to him and he became their son. Lazier left the orphanage in exchange for a good-sized bedroom, a new bike, and a dog, which he negotiated as part of his adoption agreement.

Always drawn by the fast life, Lazier began to race cars. He worked his way up through street racers and stock cars until he became an Indy car racer, competing in the 1981 Indianapolis 500 and becoming racing's "Rookie of the Year" at the age of forty-two.

After eight accidents caused by equipment failure, Lazier put auto racing behind him and became a developer of commercial real estate. He was riding high with a hotel in Vail, which he had visited with his new bride and had decided to stay and stake a claim to. He also had a number of successful developments in other western states. Eventually his son Buddy Lazier would also pursue a racing career, winning the Indy 500 in 1996, only nine weeks after surviving an accident at the Phoenix 500 that broke his back in twenty-five places. Bob Lazier had a lucky and tenacious bloodline.

Lazier was impressed by the *Whydah* project. He listened to the story of Black Sam Bellamy and his treasure-laden ship with the fidgety impatience of a man who is wealthy and curious about the world around him. Although he was obviously a master at making money and had a fortune estimated at $25 million, Lazier was not all that interested in the moneymaking possibilities of the *Whydah*. What impressed him was the way the study of pirates could change history.

"These guys were floating democracies," declared Lazier, excited about the fact that pirates elected the people who ran their ships. "Just think, it may have been that the Constitution of the United States was influenced by the men who flew the Jolly Roger."

The thought that we could rewrite history was a moving one for Lazier. He immediately began to talk about a pirate museum, in which the artifacts of these early democrats could be displayed for all to see. He's miles ahead of me, I thought. I just want to bring this stuff up. Lazier already has it in a museum. As Lazier paced his penthouse and talked, he swept by a writing desk and picked up a legal pad. In a moment he sat down and began jotting down the details of the *Whydah* financing.

To begin with, he didn't think we were asking for enough money. Considering that I needed a crew of technicians, divers, deckhands, a historian, and archaeologists, he reasoned that a large amount of the money would be eaten up by salaries that first season. Then there was the equipment needed to dive over such a treacherous site, including a large and stable boat, a magnetometer to map the area, and dive equipment and dry suits for divers to stay down on the bottom for long periods of time. When the artifacts were brought up, we would have to restore them in a laboratory before the fresh air dried out the salt water and rotted the metal like the undercarriage of an old car in snow country.

"Going into something like this with too little money can be dangerous and demoralizing," he declared. "What if you are close to finding the treasure and run out of money? You will have to stop and try to raise more. It could knock you out for the season and derail the entire project."

I knew what he was saying, but in my mind a quarter of a million dollars seemed like the magic number. Raising more than that, a half million or a million, for instance, seemed an unattainable goal. A quarter million seemed easier to raise and would give us one strong season, which is all the time I thought we would need.

"I'll tell you what," I said to Lazier. "I'll work mainly for stock in the company. That way more money will go to equipment and personnel and no one can argue that I am taking an outrageous salary."

Lazier shrugged and returned to his legal pad. I remember looking at the clock and seeing that it was 10 P.M. As Lazier sat at a table and worked and talked, we gathered one by one around him. The next thing I knew it was 1 A.M. All of us were exhausted by the money discussion.

"I'm going to bed," said Lazier, throwing down his pen and marking an abrupt end to the meeting.

Everyone else agreed, and we drifted off to our respective rooms in the penthouse. I tried to get comfortable but soon found that sleeping was an impossibility. No matter how hard I tried, the excitement of realizing my dream kept me awake. At 3 A.M., I got dressed and went into the living room. Bob Lazier was sitting at the table, looking at the figures on the legal pad.

"I couldn't sleep, either," he said, pushing a chair out with his foot for me to sit down. "Let's figure this out right now."

By 4 A.M., we had structured the deal and were ready to lay it out for the others when they got out of bed several hours later.

A private-placement stock corporation would be formed called Maritime Explorations. I would keep one-third of the stock as president of the company. About fifty percent of the stock would be kept in reserve. The rest of the stock would be sold in $10,000 increments to investors to raise the $250,000.

Lazier liked the idea of a stock corporation because it was more democratic. "Everyone who owns stock gets to vote on the future of the company," said Lazier. "That gives everyone a chance to be in on the decision-making process."

I began to compile a list of possible investors in Cape Cod, people who had an extra $10,000, knew the legend of Bellamy, and might want to own a piece of local lore. The list was depressingly short and not very promising.

Lazier described the type of person who would invest in such a venture. "Investors in this project are more interested in adventure than they are in returns," he said. "Everyone wants to make money, and we all hope that everyone does. But these people want a story that they can tell their friends. They want to be a part of history."

Lazier thought that a sea hunt for pirate treasure would sell best to investors in Colorado, where sea adventure was a distant fantasy. "A person's backyard is not where they imagine adventure taking place," he said. "Something like this will be exciting to the kind of people who hang out in Vail."

Following this strategy, Lazier compiled a list of twenty-five possible investors and invited them to his penthouse. Included were Howard Head, founder of Head Skis, and a lovely woman weighted so heavily with diamonds, emeralds, and gold that she looked like an open treasure chest. We made a sales pitch that included all the information we had to date, including the story of Black Sam Bellamy and Maria Hallett. The potential investors were fascinated at the prospect of turning this myth into fact, or at least working toward it.

At the end of the pitch, seventeen in the group wrote $10,000 checks. "We're almost there," said Lazier. He pulled together another investor group, and we pitched again. This group was equally excited about the opportunity to rewrite history. They were fascinated by the fact that pirates were democratic in the way they approached shipboard life. A number of the people in this group bought shares, too. "We're right around the corner," said Lazier.

Lazier called on a few more friends. At midnight on January 12, 1983, we received our final check. Just as easily as it sounds, we had raised $250,000. The search for the *Whydah* could now begin.

Lazier was ecstatic. "I hope finding the *Whydah* is as easy as raising this money," he said when it was all over.

"I think it will be," I said. "I know right where it is. We'll have piles of gold and silver in a few months."

I was on top of the world. On the morning that I left for the Cape, I stood at Lazier's window and admired the mountain view. The sun was coming up on a bright and clear day, casting a yellow glow on the saw-toothed mountains of Vail.

I took a sip of coffee and felt the power of a new day, the power of the caffeine, and the power of my own soon-to-be-fulfilled dreams. A quarter of a million dollars! Nothing could stop me now.

As the sun rose higher and my future seemed brighter, it was everything I could do to keep from whooping with joy.

BOOK II

✳

THE BIG TIME

14

A Crew with No Boat

Stretch Grey, left, was the first to join my crew, shown here with John Beyer.

❋ Stretch Grey, whose lobster boat I had rented for Mel Fisher when he came to help me mag the *Whydah* site, was my first crewman. He said he became hooked on treasure hunting the moment Mel Fisher dropped that gold bar on the floor of the Red Inn. He quickly accepted the offer I made to him to captain the exploration boat I didn't yet have. Although Stretch was my first crewman, I often joke that he was my first *two* crewmen because of his massive size—six feet, ten inches tall and 325 pounds.

He would make the perfect captain. As a transplanted Rhode Islander, Stretch lived to fish. He thought nothing of spending days out on the North Atlantic, even in winter, catching whatever would bite.

One story illustrates his love of the deep blue sea. Many years after we met, Stretch was sixty miles offshore fishing for tuna with his two young sons when the radio reported that a surprise storm was coming out of the west. Reports estimated its wind speed at nearly one hundred miles per hour, and Stretch wanted no part of it.

Opening his throttle full, he turned his thirty-five-foot boat toward the storm and began racing for shore. Even though the boat was capable of twenty knots, Grey knew he was on a collision course with very bad weather. About fifteen miles from shore, the storm hit him head on. The waves began to toss the boat and then, as the wind delivered its full force, the sea flattened out. Boring headfirst into the wind and rain at full throttle, Grey found that the boat's forward progress had been reduced to about one knot per hour. At one point, his youngest son, Sean, asked, "Dad, are we going to make it?" To which the ever-honest Grey replied, "Probably."

After several terrifying hours, the storm passed and the sun cracked through the clouds, radiating on an ocean that had now flattened out like a liquid runway. To the surprise and shock of his children, Grey turned the boat around and headed back out to sea.

"Both of the kids were as scared as hell until we started catching fish," he told me. "Then they loved it. There's nothing like a low-pressure zone for catching fish."

Grey's love of fishing presented a problem for his father, who always wanted his oversized son to take over the family's business, a major consumer lending corporation. But Grey had no interest in working in an office. When his father asked him to try the business for one year, Grey agreed, only to resign one year to the day after first sitting down at his new desk.

He walked out of the office, drove to Cape Cod, and eventually took a job with a crusty old salt who was known as one of the most demanding fishermen on the Cape.

The work demands of this tough captain, combined with the rough seas, caused Stretch to vomit every day the boat rounded the Cape and headed into the churning Atlantic.

This daily seasickness continued for nearly two years without the captain's saying a single word. Then one morning, with the sun coming up and Grey heaving his breakfast over the rail, the captain stuck his head outside the wheelhouse and shouted a harsh opinion at the back of the big man.

"Hey, big boy, maybe you aren't cut out to be a fisherman."

From that day forward, Grey was never seasick again.

When I hired Grey, he was making good money as a lobsterman. A couple of times a week he would string his traps "along the backside" right over the wreck site. He had done this for years, never suspecting that anything was down there besides lobsters. Now he was ready to try something else, searching for treasure that didn't crawl.

The second person on board was John Beyer, who became a crewman of the *Whydah* expedition by default. Beyer had come to work for my salvage business a couple of years earlier, when I was preparing to salvage the propeller from a freighter that had sunk off the coast of Martha's Vineyard. A propeller is worth a good deal of money, especially one weighing several tons, as this one did. If I retrieved this object I could sell it for as much as $25,000. If I didn't, I would be in good company. Others had tried to bring the propeller to the surface and all had failed, largely because the ship was resting in 120 feet of water, which makes salvage a dark and risky proposition.

John Beyer was the second to join the *Whydah* team.

I was preparing my boat for the salvage operation when a man came striding down the dock. I looked up for a moment and returned to my equipment, thinking he was just another happy-go-lucky tourist. When his footsteps stopped next to my boat, I looked up again.

"I'm a diver and I'm looking for work," he said with a buoyant grin. "Someone in town said you need help."

This time I looked at him more closely. He had the look of an athlete, with supple muscles and a graceful stance. He was tanned and handsome and seemed to be someone who was easy to get along with.

"Are you certified to dive?" I asked.

"I sure am," he insisted. "I learned how to dive down in Florida."

I had learned to check out divers before hiring them after the navy SEAL incident, which had happened a few months before. I had hired a man who claimed to have been a member of the SEALs, the navy's elite underwater reconnaissance team. He talked a good game on shore, but when we suited up for a salvage dive and he got underwater, he panicked and had to return to the surface. I went up with him to calm him down. I told him to go back to shore, where he crawled across barnacle encrusted rocks that cut his arms and legs like razors, a mistake that no self-respecting SEAL would ever make. He had been lying to me and had learned everything he knew about SEALs from the movies.

I was desperate this time, since I had a buoy tied to the propeller and wanted to bring it up before someone else figured out what I was doing and used my own buoy to get the propeller ahead of me.

"Okay, you're hired," I said to the man, who introduced himself as John Beyer. "Tomorrow we are pulling up a propeller."

In the morning, we boarded my dive boat and headed for the site. Beyer put on his wet suit like a pro, but when he turned the regulator something didn't seem right. Like a high school coach who can spot a baseball player by the way he picks up the ball, I could tell that Beyer knew little about dive equipment.

"Before we go down, John, I want to tell you a story," I said. I told him about the SEAL imposter and asked if he had more experience than that man had.

"Not really," he said, with a smile that could be described as prizewinning. "But I'm willing to try."

He later confessed that his only "diving" had been in a swimming pool in Miami where he photographed swimsuit models for a calendar. He did okay for the day, though. I told him just to hang on to my belt until we got to the propeller and then I would show him where to put the wrench and how to twist it.

As we descended, I could see Beyer's eyes grow larger as the environment around us became darker. At one hundred feet, there is less light penetration than in a forest at midnight, and I thought that the first-time spookiness of such a descent might make Beyer bolt for the surface. It didn't. I learned that day that John Beyer doesn't flinch.

When we brought the propeller to the surface later that day, I asked if Beyer wanted a full-time job.

Eventually he became my right-hand man in both my salvage and construction businesses. Beyer was a self-starter and always had been. As a track athlete at Boston College, he was distressed to find that there was no money to coach pole vaulters. Rather than take up another sport, he became the only non-coached athlete at the college, even paying his own way to track meets.

By doing that he had become a great scrounger, able to beg and borrow things he needed. Had he been a less pleasant person, John Beyer would have made a great Sergeant Bilko. As he was, he made a terrific addition to the expedition team.

Both Beyer and Stretch Grey were ready to crew on a boat that I didn't yet have. In fact, I was shy more than a boat. I had none of the gear necessary to search for sunken artifacts. Although the dive boat I had been using in Martha's Vineyard was perfect for salvage work, it was too small for a large-scale operation like the search for the *Whydah*. I was looking for a boat large enough for as many as a dozen crew members and divers to work comfortably, with powerful engines that could push a high volume of prop wash through mailboxes, and a crane that could lift artifacts weighing several tons from the bottom of the ocean. Yet the boat had to be small enough to work in the shallow waters close to shore.

I considered a wide variety of boats, including some of the fishing vessels that graced the harbor of Provincetown.

While I was scouring the classified ads in *National Fisherman,* I found an ad that caught my eye. The Gammage Boat Yard in Bristol, Maine, was advertising a sixty-five-foot sonar chaser that had been built for the navy by the yard's namesake, Harvey Gammage. For a sailor, finding a boat built by Gammage was like an architect finding a residence built by Frank Lloyd Wright. I could hardly believe my good luck.

When Grey came by later that afternoon, I showed him the ad and we decided that he should drive up to Maine to make a closer inspection of the boat.

"This looks good on paper," I said, waving the page at Grey. "See if she has any possibilities."

When Grey left to look at the boat, I felt I was well on my way to crossing the path Black Sam Bellamy had pursued so many years ago.

Bellamy probably left England for the New World to search for employment. The War of the Spanish Succession, which involved most of the European powers, had ended, and its end had meant the loss of thousands of jobs for English sailors of all stripe. The Royal Navy released forty thousand officers and seamen, leaving the streets of many English seafaring towns teeming with sailors.

It was from these ranks of the nautically unemployed that Bellamy probably came, arriving in Provincetown in the spring of 1715.

About the time that Bellamy arrived in Provincetown, the wreck of the Spanish Plate Fleet took place on the coast of Florida. This massive shipwreck, which nearly bankrupted Spain, created a moneymaking opportunity so great that historians have compared it to the California Gold Rush of 1849. It was most certainly the event that marked the peak of the golden age of piracy.

On July 24, 1715, the first shipment of Spanish gold and silver to be sent to the king in more than eight years left Havana, Cuba, for Spain. Gold and silver from the mints of Peru and Mexico had been secured in the treasure warehouses of Cuba because of concern that any treasure shipments to Spain might be intercepted by English warships. With the end of the war in 1714, Spain was desperate to bring back the precious metal to eliminate some of her wartime debt, a desperation that forced the treasure fleet to attempt a risky crossing during hurricane season.

The journey to Spain began well. As the wharfs of Havana bustled with well-wishers, fleet commander General Don Antonio de Echeverz y Zubiza ordered a cannon fired that signaled all of his ships to unfurl their sails and begin the two-month journey to Spain. Orders were shouted, anchors were raised, and the only clouds that could be seen in the sky around Havana were the clouds of canvas that billowed with the wind, tugging the Spanish ships into deep water. As the ships passed the ramparts of El Morro castle, a black-robed archbishop blessed the fleet to the tattoo of beating drums and the thunder of cannons fired in salute.

The route would take the treasure fleet northward through the straits between Florida and the Bahamas known as New Bahama Channel. Around the Carolinas, they would turn eastward for the lengthy Atlantic crossing.

PIRACY WORLDWIDE

Contrary to impressions from novels and movies, few pirates confined themselves to the West Indies. Most moved throughout the Atlantic, and sometimes even farther. Indeed, the itinerary of a pirate crew often followed a predictable pattern to take advantage of currents and seasonal trade winds.

After wintering in the Caribbean, many crews moved northward out of the West Indies with the Gulf Stream. Their prey was transatlantic British shipping, which began arriving off the Carolinas, Virginia, Pennsylvania, and New York by early spring. Such vessels carried cargoes of goods that were prohibited from manufacture by the colonies themselves so as to ensure a strong market for British-made goods.

These monopolistic policies inflated prices so much that at least a few colonial merchants were eager to trade with pirates, who sold goods from plundered ships at ridiculously low prices.

A pirate ship was usually off the New England coast by early to mid-summer. After molesting ships bound for Boston, she'd steal away into a quiet Maine cove for fresh water and a quick refitting. By late summer, the pirate vessel would be off Newfoundland attacking homeward-bound fishing fleets.

As the northern latitudes cooled, the pirates either returned to the West Indies by way of Bermuda or moved southeast to the Western Islands and the African coast. The Azores, Madeira, and the Canary Islands attracted predators anxious to attack their numerous wine ships. Farther in-shore, off the African coast itself, inward-bound cargoes of small arms, gunpowder, and liquor were prizes welcomed by any pirate—as was gold from Africa.

From there a vote was taken on which of two possible routes to pursue. They could round the Cape of Good Hope and enter the rich hunting-ground of the Indian Ocean, or they could sail westward from Africa to Brazil. If the voyage was timed properly, the pirates could intercept Portuguese ships laden with rich cargoes of sugar, tobacco, gold, and diamonds. From Brazil, it was an easy sail northward back into the Caribbean by way of Cayenne, where the entire cycle would start over.

A Coin's Journey

Working in dangerous mine shafts as much as nine hundred feet deep, Indian slaves hammered silver ore loose from rock walls, lugged it in baskets through narrow tunnels to the surface, and ground it into fine powder for refining. Mercury was then mixed with the powder to amalgamate with the silver, which was then removed by cooking the amalgam until the mercury boiled off. Cast into discs, bars, or ingots, much of this bullion was then converted into coins.

From the ends of flat strips of silver, coin-sized slices were chiseled or clipped. These cobs, as they were called, were then hand-struck between two dies, embossing them with the royal coat of arms on one side and the cross of Spain on the other. The assayer would check the coins for correct weight and clip off any excess—thus none were exactly alike. They were struck in denominations of one-half, one, two, four, and eight reals—the largest being known as a "piece of eight."

The treasure was transported across the isthmus of Panama either entirely overland, by mule on dangerous mountain trails; or partly by water, down the jungle-choked Chagres River to the fever-infested Caribbean town of Portobelo, where a large month-long trade fair would be held to celebrate its arrival.

How might this coin have come to the pocket of a pirate?

Ravaged by decades of war, Spain's merchant fleet was unable to adequately supply her colonies with the goods they needed. As a result, a lively smuggling trade sprang up between British colonies and Spanish colonies. Perhaps aboard the *Whydah* at the time of her capture, the coin illustrated above may well have been part of a Spanish payment for a British cargo of captive humans.

That we have selected a coin in the shape of a teardrop is therefore no accident.

The ships made good time, traveling at speeds of six knots during the day. They moved slower at night so the helmsman would have time to react to any shoals that the double lookouts might spot. The crew took depth soundings every fifteen to thirty minutes, a frequency that showed the care with which these ships were sailing and emphasized the importance of the fleet's cargo.

Five days out, some of the veteran seamen complained of aching joints and headaches, a sign that bad weather was coming. By the sixth day at sea, a milky haze obscured the view, and the ocean became calm, almost leaden. By evening, the wind had slackened and rain squalls dotted the horizon. Commanding General Juan Ubilla took all of nature's signs seriously. He ordered full sail to be raised and the frequent depth sounding to be stopped. The events surrounding them were signs of a gathering storm, and Ubilla knew that the New Bahama Channel was no place to be in truly bad weather.

The tight fleet formation, which must have resembled a caravan of elephants walking nose to tail, began to break up as all the ships made a run for it. Hatches and ports were closed and battened down, and sails were raised to increase speed.

It had grown so dark by mid–afternoon of July 30 that the stern lanterns were lit so the ships could see one another. By late afternoon, the ships were staggering through rough seas and no longer obeying their helms. The forces of nature had turned the bows of the eleven ships into the wind, where they sat, pounded by the elements.

Records show that by midnight the ships were assaulted by five separate gales, which were working the beams loose, allowing water to pour into the hulls. Pumps were manned constantly belowdecks as desperate deck crews climbed the rigging to lower sails in the faint hope that the ships could be brought under control and sailed back out to sea.

At 2 A.M. on July 31, a hurricane struck that ripped the masts from the decks of several of the ships. As the wind velocity climbed to at least seventy-five miles per hour, few sailors thought of keeping the ships at sea. Since they knew they were going to wreck, they began to jettison cargo to lighten the vessels so they would float closer to dry land. Over the side went cannons, anchors, livestock, anything that could cut the ship's weight.

The *Capitana* was the first to hit shore. She struck with such force that the lower hull sheared away, leaving a gaping wound through which poured cannons, cargo, passengers, and 120 tons of registered silver. More than 220 people drowned.

Next to strike bottom was the *Santo Cristo de San Romain.* The 450-ton ship lost her hull first and thousands of pounds of registered silver with it. The deck and forecastle broke loose, floating toward shore and breaking apart in the heavy surf, leaving 120 people dead on the beach. Two frigates were torn apart, but on one, the *Nuestra Señora de las Nieves,* more than one hundred survived by riding the deck to shore after it floated away from the hull.

General Echeverz's flagship was among the lucky vessels. Her load lightened sufficiently by the crew, the *Nuestra Señora del Carmen* ran aground near shore with little loss of life. Although Echeverz survived, his son, captain of the *Nuestro Señora del Rosario,* drowned when his ship was completely destroyed south of his father's, with the loss of 124 lives.

All told, eleven ships were wrecked, more than seven hundred people died, and more than fourteen million pesos were left sitting on the floor of the shallows off the east Florida coast. Surprisingly, given the storm's severity, fourteen hundred people survived.

News of the Spanish shipwrecks traveled fast. Governor Spotswood of Virginia wrote to the king of England, apprising him of the golden opportunity to be found in the nearly unprotected wrecks.

"There is advice of considerable events in these parts that the Spanish Plate Fleet, richly laden, consisting of eleven sail, are, except one, lately cast away in the Gulf of Florida to the southward of St. Augustine," he wrote in an intelligence dispatch to the king. "I think it is my duty to inform his Majesty of this accident which may be improved to the advantage of his Majesty's subjects by encouraging them to attempt the recovery of some of that immense wealth."

Good news travels fast. By the time the letter reached the king, the rush had already started. From Jamaica came Captain Edward James and Captain Henry Jennings, commanding a small flotilla of ships aimed at salvaging the sunken treasure. From the Bahamas came Benjamin Hornigold, a noted English pirate with a hatred of the Spanish and a patriotic refusal to attack any ship that flew the Union Jack. He left Providence, Nassau, in a sloop named *Mary* and sailed hard for Florida. From other parts of the colonies and the Caribbean basin came hungry sailors eager to make a score on the sunken treasure ships. They came in galleys, sloops, pinks, and even periauguas—large, flat-bottomed canoes that were barely oceangoing.

Word of the Spanish Plate Fleet wreck arrived in Provincetown just a few months after Bellamy immigrated from England. What he was doing for a living at this time is anybody's guess. The notion of fourteen million pesos sitting on the ocean floor would have to have been a heady one for the broke yet entrepreneurial young Brit. This must have seemed like the opportunity of a lifetime.

Bellamy had just one problem: *Who could he get to finance his venture?*

15

The Vast Explorer

The bay next to the Great Island Tavern, where Bellamy most likely launched his unintended pirate career.

❋ A spit of land that juts into Massachusetts Bay like a crow's beak, Great Island is a peninsula that must have been named at high tide. When the moon is full and the tide is at its peak, this heavily wooded promontory is cut off from the mainland by salt water that oozes from the porous marshland.

Indians lived on this part-time island for hundreds of years, and nature worshippers (better known as "witches") danced beneath the full moon at sites that can be identified today. Despite its natural beauty, few white settlers ever lived there, probably because of the aforementioned occupants. In fact, few people ever even seemed to *visit* Great Island, regardless of creed or color. It was just too far out of the way, which made the existence of the Great Island Tavern even more mysterious.

Built around 1712, the remote yet somehow thriving tavern had been purchased by Israel Cole shortly before Bellamy came to the Cape. Little is known about Cole. Historians have recently concluded that he was married to a cousin of Sam Bellamy's. If true, that would explain much about the financing of Bellamy's career and may even explain some of the mystery surrounding Maria Hallett.

It is certain that Cole died rich, since an inventory of his estate filed with the court in 1724 shows that at his death he had £10,000 in the bank and owned a large quantity of land and other chattel. These financial facts were reported by none other than Benjamin Franklin, who wrote an unflattering poem about Cole for the August 10, 1724, issue of his *New England Courant* newspaper.

> *Here lies old Cole; but how or why*
> *He lived, or how he came to dy,*
> *His Son and Heir may best declare it,*
> *Who's doubly blest with Father's spirit;*
>
> *And who, when e'er he comes to breathe all*
> *His useless Breath away, and leave all*
> *To such another Son and Heir,*
> *He may be thrown—but God knows where;*
>
> *Perhaps in some black dark Hole*
> *Where out of wood he extracts Charcoal.*

These are harsh words from so powerful a man as Franklin for an ordinary innkeeper. But Cole was not an ordinary innkeeper: he was a smuggler who ran a smuggler's den.

Although many of the goods the smugglers fenced were stolen, most of them were probably stolen from British sources, which, given the attitude of the day toward England, made it a far lesser crime than theft from a neighbor. By the same token, goods smuggled in on ships might not have been stolen, but their sale evaded taxation.

The notion of salvaging the Spanish Plate Fleet was most likely discussed at Great Island Tavern. I can imagine the Coles and the Browns and the Paines, all related through marriage and occupation, sitting around the tavern considering the possibilities that a sunken treasure fleet might offer. With fourteen million pesos on the shallow ocean bottom, all a treasure hunter would have to do was snag one casket of coins and he would be rich beyond his dreams.

By the end of these speculations, there were at least two people who were convinced that the Silver Plate Fleet could be had: Bellamy and Paulsgrave Williams.

Williams was the middle-aged son of a former Rhode Island attorney general. Married with two children, he was a moderately successful jeweler. He had come to the Cape to visit relatives and began spending time with Bellamy. Williams saw the good sense in pursuing sunken treasure.

Exactly what transpired is not part of the historical record, but we do know that Williams put much of his personal wealth as well as his life into the hands of Sam Bellamy. During the next several weeks, they acquired a boat, probably a small sloop, and assembled a crew of about a dozen men.

During these days of planning, Bellamy met Maria Hallett. There are many different versions of the story of Sam and Maria, including the one told to me by my uncle Bill. But the written version I was most familiar with was that laid out in Elizabeth Reynard's 1978 book *The Narrow Land*.

As Reynard tells it, Bellamy emerged one night from Higgins Tavern in Eastham to clear his brain of the ale he had been drinking. Deciding to walk it off, he took a stroll through the cemetery. As he was about to turn around, he heard the lovely voice of a girl singing to herself. Then, wrote Reynard:

> He traced the song to a circular hollow surrounded by trees, and coming to the edge, saw, below him, a white cloud floating. From the cloud rose a song. He strode downslope, through 'Tarnity Briars, and found that the cloud was a flower apple tree. Under the tree stood Maria Hallett, a (bouquet of flowers) in one hand and blossoms in the other. She was fifteen years old; her hair glistened like corn silk at suncoming; her eyes were the color of hyacinth, like the deeps of Gull Pond. Black Bellamy made masterful love, sailorman love that remembers how a following wind falls short and makes way while it blows. Maria Hallett had never seen a man as handsome as Sam Bellamy; just out of the West Country, his black hair curly, his fortune buckled in his three-cornered pocket, and mighty dreams in his eye. Love was settled between them in no time at all, under the apple tree by the Burying Acre, and Sam sailed away with a promise to Maria that when he returned he would wed her by ring to the words of the Rev. Mr. Treat, and in a sloop laden with treasure, carry her back to the Spanish Indies, there to be made princess of a West Indian isle.

The truth about their brief relationship will always remain shrouded in speculation. What Sam Bellamy did next, however, became a well-substantiated part of world history.

★ ★ ★

"Barry, this boat is awesome."

Those were the first words from Stretch Grey's mouth when I picked up the telephone. He had taken the long, lonely drive to Bristol, Maine, to examine the *Vast Explorer.* It was obvious from his voice that he was happy with what he saw.

"What's so good about it?" I asked.

"Well, for one thing, she isn't a fishing boat." He laughed. "She is built to be a research vessel."

I was elated because Grey was elated. As a man who was born to be on the water, Grey knew a good boat when he saw it. The excitement in his voice told me that this was the boat we needed and that we would not have to look any further. I packed a bag and drove up to Bristol to see what we were buying.

The Gammage Boat Yard was a legend, a place where the beautiful trees of Maine and other parts of the world were crafted by nautical engineers into some of the most revered vessels to sail the seven seas. Harvey Gammage himself had passed away several years earlier, and his boatyard was dying a slow technological death. Builders could not compete with manufacturers who used cheaper materials like fiberglass that allowed faster methods of construction. Gammage's grandson, Linwood, was converting the fabled facility into a marina by refitting the huge boat dock to accom-

The *Vast Explorer* at the Gammage Boat Yard in Maine.

modate pleasure boats. Because of the construction, there was only one boat at the Gammage dock the day I arrived, the *Vast Explorer*. Standing alone, I gazed at the black-and-white beauty rocking at her berth. There was no question that Grey had summed her up with that one word, "awesome." She was perfect.

"Hell of a boat," came a decidedly Maine voice from behind me.

"That she is," I said, surprised to see a powerful yet undeniably ancient man approaching. He introduced himself as Corliss Ferron, a former captain of the *Vast Explorer*. I shook his hand and was shocked by its feel and grip. It was like grasping the thick branch of a sturdy oak tree—an effect produced by the fact that Ferron had pulled eighty lobster pots off the ocean floor each day for the last twenty seasons when he wasn't captaining the *Vast*. This man was tough and smart and clearly knew boats.

Ferron took Stretch and me on board the *Vast* and told us why she was a good treasure-hunting ship and how she could be made better. Constructed of solid pieces of white oak, her hull was thick and seemingly unsinkable. Because she was wooden, there would be none of the interference with the magnetometer that a metal hull would present. Her deck was covered with thick tiles that made an excellent non-slip working surface, and her superstructure was built like an oil derrick and fitted with a hoist that could lift two tons.

Twin diesels crowded the engine room, but not so much that we wouldn't be able to dry plenty of dive gear by hanging it in the passageway between the engines, and put our scuba tanks in the tool locker. An enclosed pilot house contained radio and navigational gear and a flying bridge gave us the luxury of steering the ship from a sunny deck when the weather was good.

A galley and galley table were below the pilot house, and in front of that were six bunks with a passageway down the middle to the ship's head, which was located in the very bow. Above the head on the forecastle was a powerful hydraulic capstan, a winch used to pull up the anchor.

"She's a great working boat," said Ferron. "Harvey built her for the navy to retrieve sonar buoys. They dropped the buoys from airplanes to keep an eye on Russian submarines that were cruising our coast. When they started to drift out of position, the *Vast* would go out and find them."

Ferron talked about the *Vast* as if she were alive, and in some ways she was for him. He had spent more time with her than anyone but his wife. The *Vast* had taken care of him in all the weather that the sea can dish out, and he had cared for her in return. Although he was sorry to see her go, he knew that the *Vast* was headed for even greater adventures. "Working for the navy was an honorable profession for her, but treasure hunting sounds like fun," declared Ferron. "You won't be disappointed."

After we bought the boat for $168,000, the employees of the Gammage Boat Yard began the task of repainting and refitting the sixty-five-footer for treasure-hunting duty. Several changes were made, but the most obvious one was the installation of the mailboxes, the metal tubes that drop down and fit over the propellers to divert their thrust straight down and clear the sand from the ocean floor. These required the engineering expertise of Bruce Etchman, the man who had designed the mailboxes for the boats of Mel Fisher's treasure-hunting operation in Florida. Made of heavy-gauge metal and requiring precision installation so they fit correctly over the propellers, these devices were tricky to attach.

With all the work that needed to be done, the Gammage people estimated that they would have the boat completed by the end of June, which was way too late. I told them that we planned to begin digging this season, and waiting until the end of June would cut our season in half.

"It'll speed things up if you leave your crew here to help," said Linwood Gammage. "Then maybe we could finish by some time in May."

I hesitated for a moment, but not because I was afraid of leaving my crew in Maine. The investors' money had not arrived from Colorado yet, and I

JFK Jr., right, and Todd Murphy watch as Stretch and Bruce Etchman adjust the *Vast*'s mailboxes at the Gammage Boat Yard.

was paying for operating costs out of my own pocket. Having made a down payment on the boat and an advance payment on the refitting, I was practically out of money, which made my wife back in Martha's Vineyard extremely nervous.

I told Grey and Beyer that I was nearly out of cash, but if they would stay and work while we waited for money to come in I would pay them the wages I owed them plus shares of stock. I felt uneasy at making the offer, especially since we hadn't started searching for treasure, let alone found any.

The response that came back was immediate and definite. "We'll take it!" declared Stretch.

16

What Now?

The crew assembles at the Captain's House.

❋ The hearts of Bellamy and Williams must have sunk when they arrived in the Gulf of Florida, since salvage efforts by the Spanish had already begun. With the efficiency of a mighty sea power, the Spanish had secured the area, leaving the looters to their unfulfilled dreams.

The treasure was saved for the Spanish by the fast action of Admiral Francisco Salmon, the highest-ranking survivor of the shipwreck.

From the *Urca* and the *Nuestra Señora de la Regla,* his men had salvaged boats, which he immediately had outfitted with food and water and manned with his most loyal sailors. Each of the boats was about twenty-four feet long and could carry as many as fifty people. One boat was sent 120 miles north to St. Augustine, loaded with women and children who had been passengers on the ships to Spain, as well as the most seriously injured.

With them he sent a desperate letter to Governor Francisco Corioles pleading for help.

Dear Sir:

I have not communicated our mishap to you before because I did not have a vessel at my disposal. I do it now with deep sorrow in my heart since this disaster has been the worst that has occurred in many a year. Not a single ship, whether from the naval escort or from the galleons, has been spared, and because my general Ubilla perished in the Capitana, I have taken his place to recover this treasure, which is something of great importance to the service of the King and to the common good. Inasmuch as I am on an island, where we became lost, and we are all so desperately in need of supplies, I am begging you to help me by sending to us as much as you can, or else everyone here will perish. In addition to food supplies, I would like to receive twenty rifles with their bullets, as much powder as possible, half a dozen axes, another half a dozen shovels and some hoes to remove the sand in order to see whether I can manage to dig out some of the silver and break open part of the hull. His Majesty's treasure and that of private persons, both of which were carried in the hold, sank with the ship in five fathoms of water, in a spot we have duly marked. I am sending my pilot along with this message. I hope and trust that you will help me as soon as possible with some vessels from your garrison. May God grant Your Lordship a long life. August 4, 1715.

Your most humble servant,

Don Francisco Salmon

The second launch was sent 360 miles south to Cuba, where word of the wreck swept the streets of Havana like a tidal wave of grief. Church bells pealed and officials read dispatches prepared by the governor's office. In short order, the citizens of Havana knew that fourteen hundred people had survived the wrecks and were now on the island of Barra de Ays, where they were suffering from lack of food and water. They also knew that Cuba's Governor Casatores was going to act as quickly as he could to rescue the survivors and salvage the treasure.

Casatores wrote a letter to King Philip V of Spain and sent it aboard the frigate *Francisco,* which was sailing for Rochelle, France. Then, in an exhibition of efficiency, Casatores assembled seven ships and loaded them with specialized salvage equipment, including grappling hooks, coils of rope, long-handled rakes, empty chests, diving bells, and glass-bottomed buckets to better see underwater. Thirty experienced Indian divers from the coast of South America were recruited and promised a percentage of every chest of silver that they found.

On September 10, 1715, more than five weeks after the catastrophe, the ships arrived at the island camp of Admiral Salmon. Fresh water and food were rowed ashore, marking the end of suffering for the castaways. During the next several weeks, the survivors were ferried to the big ships and eventually taken back to Havana, where they would be deposed by officials who were hungry for the details of the wreck.

Back in Barra de Ays, meanwhile, salvage work had begun. Divers had found the remains of the *Capitana* and the *Almiranta,* in which the majority of the treasure was being transported, and now they were racing the onset of bad weather to collect as much of the sunken treasure as they could.

Led by a Spanish diving engineer named Clemente, the Indians dove in the treacherous water, where they found chests of silver stacked in rows inside the hulls that had carried them. The moment of impact had been so violent that the hulls sheared in half and simply dropped to the bottom, cargo intact.

Clemente himself made three dives and found boxes of silver piled on top of ballast stones and shattered timber. Despite his good fortune at finding so much booty, Clemente was concerned about the weather. Autumn was descending, bringing the violent seasonal churn of the North Atlantic. Soon, punishing winds would come from the east and with them the waves that would make retrieval of even the easiest objects a deadly occupation.

Ordinarily the veteran diver would have ordered his men to wait until spring, when calmer weather would allow for safer and more leisurely salvage. Already, however, English ships had passed the site and Clemente and his boss, Hoyo Solorzano, knew that more would be coming to get what they could. It was clear that these two men saw more danger above the water than below, because that would be the only reason for diving in so rough an ocean.

As cutters and longboats fought for position over the wrecks, the Indians dove naked to search blindly for the treasure chests. With visibility less than an arm's length, the divers felt the bottom for the chests. In some instances, the chests could be easily lifted and raised to the surface. Other times, the Indians had to use crowbars to pry them loose from obstructions.

As near as can be determined, none of the Indian divers drowned in the first two weeks of salvage, although three were killed: two by falling chests and one by a hungry shark.

With much of the easily accessible treasure recovered, the divers ripped the ships apart with crowbars and grappling hooks to get at the rest of the booty. After several weeks of salvaging, probably during the time that Bellamy and Williams were on their way to the site, the Spanish had recovered a large portion of the treasure, possibly as much as 80 percent. Most of this treasure made it back to the storehouses of Havana, but some did not. English privateer Henry Jennings, sent to sea by the governor of Jamaica to search for pirates, landed three hundred men at Barra de Ays and stole sixty thousand pieces of eight after overpowering the sixty soldiers guarding the storehouse.

There is a chance that Bellamy and Williams were able to grapple for some of the Spanish treasure, but highly unlikely that they had much luck. The Spanish had so thoroughly swept the area of treasure that what was left would not be found for more than 250 years, when treasure hunters like Mel Fisher began to comb this area with modern salvage techniques. Bellamy and crew may have grappled the sites or dragged a rope between two ships in hopes of snagging something of value, but they must have realized that the Spanish had beaten them to the gold.

At some point the two sailors must have wondered what their future held. A return to the colonies as failures would make them the laughingstocks of the Cape. They might also have been indentured to others like Israel Cole, who may have put money into the venture and would be furious at the loss of investment dollars.

As their tiny boat pitched and creaked with the wind and waves, the entrepreneurs sat with their heads together and realized that their venture was broke. Making the decision to go pirate may have been their best choice.

For me, the project was full speed ahead. It was spring of 1983 and my preparations were moving forward faster than the money was coming in from the investors. This situation made my wife nervous, who watched in horror as our finances rapidly poured into the project. She could not understand my fascination with a shipwreck that had taken place more than two hundred years ago and could not believe a group of wealthy men in Colorado might have an interest in a Cape Cod pirate, let alone invest in a project to find his ship's remains. She thought I had lost my mind along with everyone remotely involved in this exploration.

"This will only take a few months," I told her, trying to minimize the impact of the expedition on our lives.

She just shrugged. She liked the comfortable and sure life we had been leading, and saw the *Whydah* expedition as a threat. It was clear to me that Birgitta and I had reached a crossroads, one that would see us taking separate paths. Before long we were divorced.

I began searching for a house to rent and found a massive colonial near Nauset Inlet, a shallow harbor out of which I planned to work with a shallow-draft speedboat. The two-story house was white with green shutters and set in a majestic grove of maples and birches. I immediately dubbed it "the Captain's House," because the place was stuffed with nautical antiques and beautifully painted portraits, including one of a sea captain whose eyes seemed to follow you no matter where you were in the living room. The owner was meticulous about the house and seemed worried about the fact that her place would be used as a base of operations for a treasure-hunting expedition. The fact that I was born and raised on the Cape seemed to figure in her decision to allow me to rent her house. As a local, she figured I would not be too difficult to track down if anything was broken or destroyed.

I discovered later that the house was located next to Jeremiah's Gutter, the narrow, marshy groove through which Cyprian Southack had rowed from the harbor to the Atlantic on his failed attempt to salvage the *Whydah*. The irony of this location was not lost on me. What Southhack had started, I was now going to finish—or at least, I hoped I would finish.

In April, before everyone descended on the house for the first season's dig, I had a vivid dream: I could see rows of men walking out of the swampy slime of the Gutter. They were dressed like pirates and covered with seaweed and sand. With menace in their eyes, they strode through the trees and across the green lawn of the Captain's House. Without knocking, they walked in the door and came up the stairs in single file toward my room.

In my dream, the door opened. I popped awake and turned on a light. I expected to see a roomful of pirates protesting the fact that I was searching for their booty, but the room was empty. The door was still closed, and there were no wet footprints or strands of seaweed to indicate that the pirate ghosts had existed anywhere but in my head. Still, the dream was so vivid that I sat up for a while and contemplated its significance.

The dream was cryptic, its meaning confusing. Examined one way, it seemed as though the ghosts were hostile and didn't want me to search for the booty that had gone down with them. Examined another way, this could easily have been a greeting party, a grim crew from the past that was coming to welcome me to their treasure lair. Ultimately I came to regard this dream as a sort of hospitality visit from the true owners of the *Whydah* treasure. Somewhere, even if only in my mind, I was being given an invitation to search for the *Whydah*.

The team members for the first *Whydah* expedition started coming together in February. In addition to Stretch and Beyer, who were still in Maine, Todd Murphy joined the group. He was a Green Beret in the army reserves who was pursuing a degree in exercise physiology from the University of Connecticut. He was in great physical shape from running and

A "formal" meeting of the dive team on the lawn of the Captain's House.

other sports that didn't require huge muscles. This emphasis on the non-weightlifting sports gave him an advantage on a crew where many of the members would be more likely to think with their biceps than their heads. Todd was a stickler for safety, and eventually filled the important role of director of dive operations. Also joining us was Charlie Burnham, a friend of mine from Martha's Vineyard who had honed his mechanical genius at Yale and was now studying robotics. Bill Dibble became a member of the crew, too. The kind of guy who would be picked as the "most likely to succeed" in his high school yearbook, Dibble had been a fighter pilot in Vietnam. As the scion of a very wealthy Greenwich, Connecticut, family with all the right connections, I would have expected him to be on the fast track to corporate stardom. It didn't work that way for Dibble. Vietnam had been hard on him emotionally and left him feeling rootless.

He was elated when I asked him to join the team. In preparation, he worked out steadily from winter until May, when we made the first magging trips to map the site. He regained much of the physique that had made him such a fine athlete in high school and at Wesleyan College, where he was voted on the Little All-American football team.

I was also called by Trip Wheeler, a throwback to my college days. Wheeler was a wild man whom I first saw in Gunnison, Colorado, roaring down the street standing upright on the seat of a motorcycle.

And, of course, there was Rob McClung. Things were not going so well for the chief of police of Aspen. He resigned amid accusations that he had improperly removed a pistol from the police department's evidence locker. McClung said he had removed it in an effort to test the vigilance of the locker's guard, but nonetheless, his days at the police department of the most beautiful city in Colorado were numbered.

McClung wanted to start a new life. He decided that new life would be as a treasure hunter.

I ignored the charges that had forced McClung to leave the police department. The Rob McClung I hired onto the project was the one I had gone to college with at Trinidad. There we had enjoyed hours exploring the wilderness, sometimes swimming the frothy rapids of the Purgatory River for an entire day, wearing nothing but shorts, sneakers to keep our feet from being cut by sharp rocks, and belt knives. To me, McClung was a Huck Finn–style companion who was always adventurous. For me the *Whydah* expedition was like a college reunion—the good old days revisited—and I was blind to the notion that ten years had changed some of my old friends a lot.

Along with McClung came John Levin. He was the district judge in Aspen who helped us arrange financing. A good businessman and a junkie for adventure, Levin liked what he heard about the *Whydah* project and asked to be made business manager of Maritime Explorations.

At the time, he seemed the perfect person for the job. A former prosecutor from New York who had worked on the Frank Serpico police-corruption investigation, Levin had long black hair and big dark eyes that led many people to say that he resembled the actor Al Pacino, who had played Officer Serpico in the movie about the affair. The more Levin heard about the *Whydah,* the less he liked his job as a judge. His marriage had broken up and his emotions were so on edge that he no longer felt he was doing a good job on the bench. In addition, he lived vicariously through McClung, accompanying him on at least one of the drug busts the head policeman loved to carry out. Now that McClung was leaving to hunt treasure, Levin decided that he wanted to join him as a member of a team of treasure hunters.

I talked to Lazier about the appointment of Levin to the post of business manager, and he thought it was a fine idea. McClung approved, too. He declared Levin one of his best friends and said that the soon-to-be-former Aspen judge would make an excellent addition to the team. But something happened between Levin and McClung between the time I hired him as business manager in Colorado and the day that they arrived on the Cape. It was near the end of February, and Levin was upset. Gingerly, he took me aside to talk about it.

"Look, I am second in command, right?" he asked me.

"Yeah, you are second in command," I said, somewhat taken aback by the question.

John Levin charms a
feathered resident.

Levin nodded and continued with his line of questioning. "That means
that I get to make all the business decisions and you get to make all of the
decisions that have to do with salvage, correct?"

"Okay, that sounds good," I replied. "You handle the business and I'll handle the salvage."

"Okay. And I get to make my first decision now," continued Levin. "I am
going to make a decision, and you're not going to block it, right? I've got
your word on it?"

He had clearly put me into a corner. "Okay, you've got my word. You are
second in command and I will not block your decision."

"Okay, I am firing McClung."

I stared at Levin with wide eyes for a moment and then chuckled at the
irony of what I had just heard.

"What are you talking about?" I demanded. "This guy is my friend. Hell,
he's your friend. He is the one who brought you onto this project."

"We may think he's our friend, but he's not," Levin insisted. "I'm firing
him. I can't work with him. I can't trust him. I am firing him, and you gave
me your word that I could do it."

I told Levin that a decision like this required some thought. After he left,
I telephoned Lazier and told him what had transpired. Surprisingly, my Vail
partner and confidant did not seemed surprised by what Levin had said. In
fact, he seemed to support his point of view.

"Maybe he's right," said Lazier, who has an uncanny sense about people
that he developed in the orphanage. "McClung seems to be trying to get
into your shoes; maybe you just don't see it yet."

Levin had reasons for wanting to dump McClung. Some conversations had taken place between Levin and McClung that made Levin realize the ex-cop would be a problem later, if not sooner. Levin would not tell me what had been said, and I am not certain that it would have made a difference in my loyalty had I known. McClung was an old friend who was down, and I was willing to give him a lot of slack.

Levin went ahead and fired McClung, but I intervened to bring him back. I told Levin that we had all helped each other up to now, and there was no reason to think that we would stab one another in the back later. Maybe McClung was just feeling powerless because of everything that had happened to him, I told Levin. Maybe he had said things that he really didn't mean to say about me.

"I'm willing to forgive and forget," I said to the judge.

We all went on with the business of treasure hunting, trying to pretend that nothing had happened. Through the smiles was an undercurrent of bad feeling that kept me on edge. It was clear that the good fellowship of our college days was melting like ice cream in the hot sun. Suddenly there was no one I could talk with openly, causing me to become more guarded.

What now? I thought one day. What is going to happen next?

As I continued to study pirates, I realized that captains like Bellamy were never fully in control of their crews. Contrary to the popular belief, a pirate captain was ruled by the collective iron fist of his crew.

A pirate captain was elected by his men to bring out the best in the crew. Election to this post gave him a cabin of his own, but the men could enter it at any time without permission. The captain received an extra share of the loot, but he did not exercise absolute rule. The only time his rule was absolute was in time of conflict, when a prize ship was being taken, for instance, or when his ship was under attack. The rest of the time, the captain was just one vote in a floating democracy in which every man on board had one vote and the majority ruled.

Part of the reason seamen became pirates was to get away from the cruel merchant captains, who did rule with an iron fist.

As an added safeguard against their captain, the pirates elected a quartermaster, whose primary job was to act on behalf of the company the way a union steward acts on behalf of his fellow union members. The quartermaster inspected weapons, administered punishment, kept track of the provisions, and—most important—divided the captured loot among the men.

The pirate captain had no need to watch his back because there were long-standing rules that governed the way pirates searched for treasure.

These rules, called simply "the Articles," were an antidote to treasure fever and the single greatest bond that held pirates together.

Evolving from a seventeenth-century congress of privateers in Jamaica, the Articles were written law that governed every known pirate company. They most certainly were adopted by Bellamy's men when the decision was made to turn pirate. A version of the Articles was probably drawn up by the newly elected quartermaster Paulsgrave Williams and signed by every man on board who wanted to stay and become a buccaneer.

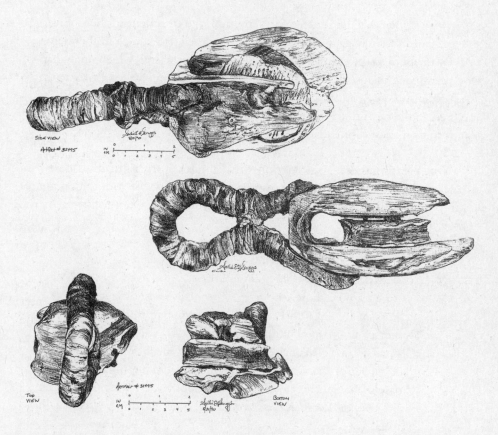

SIDE VIEW
Artifact # 32495

TOP VIEW
Artifact # 32495
BOTTOM VIEW

THE BOSUN AND THE TACKLE

The boatswain, or "bosun," was the ship's general foreman, and often as feared as the captain. His most important duty was keeping the rigging shipshape. He was usually picked from the most experienced and knowledgeable able-bodied seamen on board. Because he enforced discipline, he was also selected for his strength and brutality.

The tackle, like this one from the *Whydah*, was a key element in the ship's rigging because it was used to hoist the sails.

Pirates invented a radical form of government for themselves. For centuries, society was governed by monarchies, and the king's rule was absolute. When you read the Articles, which follow, notice how closely they resemble documents like the Declaration of Independence and others that form the backbone of democratic society. The Articles featured checks and balances, separation of powers, and federalism.

The Articles were popular among the men because, as pirate captain Walter Kennedy explained at his 1721 trial,

> Most of them having suffered formerly from the treatment of their officers, provided carefully against any such evil now they had choice in themselves. By their orders they provided specially against any quarrels which might happen among themselves, and appointed certain punishments for anything that tended that way; for the due execution thereof they constituted other officers besides the captain so industrious were they to avoid putting too much power into the hands of one man.

This paraphrased reconstruction of a "pirates' constitution" is based on rules and customs that were common to most crews of the golden age of piracy—as well as on specific practices known to have been followed by the crew of the *Whydah*.

I. Every Man shall obey Civil Command.

II. Every Man who has signed these Articles is to have a Vote in Matters of Importance. Those who have not signed shall not vote.

III. The Captain and Officers of the Company are to be chosen by the Majority upon the commencement of a Voyage, or on such other Occasions as the Majority of the Company shall think fit.

IV. The power of the Captain is Supreme and Unquestioned in time of Chase or Battle. He may beat, cut, or shoot any Man who dares deny his Command on such Occasions. In all other Matters whatsoever, he is to be governed by Vote of the Majority of the Company.

V. Every Man is to have Equal Right to the Provisions, or Liquors at any Time, and to use them at Pleasure unless Scarcity makes it necessary to vote a restriction for the Good of all.

VI. Every Man is to be called fairly, in Turn by the List of our Company kept by the Quarter-Master, on board of Prizes. Each Boarder on such occasions is to receive a Suit of clothes from the Prize. He who first sees a Sail, shall have the Best Pistol, or Small-Arm, from on board her.

VII. The Quarter-Master is to be the first man on board of any Prize; he is to separate for the Company's use what he thinks fit, and shall have Trust of the Common Stock [the pirates' treasury] until it be Shared. He shall Keep a Book showing each Man's share, and each Man can draw from the Common Stock against his Share upon request.

VIII. If any Man should Defraud the Company, or one another, to the Value of a Pound, he shall suffer what Punishment the Majority shall think fit.

IX. Each Man is to keep his Musket, Pistols, and Cutlass clean and fit for Service upon inspection by the Quarter-Master.

X. No Woman or Boy is to be brought on board ship.

XI. No married men are to be forced to serve our Company.

XII. Good Quarters [the opportunity for enemies to surrender with expectation of good treatment] to be granted when Called for.

XIII. Any Man who Deserts the Ship, Keeps any Secret from the Company, or who Deserts his Station in time of Battle, shall be punished by Death, Marooning, or Whipping, as the Majority shall think fit.

XIV. Not a word shall be Written by any of the Company unless it shall be Nailed Publickly to the Mast.

XV. If any Man shall strike or abuse one another of our Company, in any regard, he shall suffer such Punishment as the Majority shall think fit. Every Man's Quarrel is to be settled on Shore with Sword and Pistol under the eye of the Quarter-Master.

XVI. All lights and candles must be put out before 8 o'clock at night. After that hour, if any man continues drinking, he must do it on the open deck. That Man who shall smoke Tobacco in the Hold without a Cap, or carry a lit Candle without a Lanthorn, shall receive Moses's Law (that is, 40 Stripes less one) on the bare Back.

XVII. No Man is to talk of breaking up our Way of Living till each of us has shared a thousand pounds.

XVIII. If any Man should lose a Limb, or become a Cripple, he is to have 800 Pounds out of the Common Stock, and for lesser hurts, proportionately.

XIX. The Captain and Quarter-Master are to receive two Shares of a Prize; the Sailing Master, Boatswain, and Gunner, one Share and a half, and other Officers one and a quarter Shares.

With their new captain elected, the Bellamy crew prowled the coast of Central America, searching for prize ships. It is not known exactly how many ships they plundered, but it is certain that several surrendered to the novice pirates.

While the boarding party stood guard over the captured merchant seamen, the captain and officers of the prize ship were brought to the pirate ship for questioning. They were interrogated separately, asked questions about the nature of the cargo and the amount of money on board. The cargo manifest and logbook were examined, and seamen were questioned about the presence of secret booty that might be of interest.

When the looting was completed, the merchantman's crew was offered a chance to join the pirates. One such recruiting speech was made by Captain Charles Johnson (believed by some to be Daniel Defoe) in the book *A General History of the Pirates.*

> In an honest Service; there is thin Commons [rations], low Wages, and hard Labour: in this, Plenty and Satiety, Pleasure and Ease, Liberty and Power; and who would not ballance Creditor on this Side, when all the Hazard that is run for it, at worst, is only a sour Look or two at choking. No, a merry life and a short one shall be my Motto.

I am sure that Bellamy was a successful recruiter, whatever speech he made when the looting was over. His success was due, in part, to his eloquence as a speaker. Another factor was the nature of the business for which he was recruiting. It was, after all, treasure hunting.

17

The First Season

Anxious to hear of any finds the crew gave its undivided attention to divers when they returned to the surface.

❋ With surveyor tools, we marked all the major hits from the magnetometer on a map of the dive site. These hits were recorded inside the boxes of a grid, with each tiny box on the map representing eight square feet. The total site was one square mile. The idea was to excavate the site one square at a time, provided the square had something in it that had caused the magnetometer to jump.

We had mapped the area using the *Crumpstey*, a twenty-four-foot Boston Whaler we used as a second boat.

The *Vast Explorer* came down from South Bristol, Maine, with Grey at the helm. His crew for that maiden voyage was Beyer, Brad Crosby, a graduate of the Massachusetts Marine Academy, and John F. Kennedy Jr., who was on summer vacation from Brown University.

I knew Kennedy from Martha's Vineyard, and he had come along as a diver on our first trip to the wreck site the previous year. He had asked if I had a summer job for him and I said yes. Some on the crew were afraid that he would be too much of a dilettante to work as hard as the rest. Their concerns were unwarranted. From the very first day, Kennedy came on the boat and worked as hard as anyone else.

Grey was one who had concerns, too. When I told him JFK Jr. was going to be on the crew, he frowned and demanded, "Is he bringing his butler with him? What am I suppose to do with a Kennedy?"

"Treat him like any other crewman," I replied. "I don't think he wants a free ride."

His first day on board, Kennedy asked Grey if there was any work he could do. Grey gave him the worst job on the boat, cleaning and painting the lazarette, a bilge-reeking compartment in the stern that houses the rudder mechanism. Kennedy worked for a week like a mole, only coming out of the compartment when the sun was down at the end of the day.

After Kennedy completed that assignment, Grey treated his new friend with great respect, not because he was a Kennedy, but because he was the only person the veteran captain had seen who worked in that compartment without complaint.

It was rare to see JFK Jr. and Stretch take a break. They were two of the hardest working crewmen.

Within a few days we were off the coast of Marconi Beach, the last known site of the *Whydah,* or so we thought. The beach, now teeming with sun-bathers, was named for electronics genius Guglielmo Marconi, the inventor of wireless communications. At one time the cliffs overlooking the water had been the site of four enormous steel towers, built by Marconi's company in 1902 to transmit radio messages to Europe. When Marconi discovered years later that radio signals could bounce off the stratosphere to their destination and not have to be transmitted from one tower to the next, the metallic edifices were abandoned. The towers were eventually toppled into the sea for safety reasons because the sand underneath them was eroding away. The metal bars that the towers were constructed from now litter the ocean floor.

This was the spot that Fay Feild had explored with the mag and part of the area to which we had laid claim with the state. Given the large hits that registered on the magnetometer, it seemed like a good area in which to start digging.

We had made a preliminary magging venture on the *Crumpstey* and marked "hot" areas with buoys. Now Stretch was left with the task of positioning the boat over the dig site.

Positioning the boat required skill and precision. First we set the anchors. This was done by pinpointing the site with the magnetometer (it is now done using Global Positioning Satellite technology). When we were positioned directly over a target, the bow anchor was dropped and the boat was backed up to sink the anchor flukes into the sand. The anchor chain was then unclipped from the nylon line and bright orange buoys were attached. They floated on the surface and marked the line's position.

The same thing was done with the two stern anchors, each weighing half as much as the 150-pound bow anchor.

Just setting these anchors was a day's work, but it was important because they marked the triangle of ocean that would be our working area. By using hydraulic winches to lengthen and shorten individual lines, we could move the boat anywhere we wanted within that triangle without starting the boat's engines.

This was good, since the engines were not used for propulsion once we were over the wreck site. Their horizontal thrust was directed downward by the mailboxes to blow a crater in the thick layer of sand that had covered the artifacts for all these years.

The mailboxes were another challenge. Guide wires from the boat's tower lowered them into the water, where they had to be pushed and prodded into their position over the propellers. A diver would then go into the water and pin them in place. For added stability, a device called a "come-along" was connected to the sides of the mailbox and cranked tight. The mailboxes were held steady against the torrent of prop wash that swirled out of the propellers and down into the sand by the pins and come-alongs.

When the mailboxes were down and in place, the *Vast Explorer* was no longer a boat, but a floating platform that could not move on its own. If we broke loose from our mooring, which could happen if we were hit by a sudden squall or a large rogue wave, the *Vast* would suffer the same fate as the *Whydah,* running aground on that terrible beauty, the beach.

This is how it was, day after day, that first, terribly dry season. We chased the hits all over the map. Sometimes we dug on large hits because we thought that maybe they were cannons or a mass of cannonballs that had managed to stay together despite two and a half centuries of rough weather. Other times we dug on smaller hits, believing that other lighter objects had scattered and we were on the outer ring of the wreck site.

What we found instead was the litter of twentieth-century warfare, objects like .50-caliber bullets and practice bombs, all from Army Air Corps airplanes that had used this lovely stretch of beach to practice for World War II.

One time, a diver rose from the bottom elated at the cylindrical object he had found in one of the pits we dug.

Murphy's military training made him especially valuable when it came time to recognizing unexploded bombs that we sometimes mistook for artifacts.

"I think it's a small cannon," he shouted, holding it up from the dive platform.

"Throw it back!" shouted Todd Murphy, the only person on board with military training. "That's a bomb!"

Things like that happened all the time. Before long we had a collection of bullets, shell casings, rods from Marconi's towers, and a variety of other contemporary jetsam.

Our lack of success made us the town joke. One night I went into the Land Ho Tavern, our hangout in Orleans, only to hear my name bandied about from the far end of the bar. I walked quietly the length of the bar and sat on the stool next to the man who was talking. He had his back turned my way, but I recognized him as a local author who had written a guidebook to shipwrecks of Cape Cod. He was loudly holding court on the fate of the *Whydah*.

". . . I wrote the book on it and I know, that ship doesn't exist," the author was saying. "Someone made up that story to sell beachfront property two hundred years ago and it just became part of Cape Cod mythology."

The man listening was not convinced.

"How about that woman in Wellfleet who has all of those coins that her grandfather gave her?" he asked.

"That doesn't mean they came from the *Whydah*," he said. "The guy might have bought those in a secondhand store."

"Maybe so, but there are a few people around here whose families got awfully rich in the 1800s for no reason at all," the man insisted. "And now their families say they found treasure on the beach."

"Yeah, right," snapped the cynical author. "They were probably moon cussers who 'found' the ship after they wrecked it."

Some people believed me to be a scam artist who had sold a myth to the investors and nothing more. Others said that they had told me where the *Whydah* was most likely located and accused me of having jumped their claim. A fellow named Billy Crockett—the second one-eyed man I would deal with—formed a company called the Old Blue Fishing Company and was trying to lay claim to a site next to mine on the outside chance that the *Whydah* was south of where I thought it was. "I know I can find it first," he insisted. "I too have done some historical research."

To the north, a third one-eyed competitor, Matt "the Rat" Costa, had made a claim on a ship called the *White Squall,* which crashed into the shore in 1867, carrying a load of tin. His alleged interest was in the tin, but Matt wasn't nicknamed "the Rat" for nothing. He didn't file his claim until I made my search for the *Whydah* formal. I suspect that, like the one-eyed man to my south, Costa was hoping that the *Whydah* lay in his claim area.

These two men watched their sites constantly. On almost any given day during that first season we could see one or both of them watching us from shore with binoculars, trying to determine if we were in our permit area or theirs.

I felt sorry for Costa, who never struck me as being a happy man, probably because of the tragic hunting accident that caused the loss of his eye. Trying to clear a shell that was jammed in the chamber of his shotgun, Costa banged the butt of the gun on the ground, only to have it fire, blowing out his eye and taking off almost half his face. The citizens of Provincetown raised money for an expensive—and at the time, experimental—surgical operation to rebuild his face. The procedure involved attaching the remainder of his face to his shoulder so it would grow, then grafting it over the patch blown away by the shotgun blast. In time, a plastic surgeon rebuilt a reasonably good face. In the meantime Costa had become wealthy, investing in a bar and a restaurant, even developing a small subdivision of homes.

Like most people on the Cape, Costa had heard the story of the *Whydah* and felt a twinge of ownership, especially when I decided to lay claim to a specific site and start searching. After that happened, he was on my back constantly.

A particularly frightening confrontation came from both of these one-eyed claimants. We were anchored offshore near the Beachcomber, a barn-sized tavern located north of the *Whydah* site. The crew had swum in to eat dinner and enjoy a few drinks, leaving Stretch Grey behind to guard the equipment.

It was a hot night, so Stretch decided to sleep naked on the flying bridge. Well after midnight, the naked giant was awakened by a loud drumming on the hull of the boat. Arising stiffly, he peered over the side of the boat to see Costa and Crockett looking as menacing as possible. Costa had some help from a shotgun he was aiming at Stretch's head.

"What the hell do you want?" asked Grey, unimpressed by the shotgun.

"You're digging here!" shouted Crockett.

Grey shook his head in disgust.

"We can't dig at night," he declared. "And I'm all alone. I'm just sleeping here!"

The two one-eyed men looked at each other and then back at Stretch.

"Get off our site!" demanded Costa.

"You get off my site!" shouted Grey, who was becoming more annoyed as he slowly awoke.

A Myth Walks the Plank

Contrary to the old "Dead men tell no tales" stories of fiction, pirates of this era seldom massacred prisoners. In fact, to set the record straight once and for all, there is absolutely no rumor—much less proof—of any pirate crew making a prisoner "walk the plank" during the early eighteenth century! This is pure invention by nineteenth-century romantic authors. Torture was usually reserved for merchant captains suspected of concealing money or maltreating their crewmen. Captives who put up a resistance could also expect harsh and brutal treatment, and pirate companies made this quite clear.

Most pirates would not shrink from violence—whether in battle or in cold blood. By modern standards, pirates were hard, brutal, and vicious men. They lived, however, in an extraordinarily hard, brutal, and vicious age, and, by the standards of their own age, some were described as decent and humane men—even by their victims.

The two men looked at each other and then back at Grey, who had no respect for them or the gun Costa was holding.

"I said get the hell out of here before I take that gun away and shoot your other eye out!" Grey shouted. "Do it now!"

Getting the message loud and clear, Crockett and Costa started the boat and cruised off into the darkness.

Despite these incidents, I stayed focused, as did most of the crew. Grey was confronted one night in the Land Ho by the man who had financed his lobster boat. Grey had missed a few payments, and the man angrily approached the nearly seven-foot-tall sailor, demanding payment.

"I'll pay you when we find the treasure," Grey declared, his face deadpan.

That seemed to mollify the man, who had impressed his friends by confronting Grey and knew that he shouldn't push any harder.

The one person who wasn't staying focused was my business manager, John Levin. He was upset that we hadn't found the *Whydah* right away. His dissatisfaction increased as the short season progressed. We were almost through the season and had found no sign of the *Whydah*. Some of his moodiness was also caused by a crew member named Eugene Burnelle.

Burnelle, a native of Maine with a heavy accent, was reed-thin and as white as a cave fish. I always marveled at how Burnelle could stay so pale while working on a ship in the sunbathed ocean.

He was a diver, and not a bad one at that. His heart wasn't in the *Whydah* project, and he let everyone know why, whether they wanted to hear or not.

"I'm tired of not finding anything," he declared.

"We just got here," I said. "Be patient."

Patience wasn't one of his virtues. He and Levin became best friends because of their mutual dissatisfaction. Brunelle claimed to have had better luck with the *Feversham,* a nineteenth-century ship that had sunk off the coast of Nova Scotia. When it crashed in a storm the *Feversham* was thought to have been transporting thousands of Gold Eagle coins.

Brunelle said he had a coffee can full of the coins, which he and some friends had retrieved from the ship a few years earlier.

"We oughta go up there and work that wreck," he said. "You don't need no goddamn archaeologists up there to go shipwreckin'. You can go up there and do anything you want and get rich while you're at it. Down here there's too many people telling you what to do."

"Shut up, Eugene," I told him when he said something like this in front of the whole crew. "If you don't like what we're doing, just leave."

One day he did just that. When everyone showed up at Nauset Inlet for the ride to the site on the *Crumpstey,* Eugene Brunelle just didn't show up.

Later that night at the Captain's House, Levin told me that Brunelle had left "for greener pastures."

"Where did he go?" I asked, knowing full well that he had left to find his fortune on the *Feversham.*

"I don't know," said Levin. "He just went."

A few days later, Levin left too, after only a few months on the project. He seemed to have lost interest in the *Whydah* expedition. The former judge had his mind on his next move. He linked up with Michael Herstadt, a Hollywood producer, and left Cape Cod.

"Do you think we'll ever see Levin again?" I asked McClung one day on the front lawn of the Captain's House. His answer gave me pause.

"Let me put it this way," he said. "I don't think *you* will ever see John Levin again."

I was exhausted from the hard work, yet unable to sleep very well. I would doze off only to awaken with my mind full of financial details or doubts about our finding the *Whydah* and my reasons for searching for her to begin with.

Late the first season, I had a dream in which I spoke to Sam Bellamy himself and he told me to search farther out from shore. I found myself standing on the deck of a ship with Bellamy. The ocean was slick, calm, and beautiful. Behind me, I could hear people laughing and screaming, and when I turned, I could tell we were at the wreck site, anchored very close to shore.

I decided to probe the pirate for information.

"Are we over the *Whydah* right now?" I asked.

He shook his head, his dark eyes boring a hole through me.

"Are we close?" I asked.

This time he nodded.

"You are close, but too close to shore," he insisted. "Things aren't the way they used to be around here. . . ."

I sat up and shook off the dream. Even though the clock told me it was 3 A.M., I decided to call Stretch Grey.

"I know where the *Whydah* is!" I shouted.

Grey hung up. I called back.

"It's farther out," I said when he answered again. "I just spoke to Bellamy in a dream, and he told me where to look."

When I told the crew about the dream some of them mumbled that I had finally gone insane. I refused to accept that explanation, and instead called it "psycho-maging," which I defined as using paranormal methods to find artifacts, instead of the magnetometer.

The crew rebelled and insisted we stay close to the shore, where we made a find that baffles me to this day. We recorded a hit close to shore and decided to blow a pit with the mailboxes on the *Vast*. McClung made the first dive. He was ecstatic when he came up.

"It's a piece of hull!" he shouted.

Beyer and Murphy suited up and went down immediately. They found long sections of timber held together with nails and iron strapping. We worked on the hull for the next couple of days, uncovering it in sections with the wash from the mailboxes.

McClung, a fine artist, drew the hull as accurately as possible. Since we did not have an expert in marine architecture on board, it was important to have accurate drawings so experts could tell us later if this find was of eighteenth-century construction. When the weather turned rough, we had to get away from the shore.

Later, we showed these drawings to an archaeologist at the Smithsonian who said the find could not possibly be from an eighteenth-century ship like the *Whydah* because such ships did not use metal strapping. I have since learned that that was not accurate, and plan to search for that section of hull again for further examination by experts. At the time, it was a disappointment because it was the only thing we came up with that first season that seemed to be connected to a shipwreck.

In September, our first season came to an abrupt end. We were shut down by the Massachusetts Board of Underwater Archaeological Resources after our archaeologist, Ted Dethlefsen, quit in a huff. Claiming that we had a "vague and inconsistent chain of command," he was also upset at the high profile the project had achieved in the media.

He felt that the dig should have been conducted under almost secretive conditions until he, the archaeologist, decided that the information could be released.

The more I spoke to the press, the angrier he became, until he resigned in September.

When that happened, MBUAR ordered the *Whydah* site shut down until a new archaeologist was hired. I thought about fighting the ruling, but Allan Tufankjian, my lawyer, pointed out that we had agreed to follow Section 106 of the National Historic Preservation Act, which requires an on-site archaeologist at all times during excavation.

"Why fight so late in the season anyway?" asked Tufankjian. "It's almost winter and you won't be able to dig, anyway. Just fall back and regroup."

Looking back on the *Whydah* project, the first season of digging was clearly the worst. We found nothing from the *Whydah* at all. Unless you count metal rods from the Marconi towers and bullets and bombs from World War II, our artifact bins were empty.

I said to Tufankjian, "Next year better turn around, or we're in trouble."

18

Wish You Were Here

Feeling anxious after the first season.

✳ "Cream rises to the top" is a phrase whose meaning became crystal clear to me after our first season. Despite a serious money shortage and no artifacts from the *Whydah* to keep us dreaming through the winter, several of the crew members were steadfast in their resolve to stay with the operation.

Bob Lazier and Mickey Salloway contributed more money of their own. Knowing now that we would need more than the original $250,000, my Colorado friends introduced me to Bucky Zimmerman, a Minnesota lawyer who planned to raise $900,000 by means of a private offering.

A member of the crew introduced me to a local archaeologist and soon the permit problems with MBUAR were behind us. The board did make one demand I felt was unreasonable. Before we used our mailboxes again, the board wanted us to conduct "remote sensing surveys" to map artifacts underneath the sand. I explained that the prop wash would not damage artifacts since most of them would be encased in a concretion of minerals, but it did no good. The archaeologists were already circling the wagons against our excavation. All I could do was to go to the site with Stretch Grey and fish for mag hits.

Grey was firmly on board, dedicated to the project despite the slow dribble of money that came, as he put it, "on a need-to-eat basis."

Todd Murphy and John Beyer were dedicated, too. Both went on "scrounging" operations, approaching corporations for items we needed but couldn't afford. Murphy made a successful appeal to Viking America for six dry suits, full-body suits of vulcanized rubber that keep the diver dry and warm. They were also successful in getting Viking to loan us an Aga diving system, which consists of highly pressurized air tanks connected by hose to a full-face mask. By installing a communications system, the diver could communicate with the surface, a great time-saver.

Allan Tufankjian, my lawyer and friend, never mentioned the substantial amount of money I owed him. In fact, he pressed on with our legal business, suing the Commonwealth of Massachusetts on behalf of Maritime Underwater Surveys to prevent the state from claiming 25 percent of our find. "You might not find anything," Tufankjian joked, "but that doesn't mean the state is entitled to twenty-five percent of it."

Without these guys, the cream of the crop, the search for the *Whydah* might have ended there.

McClung was not part of the cream. He had grown steadily more morose as the season wore on. Toward the end of the season he was frequently missing from the dive crew. So much so, in fact, that a crew member nicknamed him "no see 'um," after those annoying gnats that buzz around campsites but can't be seen.

Finally, as the crispness of October gave way to the chill of November, McClung said that he was leaving.

"Where are you going?" I asked.

"I'm moving to Malibu to start a movie production company with Levin," said McClung.

I was as stunned as I was amused.

"You mean the guy who fired you?" I asked, thinking he had suddenly forgotten the last three months.

"That was in the past," said McClung. "We get along just fine now. Anyone can get over a misunderstanding."

"It takes a lot of money to make movies," I said. "Where are you getting that?"

"Michael Herstadt," he said, a sheepish grin spreading over his face.

Herstadt was one of McClung's multimillionaire friends from Aspen.

"I thought you didn't like him," I said. "And what do you know about making movies, anyway?"

"He's got money and I know a hot starlet when I see her," he said.

I was stunned by the defection. "I thought you were dedicated to the search for the *Whydah*," I said.

"I'm sorry about that," he said. "There is nothing here for me. We haven't found any treasure yet and we might never find it. Sorry."

About one month later, as I thumbed through the mail, I found a home-made picture postcard from McClung. He was wearing a black wig and standing with his arm around a bikini-clad beauty. Behind them was Herstadt's China-red Ferrari. "Going great guns," McClung had written on the back. "Wish you were here."

Grey and his wife went to California on vacation later in the year and stopped in Malibu to see McClung. He was living in Herstadt's Malibu digs, one of those saltbox-style beach homes built on the very rim of the Pacific Ocean. When McClung answered the door, he was wearing the wig he had sported in the postcard. He thought it looked better than his own bald pate, but Stretch laughed at him until he took it off.

"So, what's the name of your company?" asked Grey.

"It's III MARs," he declared, handing Grey a business card identifying him as executive producer. "That's Rob Alexander McClung spelled backwards. The 'III' refers to me, Levin, and Herstadt. Neat, huh?"

Bellamy's first base of operations was off the coast of Belize in Central America. Among his men, he counted at least one Mosquito Indian, a man named John Julian, who was from that area and may have been qualified to act as a guide.

Shortly after turning outlaw, Bellamy and Williams traded in their salvage boat for two periauguas. A fast and very large seagoing canoe common to Central America, the periaugua, made from the hollowed trunks of two balsa trees, was popular among pirates who wanted to make lightning-fast raids. Its modern-day equivalent would be the PT boats used to fight in the Pacific during World War II. Loaded with a few dozen men and defended by swivel guns, Bellamy's periauguas were surely a frightening sight for the ships he took.

The months the pirates spent cruising the Central American coast were good ones for the Bellamy command. Records show that several sizable

BELLAMY'S FIRST PIRATE VESSELS

Sam Bellamy's first piratical command consisted of two periauguas. A periaugua was an undecked, flat-bottomed sailing canoe used mostly in coastal waters and large enough to carry a few swivel guns and several dozen men.

ships were plundered and a number of new crewmen came from them. Among the most prized of the new recruits was Peter Cornelius Hoof, a thirty-three-year-old Swedish sailor who had spent the previous seventeen years sailing Dutch traders along the Spanish Main. His addition to the crew represented a great increase in its navigational knowledge.

In the Yucatan Channel, Bellamy's flotilla encountered a Captain Young. The freshman pirate forced Captain Young to tow the canoes to the western end of Cuba, where ship traffic was heavy and the pickings were good.

While crossing the channel, Bellamy met up with Captain Henry Jennings, the privateer who would become his first mentor. Jennings was just leaving Jamaica after successfully fencing goods stolen from the Spanish salvage expedition off the coast of Florida. His flotilla consisted of five small vessels. There is no record of why he conspired with Bellamy. Perhaps he saw potential in the newly declared pirate, or maybe the Bellamy flotilla represented manpower Jennings needed to pull off his next attack, a ran-sacking of Baya Hondo, a port on the north coast of Cuba.

Whatever the case, the pirate flotilla arrived at the bay on April 3, 1716, and spotted a large ship anchored deep in the V-shaped harbor. Jennings sent a small group of men in a canoe to gather information about the ship. Their cover story was that the flotilla had come into the harbor to replenish wood and water stores before continuing on its journey.

Suspicions allayed, the crew members of the large ship divulged the sort of information that pirates like to hear. The ship was a French merchant-man, the *St. Marie,* commanded by a Captain L'Escoubett. The French were selling expensive goods to the Spanish locals in violation of Spanish trade laws. That meant they were smugglers, which was good news for the Jen-nings flotilla, since capturing a smuggler was not considered an act of piracy in those days.

The bad news was that the *St. Marie* mounted sixteen cannons and car-ried a crew of forty-five men.

Jennings suddenly became cautious. Attempting to take an armed ship could result in bloodshed and failure. Jennings did not want to be captured and possibly turned over to the Spanish. He had pillaged the Spanish Main as a privateer and knew that the Spanish would not treat him kindly if he fell into their hands.

Jennings called a council of all of the sailors in his flotilla, including those in Bellamy's periauguas, and expressed his concerns. If he went alongside the *St. Marie* in his sloop, the French would certainly sink him with their superior cannon fire. He felt that they should think twice about attacking the French ship and possibly not attack at all.

Some of the men agreed with Jennings's caution while others were out-raged by it. Two of Jennings's quartermasters, George Dossitt and Francis Charnock, began to grumble at their captain's lack of courage. Then some of the sailors in the crowd began to voice their dissent more vocally.

"What are you come out for?" shouted one of the men.

"Yeah. What are you come out for?" shouted another. "To look upon one another and return with your fingers in your mouth?"

Jennings once again expressed his concern about the *St. Marie's* supe-rior firepower, but his speech was cut short by a crewman shouting "one and all," that most piratical of sayings that confirmed solidarity in the face of battle.

Jennings had no choice but to attack, and attack they did. Bellamy's peri-auguas preceded both Jennings's and John Ashworth's sloops into the har-bor. By 10 P.M., the four vessels were within pistol range of the *St. Marie.*

Perhaps to add visual effect, the men in Bellamy's periauguas stripped off their clothing, until, as one witness described it, they were "all in their skins or buff, with [naught but] their cartridge boxes and naked cutlasses and pistols." Then, with a rousing cheer, the pirates began to row like madmen toward the French ship.

A lookout on the *St. Marie* heard the ruckus and peered into the darkness to see the naked rowers digging hard for his ship.

"What are you come out for?" he shouted in flawed English.

"Aboard, where do you think?" responded someone from Bellamy's crew.

Someone climbed down the side of the *St. Marie* and tried to escape in a canoe that was tied to the side of the ship. He was immediately captured by one of the hard-charging periauguas. The sharp report of a cannon being fired ripped the night. An angry cry went up from the pirates in the second periauga, who were now boarding the French ship.

"Who fired it?" demanded someone from Bellamy's crew.

"It was an accident," shouted one of Jennings's men. In his excitement, a gunner on one of the pirate ships had accidentally fired a cannon.

"Do not fire," came a voice from the *St. Marie,* possibly one of the French sailors. "All is well."

One of Jennings's men, who was later captured by the British, said that members of Bellamy's crew "would give no quarter" to the French had they fired the cannon that night. In pirate terms that meant that no mercy would be given and no prisoners taken.

At first, the pirates were disappointed with their new catch. She was loaded primarily with fine French linen, which held little interest for the pirates. Then the pirates found the ship's manifest, which recorded the presence of thirty thousand pieces of eight. Confronted with the hard facts, Captain L'Escoubett admitted that there had once been such a fortune on board, but said he had taken the coins ashore and hidden them for safety reasons.

Although the French crew confirmed the testimony of their captain, the pirates didn't believe them. After a good night's sleep, the French crewmen were interrogated by the pirates. Their specific manner of questioning was not discussed in the historic record, which consists of depositions taken by the British legal system. Captain L'Escoubett said the pirates "tormented the crew to that inhumane degree that they extorted after the vilest manner from them a discovery where they said the money lay."

The treasure amounted to 28,500 Spanish pieces of eight, of which Bellamy and his crew most likely received one-third.

While the pirates were relaxing on the French ship after plundering it, a canoe came into the bay and passed by the *St. Marie.* The pirates captured the boat and were told by its crew that another French smuggling vessel, the *Marianne,* was trading at Porto Mariel to the east.

Captain Carnegie of the Jennings flotilla immediately sailed with his sloop and one of the periauguas to see if they could capture her. By the time they arrived, the ship had been taken by another pirate, Benjamin Hornigold.

The last thing Carnegie wanted to do was to go up against Hornigold. If there were a rogues' gallery of pirates in the British Museum, Hornigold's portrait would occupy a prominent spot. Hard-bitten and crafty, Hornigold had been a privateer for England in the War of the Spanish Succession. There were few things he didn't know about robbery on the high seas, and few ships he wouldn't tackle. He was the dean of buccaneers. Some historians speculate that at least a third of pirates operating during the golden age of piracy were trained by Hornigold.

Carnegie's group returned to Baya Hondo, where Jennings was told that Hornigold had beaten them to the booty. Jennings, emboldened by his success against the *St. Marie,* readied two sloops and weighed anchor to search for Hornigold. Bellamy and his crew were left to guard the treasure of the *St. Marie.*

As soon as Jennings left the bay, Bellamy ordered the treasure loaded into one of his periaguas and left for points unknown. When Jennings returned to the Baya Honda without having found Hornigold, all that remained was Bellamy's other periagua and a flustered Captain Young, who had been unable to stop Bellamy from leaving.

In a rage, Jennings sank Bellamy's boat. Then, to further satisfy his anger, he sank Young's sloop, too. Finally, cursing his error in judgment, Jennings ordered his remaining flotilla to sail from Baya Hondo.

In the middle of winter, III MARs was cut down to II. Herstadt was murdered. While attending a trendy party in Aspen, he had gotten into a fistfight with a man who was humiliated by his defeat. The man left the party, returned with an M-16, and pumped about twenty bullets into Herstadt, abruptly ending his film career. Just like that, McClung's film production company wasn't worth the cards that his title was printed on. The house in Malibu was gone, as were the Ferrari and the firmly packed starlets who graced his homemade postcards.

By the end of winter I received a call from McClung. His voice sounded sheepish as he told me that he was jobless again.

"What happened to Levin?" I asked.

"He left and went to Nova Scotia with Eugene Burnelle," said McClung. "The two of them are going to look for the *Feversham*."

"So, what does all of this mean to me?" I asked McClung, sure that the answer would have something to do with the *Whydah*.

"It means that you get me back," he said, a sort of pleading in his voice. "I think we can find it this time."

I agreed to give McClung another chance. Maybe things will be better this year, I thought. Maybe the movie business has taught him a lesson.

What the hell, I thought. The truth is, I need crew.

19

Iron and Gold

A pensive moment before elation, as one of the divers announced that he "thought" he found three cannons. It was true, and this marked the beginning of a steady stream of artifacts from the *Whydah*.

✳ The second season was shaping up to be as disappointing as the first. Beginning in late May of 1984, we again spent two months salvaging only the remains of World War II training exercises, pieces of the Marconi towers, and that mysterious hull. Although autumn was still a few months away, the weather was exhibiting periods of moodiness that foretold the kind of extreme change in conditions that would prevent us from anchoring over a search site.

The crew members were exhibiting periods of moodiness, too. Our artifact bins were still empty and most everyone was totally frustrated by the *Whydah* project. There was grumbling about the hard work and some backstabbing was in the air as well. McClung began to tell everyone how he "would do it better" if he were in charge.

I heard about his complaints from other members of the crew.

"He bitches about you all the time except when you are within earshot," said one of the crew members. "Now I know where that old saying came from, 'Keep your friends close and your enemies closer.' You should keep that guy chained to your belt."

I had thought that McClung would be less hostile with Levin absent from the scene. To me, Levin had been the catalyst for McClung's bad behavior. I was beginning to realize McClung needed no catalyst.

If the *Whydah* expedition crew was testy and almost at the end of its collective rope, then the *Whydah* project itself was already there. I had not told anyone, but we were out of money. I had managed to stretch the initial $250,000 investment through most of the second season, but now there was nothing left.

I had seen the amount in the checkbook dwindle from several thousand dollars to just a few hundred. My remaining cash would finance food and fuel for less than a week.

I told Grey the situation and he just shrugged and offered his solution. "Buy the essentials and let's go until we can't go anymore."

So that's what I did.

On July 20, we anchored the *Vast* over an unexplored site. Dropping the mailboxes, we blew a big hole and waited for the sand to settle.

We had a camera crew with us from NBC, headed by Nancy Fernandes, an excellent correspondent who had been pushing us the last few days so she could get the shots she needed. I have to admit that had she not been there, we would not have been out on the water on this particular day.

In order for the camera crew to get some footage, we suited up a new guy, Mike Kacergis, and sent him down. He was young and excited and ready for action. The rest of us were tired, burned out, and somewhat cynical. It was probably the fiftieth hole we had blown and examined since the excavation started. None had contained artifacts. We expected the same would be true of this hole, too.

No sooner had Mike gone to the bottom than he came right back up. From the look in his eyes, some of us thought that he had seen a shark or maybe a large ghost of Sam Bellamy. What he had seen was just as surprising to us at this point.

"Hey, you guys!" he shouted after ripping out his mouthpiece. "There's three cannons down there!"

A jolt of electricity ran through the crew, and along with it, caution. We'd had our hearts broken before and we weren't ready to fall for just any artifact again.

"Rob, suit up!" I shouted. I would have dived myself but I had just been told by my doctor not to dive because of progressing nerve damage in my ear. I didn't quite believe what I was hearing. I thought maybe he had found some bombs from the bombing range or something else he had mistaken for cannons.

Rob needed no help in getting into his wet suit. He pulled it on in a rush of rubber and weight belts and was in the water in a splash.

The NBC cameras were rolling, capturing everything on film for a segment that would make it on the evening news for sure.

In a few moments, McClung came up with a big smile on his face. Kacergis had indeed found three cannons, he confirmed. In his hands McClung carried an intriguing chunk of encrusted salvage. As the cameras rolled he raised it over his head and handed it off.

Someone pulled the find from Rob's hands and put it on the deck. Then we all stood over it and stared.

"Let's take a look at it," said Murphy, our archaeologist.

I held the concretion while he tapped it slightly with a hammer. A chunk of concretion broke off to reveal a cannonball. I picked up the part of the concretion that fell off. I held it up and looked inside the rough, cuplike formation. There, at the bottom, looking like a silver seashell, was a coin. A little wiggle and it was free in my hands. From its uneven edges and the markings on its face, I could tell that it was a Spanish piece of eight. I flipped it over to reveal a Spanish cross with markings that clearly indicated it was from 1688.

"I think we have a pirate ship here," I said, holding the coin up for everyone to see. There was an eruption of unrestrained joy as the hardworking crew realized that at last, we had found proof that the *Whydah* was below us. We were hugging each other as though we had just scored the winning touchdown, and passing the coin around like it was the game ball.

Until now the sky had been clear, with the exception of a small black cloud that had lingered on the horizon most of the day. In the frenzy of dealing with the artifact, no one had noticed the cloud move over our boat and become darker. As soon as I declared the presence of the pirate ship, the cloud made itself known with a bright flash of lightning, a loud clap of thunder, and a quick but definite cloudburst.

"It's Sam Bellamy," said a crew member.

"The pirates don't want to be found," said Grey.

When the rain ended, Grey went to the refrigerator and produced a bottle of champagne. It had been brought on board to celebrate the discovery

EAK-86-MEI

ROYAL STRIKE

Specially minted, this coin is known as a "royal strike." That its exceptional craftsmanship was valued even then is shown by the drilled hole so that it could be worn around the neck as jewelry.

A simple object can sometimes speak volumes. To the left, the coin contains a shield that represents provinces subject to the Spanish monarch, King Philip IV.

The "tic-tac-toe" design on the opposite side of the coin carries an elaborate message. The two central columns rep-

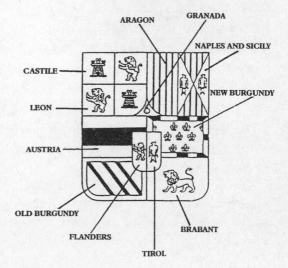

resent the Pillars of Hercules, a reference to the Straits of Gibraltar, once considered to be the end of the world, or a sea road into the unknown. The middle three horizontal spaces contain the Latin phrase *plus ultra*, meaning "more beyond." The message reads, "Across the Atlantic, past the Straits of Gibraltar, lies a New World which belongs to Spain."

In the upper left and the lower right corners, *P* stands for Potosí, Peru (now Bolivia), where the coin was minted. In the upper right and the lower left is the assayer's monogram. The central square in the uppermost row contains an *8*, meaning that it is an eight-real coin, while the *93* on the central space of the bottom row is the year of minting—1693.

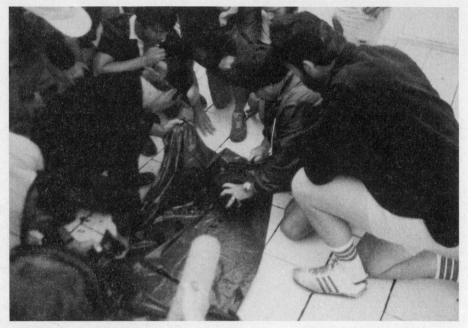

Huddled around the first artifact, a cannonball that would yield the first coin.

of the first artifact. I had hoped that we would drink it earlier than this, but late was better than never. I popped the cork and we all drank the champagne as though we had experienced a final victory.

We hadn't, of course.

This artifact represented only a beginning for us. Still, July 20, 1984, was a heady day for us. From now on we knew that we were digging in the right area and could actually start finding the things we had come for. We passed around the cannonball and coin for several hours, elated at having found an authentic piece of the *Whydah*.

Before newspapers could get wind of the story, NBC showed the joyous moment on the evening news—a scene of utter chaos as we hugged one another and passed our *Whydah* find around the boat as though we were passing a newborn baby around a room.

Some of us watched the news story from the Land Ho in Orleans, the expedition's official hangout, mainly because the owner allowed us to carry a large tab. I was surprised he didn't cut us off that night. We added several hundred dollars for the libation alone, drinking, laughing, and patting ourselves on the back for the good fortune of our find, and most of all, the luck of having a team of television reporters on board.

"We did it!" I shouted to the handful of detractors who sat at the bar with their backs to us. "We found the *Whydah* and it's on the evening news!"

No one else in the Land Ho was ignoring us. They were living vicariously through our success, and seemed to be so excited they could have been taken for members of the crew.

Over the next several days, the find received enormous play in newspapers all over the country. The *New York Daily News* ran a photo of Todd Murphy and me whooping it up at the Land Ho above a headline that read: PIECES OF 8 ADD UP TO PIRATE TREASURE.

Another story, this one in the *Boston Herald,* carried a picture of me reading a book and the headline: BOY DREAMED OF GOLD & FOUND IT.

Of course, our success inspired some nasty comments from our detractors. One of the people who had filed a claim next to ours declared that NBC was in cahoots with us, and that the underwater footage they aired appeared to be "rehearsed."

This claim resulted in an angry denial from Fernandes, the NBC correspondent, who said, "It's absolutely false and irresponsible for anyone to make such a statement. It's a real coincidence, we were at the right place at the right time."

She couldn't have said it better. We were at the right place at the right time, period.

A couple of days after celebrating the discovery at the Land Ho lounge in Orleans, Lazier and I put our heads together and wondered where we would get enough money to continue. We had to get it soon, because we were broke.

Despite the lack of money from investors, we couldn't stop. Lazier loaned more money to the project and we kept digging. As we dug, we found thousands of artifacts, including cannonballs, pewter plates, forks, and shot, grape-sized pieces of lead meant to be fired from swivel guns mounted on the stern section of the ship. Every hole we dug with the mailboxes contained a bonanza of historical relics.

And then, of course, there was the gold and silver. It seemed to be everywhere. John Beyer brought up the first dive bag full of silver coins. When he brought them up on deck, we all just stared at them. Silver coins from the bottom of the ocean don't look like the silver dollars you get from the bank. Years of exposure to the elements leave them gray and corroded with oxidation. Since these were pieces of eight, they were not round, but uneven from having their rims clipped by coin makers trying to achieve a weight of approximately one ounce.

"They look like seashells," said Grey.

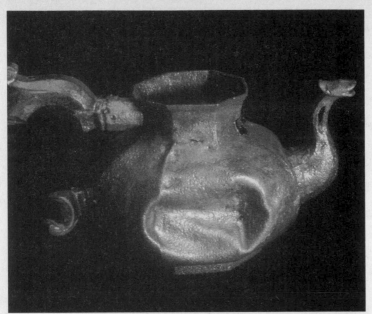

Tea kettle.

Tea kettle
under water.

Mickey Salloway, an investor, stands next to a typical day's yield of coins. The bowl that looks like olives in the foreground is lead grapeshot fired from cannons.

"Yeah, but they clink like silver," said Murphy.

I picked one up and rubbed it until the Spanish cross appeared, clear proof that we had pieces of eight.

"There's a lot more where those came from," said Beyer.

He was right. In twenty minutes one day, I found 280 coins. They weighed almost twenty pounds. I could have tied them to a line and raised them that way, but I did not want to let them leave my hands. These coins were the heart and soul of the *Whydah* and the primary reason that her pirates had become pirates. I wanted to hold them close for the secrets they could tell me.

The gold artifacts emerged from the depths looking the same as they had the day they had spilled into the sea. There were several *escudos*, tiny gold pieces used by the Spanish, that came up looking bright and shiny. Then, of

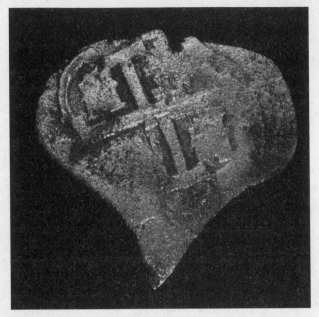

Piece of eight worked into a heart shape.

course, there were the gold bars. They appeared in various sizes and shapes, looking as if they had been poured into ingots and dropped into the sea only the day before. Some had blade marks on them, a sign that Bellamy's quartermaster had tried to cut them with a knife or sword to divide them up between the men. Others had been severed, hacked clean through by a hard whack of the blade.

One day Beyer was on the bottom when he noticed gold dust layered in the wall of a pit like chocolate in a marbled cake. He tried to pinch some out with his fingers and it dispersed into the water. After a couple more tries, he came back to the surface.

"Hand me that turkey baster in the engine room," he shouted to Grey, who was not diving that day. Stretch retrieved the instrument, which was used to prime the engines, and handed it over the side.

"Why? Doing some cooking down there?" he asked.

"No, there's gold dust in the sand," said Beyer. "Give me one of those sandwich bags, too."

Grey thought Beyer was being a wise guy, until he came up several minutes later with the sandwich bag partially filled with the dull glitter of gold. From that point on, the turkey baster took its place with the mailboxes and magnetometer as a tool of treasure hunting.

It was our guess that the *Whydah* was carrying bags of gold dust along with the coins and ingots of silver and gold. These were shuffled under the sand like all the other heavy artifacts. When the bags disintegrated, the dust had been held there, spreading throughout the sand and even sinking down into the clay subsurface. Now it seemed to be everywhere.

We found several cannons, their iron bodies so heavily concreted that they looked like elongated boulders. These presented a special problem for us. Concreted items need to be stored in vats of seawater until proper conservation can be done. If allowed to dry out, they become brittle and break like sandstone. Since we didn't yet have a conservatory, or even a warehouse, there was no place to keep them on the surface. So instead of hoisting the cannons up, we marked their locations with subsurface buoys and covered them with sand. They had been safe there for 267 years, we reasoned; another few months on the bottom of the ocean wouldn't make any difference.

Although the gold and silver were foremost in everyone's mind, I made it clear from the beginning that all the artifacts were important.

"Iron and gold get the same treatment," I told a reporter, explaining the difference between a treasure hunter and an archaeologist.

"You don't have to have an archaeology degree to care about the artifacts from a pirate ship," I said. "The gold and silver is what the pirates were after, but they chased it with devices made from iron and wood."

I had been adamant from the beginning about my goals: I wanted to conserve the artifacts and display them in a pirate museum. Given that this

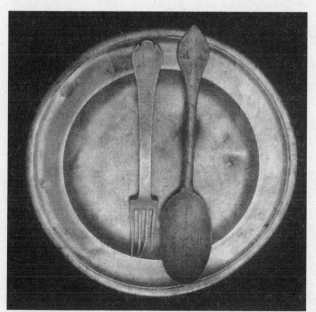

Plate with fork and spoon.

was—and remains—the only pirate ship ever found, I felt that the best way to understand this mysterious subculture would be to put all the artifacts on display so the full presence of their history could be felt.

I was not a treasure hunter, although I was obviously hunting for treasure. I was a history hunter, an undersea salvor with a driving interest in bringing a great historic period back to life in a responsible way that a working man could appreciate as well as a historian.

Surprisingly, my ringing endorsement for preservation did not win me any friends in the archaeological community. They didn't like the notion of

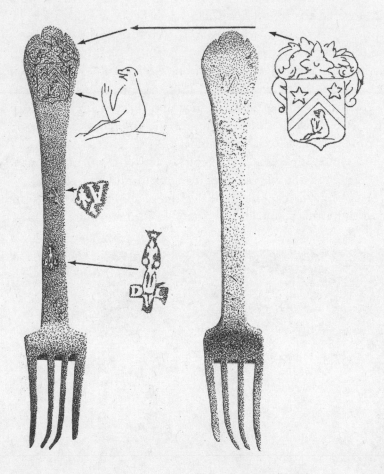

FIT FOR A PIRATE

The trifid end of this four-tined fork indicates that it was probably made sometime between the late 1660s and 1700. The fleur-de-lis, as part of both proof mark and maker's mark, indicates that it's probably French. The unusual owner's mark has not yet been traced.

a private individual launching an archaeological project in the first place. Now that I was declaring myself one of them, they liked the *Whydah* project even less.

At the next meeting of the MBUAR, it was obvious that I was going to be held to even stricter preservation standards. Dr. Paul Johnston agreed to let the meeting be held at the Peabody Museum in Salem, where he was curator. Johnston had been one of the academic archaeologists who didn't mind speaking out publicly about the *Whydah* project. Before I started the search, he told the press that the *Whydah* never existed, that it was only myth, the type that can be found in any town up and down the Eastern seaboard. Now that artifacts had been found, he was the first with credentials to tell the press that there was no proof that I had found the *Whydah*.

So disparaging were many of his comments that my lawyer, Allan Tufankjian, took it upon himself to write a letter warning the directors of the Peabody that their curator was close to slander in some of the things he said about the *Whydah* project. I was not enthusiastic about Tufankjian writing such a letter, hoping instead that archaeologists would see the conscientious work we were doing and give us credit for a job well done. Tufankjian replied that the world does not work that way.

"If we let them slander us and don't respond, then what they say becomes truth," he said. "And if what they say becomes truth in the eyes of the public, you will become an outlaw and it will be hard to get support of any kind, moral or financial."

It turned out Tufankjian was correct. In front of a packed house, I was applauded by the board, who felt that the discovery of the artifacts was "significant" and proved that I had indeed found an eighteenth-century ship. However, said Joseph Sinnott, director of the MBUAR, there was no artifact, "such as a piece of wood with '*Whidah*' written on it," to prove conclusively that the ship had been found.

I was stunned. I looked at my friend Robert Cahill, one of the board members, but he would not make eye contact with me. From the way he had spoken to the newspapers, I thought he was even more convinced than I was that our find was the *Whydah*. In the newspapers he had made the remarkable statement, "If anyone, after seeing this stuff, still has doubts that this is indeed the '*Whidah*,' I don't know what would convince them."

It was only later that I learned that Cahill had been reprimanded by his fellow board members for declaring we had found the *Whydah*. Now he just sat nervously, waiting for the bad news he knew was coming.

"We have been unable to prove beyond a shadow of doubt that the ship you have found is the *Whydah*," declared one of the board members.

"It's an early wreck, it's an important wreck, it has some of the same characteristics as the *Whydah* may have," said Jim Bradley, a member of the MBUAR and the Massachusetts Historical Commission's board. "But to say it's the *Whydah* is premature at least. That area of the Cape has one of the highest densities of shipwrecks of any place on the East Coast. There are hundreds and hundreds of wrecks out there."

As a student of Cape Cod shipwrecks, I knew what he said was true, but there were no ships other than the *Whydah* carrying gold bars and pieces of eight dated from the eighteenth century.

I tried to explain. They were not willing to hear what I had to say.

"There's no doubt you've found an important wreck, which might well be the *Whydah*," said Cahill, choosing his words carefully. "Some of us, though, feel we should wait for further evidence before making formal recognition."

There had clearly been disagreement on the board about what proof they should require. Some, like Cahill, knew the area and was aware that the objects we had found could only be from the *Whydah*. Others wanted written proof. One of the board members, I discovered later, had declared that only "a quarterboard that says '*Whydah*' would make me believe these guys."

I knew I had the *Whydah*, and frankly I didn't care what the board thought. Their next bit of news hit me like a load of bricks.

"The only way to answer this doubt satisfactorily," said Sinnott, "is to conduct a full archaeological examination of the site before another coin is disturbed. Such an examination is the responsibility of Maritime Explorations."

Suddenly I was reduced to desperation. A full archaeological site examination is an expensive procedure, and I barely had enough money to pay for essentials for the next two weeks.

"What are we going to do?" I asked Lazier.

"There's nothing we can do except what the board tells us to do," said Lazier. "They are controlling the site permits."

"I realize that, but a survey would put a dent in the best-financed operation," I said. "And we don't have any money."

"I guess I'll have to spring for it," said Lazier. "Frankly, if we don't, the project is probably dead."

Lazier agreed to write a check for $50,000, which would cover operations for the rest of the summer, including the cost of the survey. Then he went searching for additional financing.

An archaeological survey is a simple thing to do on archaeological sites such as those in the deserts of the American Southwest, where archaeologists survey ancient Indian sites with great precision. The archaeologists' first move is to determine the perimeter of the site they plan to survey. They will pound stakes into the ground and string rope between the stakes to mark the boundaries of their dig. Then they divide the interior of the site into a grid, pounding stakes into the ground at regular intervals and weaving string between the stakes. This string grid allows archaeologists very accurately to uncover, record, and photograph objects and their locations.

This method of pinpointing artifacts is quite useful. In the case of, say, an Anasazi Indian site in New Mexico, the artifacts are in exactly the same place they were left more than a thousand years ago, when this tribe dispersed to points unknown. The location of artifacts can give you a lot of information about how people lived, but only if the site is in a stable location where little has changed.

Working the site before the state forced us to conduct a futile archaeological survey.

That was the problem with doing such a survey on the *Whydah* site. Nothing was the same. The sands of the Cape are constantly changing. Sometimes, when the current is strong or the water is rough, you can sit on the bottom and watch the sands shift like the Sahara Desert in a windstorm. Coastal experts say that the sands of the *Whydah* site are completely replaced every fifty to sixty years. The truth of that is evident in the fact that the Cape itself is bending toward the Northwest at a rate of about three feet per year.

What this means, of course, is that only the heaviest items from the *Whydah* would remain close to where they were dropped.

In addition, the *Whydah* is an "exploded" site. That means the ship hit the shoreline with such force that it broke up and scattered, the same way an airliner would if it had crashed in the same spot.

With these conditions, the location of artifacts didn't mean much in the overall scheme. It wasn't as though we had found an intact ship in the sand. The *Whydah* was all over the place, churned and spread by that natural washing machine known as the surf zone.

Of course, the savvy members of the board knew that forcing us to conduct the survey would be a major hurdle to our economically strapped operation. With Lazier's financial rescue, we decided to conduct the best survey we could.

We eventually hired a company called Maritime Archaeological and Historical Research Institute, run by Warren Riess. He was our second professional archaeologist. The first, Ted Dethlefsen, was president of the National Society for Historical Archaeology. Pressured by members of his organization, who felt he should not do business with a private archaeological venture, and frustrated by our poor relationship, he had finally jumped ship, literally. One day he dove overboard and swam fifteen hundred feet back to shore, never to return to the site. Riess was a lanky graduate of the Institute of Nautical Archaeology in Texas. There he had been a student of George Bass, who had a disdain for private archaeology. Despite pressure from his mentor and from other members of the archaeology community, Riess took the job.

With cord in hand, Riess showed the crew how to lay a grid pattern. They sat in stunned silence as he carefully described how to drive stakes into the sand and string the cord.

"And then what are you going to do?" asked Murphy.

"We are going to excavate each square and mark the precise location of the artifacts that we find," said Riess.

"Better move fast," said Grey. "The ocean waits for no man."

The *Whydah* divers did their best to lay a string grid over the site. They strung cord and pounded stakes and squared off the bottom until it looked like grid paper from an office supply store. Within hours—sometimes minutes—of stringing a line, the current would bend it or the sand would cover it up or the stake would be swept away. It became clear almost immediately that this approach to retrieving the *Whydah* was not going to work.

Members of the board insisted on coming out to make sure we were following their regulations, and I gladly accommodated them. They stood unhappily on the pitching deck of the *Vast,* the rolling sea making some of them sick, and saw firsthand that the grid system wasn't working.

I got the idea from these on-site visits that most of the board members were sympathetic to our plight. They realized how difficult it was to search for an ancient shipwreck trapped underneath several feet of sand and would have gladly let us do that had it not been for the influence of some of the academic archaeologists. Opposed to private archaeology of any kind, these academics consider themselves the public stewards of archaeological resources, and feel that degreed members of their community should be the only ones allowed to search for the relics of history. They also feel that government and certain educational institutions should be the only ones allowed to possess these relics of history.

They are also opposed to the commercial exploitation of archaeology. This meant the selling of artifacts from the *Whydah,* which I had already gone on record as opposing. As they continued to voice objection to "commercial exploitation," I realized that they were including the display of artifacts in *private* museums, like the one I wanted to build.

I found their opposition ludicrous on both counts.

As far as I could tell, they had appointed themselves the gatekeepers of history. I didn't see why responsible individuals who were willing to take the chance could not act "on behalf of the public" in the same way the extremist academic archaeologists do. Although I was also opposed to the sale of artifacts, especially before they were studied and properly curated, I could not see why a private museum should garner so much opposition. Didn't academic archaeologists charge admission to their museums? Although these museums may be "nonprofit" organizations, they certainly make a lot of money from the "commercial exploitation of archaeology." Not that they shouldn't. As I had found out, archaeology is an expensive venture.

The academic archaeologists, I felt, were making the *Whydah* a rallying point. I have always been amazed that my most vocal academic opponents don't even bother to examine the conservation we have done over the years or the careful methods we have used in retrieving the artifacts. If they did, I think they would modify their stance.

Their stance at that time was compliance with the Society of Professional Archaeologists' guidelines. And those guidelines were not working effectively at the high-energy site, where currents and shifting sands created an almost constant underwater sirocco.

When everyone finally agreed the string grid approach had failed, Riess came up with another idea: a cofferdam. The cofferdam he had us construct was a large iron box that was open on two sides. It worked on the cookie cutter principle, pressing through the porous sand like a cutter through dough. Once it was stuck into the ocean's clay bottom, divers could work inside the eight-foot square, finding and recording the artifacts that were trapped within its confines.

Though it sounded great in theory, in reality it never worked. For one thing, the ocean bottom is not smooth like rolled-out cookie dough, but uneven like a riverbed. The cofferdam would not make a tight seal against the ocean floor, and sand granules would pour into the metal box from underneath.

Also, the moving sands of the Cape tend to drift over any object on the bottom. If we left the cofferdam underwater overnight, it would almost invariably be covered by a mountain of sand in the morning.

Finally the cofferdam got wedged in the rocky bottom. For days we tried to bring it up, but it was stuck solid, apparently for good.

We soon figured out how to use the stuck cofferdam and appease the board at the same time. Todd Murphy used the cofferdam to establish one precise geographic point that he was then able to locate on a grid pattern on a computer screen. From that point on, we marked the location of a hole by measuring its distance and direction from the cofferdam. The objects would then be marked on the map, assigned a field number, and photographed when they reached the deck of the *Vast* and again when they were taken to the lab.

This method was surprisingly accurate. Years later, we compared our accuracy to the amazingly precise global positioning system, the Trimble DGPS, that we now use and found the old method to be accurate within feet. At the time, our method of creating the real treasure map was a revolution in the field of underwater archaeology.

A demonstration of the newly developed method impressed the board, and we were allowed to get on with the excavation. Despite the holdups and the expenditure of an extra $30,000, it proved to be an amazingly fruitful season.

We recovered 12,107 artifacts that season and 7,309 the next, for a total of 19,416.

CONCRETED TEA KETTLE

While merchant and naval officers occasionally enjoyed the luxury of hot tea, crewmen usually quenched their thirst with a daily ration of about a gallon of strong beer.

The base of the large tea kettle depicted here was offset to fit in a recess of the ship's stove. This kept it from toppling over in heavy seas. Heavily concreted, it is currently undergoing conservation treatment. It is hoped that it may still contain tea leaf residue.

Lazier found more financing through a Minnesota investment lawyer who put together a private stock offering that raised nearly a million dollars. This continued to underwrite the operation and allowed us to rent a large warehouse that we converted into a lab. There, newly hired conservators faced the daunting task of restoring the heavily concreted artifacts to something close to the luster they had had in 1717.

Conservation is one of the slowest, most meticulous jobs known to man. Yet, thanks to the excellent conservators we have had over the years, thousands of objects from the *Whydah,* including even leather and cloth, have been splendidly conserved.

With the exception of silver, gold, and lead, which suffer very little from hundreds of years underwater, all the objects we find are permeated with the corrosive salts of seawater. Most of them, especially iron, are caked with a concretelike covering of salts and other minerals that have to be neutralized. This is done by placing the objects in a tank of fresh water wired with DC current. The process functions like electroplating in reverse. Eventually, after weeks or years, the encrustation falls off to reveal the object under-neath. When most of the salts have been removed, helping the object to lose its brittleness, the conservator continues the process of restoration, which might involve extensive use of dental tools to scrape off the remaining encrustation.

The object is then polished and coated with wax to protect it from the oxidizing effects of air. Finally, it is photographed and drawn for the annual report that we have to file with several entities, including the U.S. Army Corps of Engineers, which monitors the excavation for the federal gov-ernment.

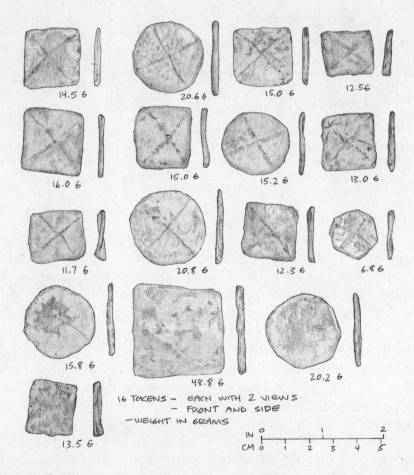

16 TOKENS — EACH WITH 2 VIEWS.
— FRONT AND SIDE
— WEIGHT IN GRAMS

FUN AND GAMES

Pirates had other pastimes besides drunken binges. These homemade gaming tokens reveal how cards, draughts (checkers), backgammon, and other dice games helped fill long hours at sea with interest and excitement.

This illustration shows what the site looked like after the sand was blown away by the mailboxes and the artifacts exposed. In reality, the pit is much smaller than the one illustrated here.

Conservation is expensive. To equip the lab cost more than $250,000. This included office space; a variety of electrified tanks ranging from those small enough for pistols to others large enough for cannons and anchors; an intricate water and electrical system; plus all of the necessary dental tools, cameras, and drafting tables. It did not include money to pay a conservator or any assistants. Nor, for that matter, did it include the cost of X-raying the larger concretions, which we did at a laboratory in Auburn.

Even though we now had a considerable amount of money in our coffers, we were spending it very rapidly on careful excavation and diligent conservation efforts. Although this was exasperating to some of the investors, especially the ones who did not realize how meticulous the art of archaeology could be, it was fine with me.

I could understand the academic archaeologists' opposition to some private ventures—I shared their misgivings. The *deBraak,* for example, a two-hundred-year-old British warship that sank off the coast of Delaware, was raised in the 1980s by cables without a cradle. The ship broke open as salvors raised it from the bottom and spilled contents back to the ocean floor. Salvors then scooped the bottom with clamshell buckets and dumped their contents into a road-construction rock sorter to sift for treasure.

This was not good archaeology, to say the least. But to use a poor effort like the *deBraak* operation as an excuse to stop all private archaeology seemed like elitism to me, a way of eliminating the competition. Already one of our archaeologists had been refused the opportunity to present a paper at the Society for Historical Archaeology on the grounds that "no paper that results from, or reports on treasure hunting" could be given.

Although we were doing good archaeology—and I had the bills and results to prove it—we were still considered thieves of history by many academic archaeologists. It did not seem fair to me, but that's the way it was.

20

Masters of Their Universe

Days like this became common as cannon after cannon was hoisted on board.

✳ Nineteen-eighty-five was a good year for archaeological finds, but perhaps the greatest treasure that year came in human form with the arrival of Ken Kinkor. Kinkor was a historian—a piratologist, to be exact. His career path was chosen when, as a child, he finished reading *Treasure Island* and wished that the book was infinitely longer. He went on to read nearly everything written on pirates, including a lot of primary source material like the depositions of merchant captains captured by pirates and military accounts of encounters with buccaneers.

The notion that a loosely knit group of men could live so successfully outside of society intrigued him. His reading told him that pirates had a spirit of "liberty, equality, and fraternity," which, he later discovered, led them to welcome people of color into their ranks. He began to see pirates in the same light as Bellamy saw them, as roguish descendants of Robin Hood.

After attending Loras College in Dubuque, Iowa, Kinkor did graduate work at the University of Iowa and then at Illinois State University. His chosen field of study was "the modern world, 1917 to the present." In 1978, while researching a historical project, he encountered some source information on pirates. The next thing he knew, he was studying Paulsgrave Williams, Bellamy's financier and partner, and using him as a focal point for delving into the golden age of piracy, roughly 1690 to 1724.

After leaving the university, Kinkor helped start a telephone sales company, a strange turn for a piratologist.

Kinkor buried his love of pirates somewhere in his psyche and devoted his time and energy to running his fledgling business. His idea, as he told me later, was to "make a lot of money, get married, and live happily ever after."

Then one day, sitting in a donut shop in Peoria, Illinois, Kinkor began flipping through the pages of a newspaper. Deep inside the first section, his eye caught a headline about the discovery of the *Whydah*. He knew the story intimately from his study of pirates, and especially from the information he had gleaned about Paulsgrave Williams. In a flash, his old love of pirates reemerged.

He wrote me a long letter recounting his own history of pirate study and asking whether there was any information we could share. After several letter exchanges, I realized that Kinkor was the type of person we needed to sort out the history of the *Whydah* and the men who sailed her.

In the summer of 1985, at my invitation, he attended a meeting about the archaeological direction of the project and got to meet Bob Lazier, Rob McClung, Todd Murphy, Stretch Grey, and the other searchers for the *Whydah*. His ability to contribute was obvious from the beginning.

Someone asked about Williams's genealogy, wondering if we knew anything about his origins. Nobody did, though we had a few people doing historical research. Then Kinkor spoke up.

"Well, I can tell you a little bit about Williams," he said, keeping us in suspense while he paused to light his pipe. Finally, smoke puffed from the bowl. "He was the black sheep son of a Rhode Island attorney general who was trying to impress his daddy by striking it rich."

Kinkor then told us the history of Williams, right down to a sighting of him recounted in the journal of a slave-ship captain who was captured by the pirate off the coast of Africa.

"I think he is buried somewhere around Jamestown, Rhode Island," Kinkor said, "but I haven't had time to prove it yet."

After the meeting, Lazier pulled me aside.

"You'd better get that guy," he said. "This project will get a lot smarter if he joins."

I offered Kinkor a job immediately and he eventually accepted, joining us in the spring of 1986.

Kinkor was so excited to start that he drove his ancient Ford Fairlane from Illinois in thirty hours of nonstop driving. When he arrived he was wired but ready and began to organize himself immediately in our South Chatham offices.

One of the most important areas of research for Kinkor was the dicey subject of the pirate crew's racial mix. Many black activists in the Boston area were upset that so much had been made of the *Whydah,* especially since she had been a slave ship. I thought it might please them to know that many of the crewmen were slaves who had been freed by the pirates and worked as equals on the ship. To my surprise, this news seemed to infuriate them even more.

Most vocal was State Representative Byron Rushing, who for ten years had directed Boston's Museum of African-American History.

"I think you should tell the story of black people in New England, but I'm not sure if I would start with gangsters, which is what pirates were," he said after one of the public forums at which we presented the history of the *Whydah* and our goal of building a museum. "To me, that's like telling the history of blacks in the 1990s and starting with drug dealers. Sure, it's part of the story, but it's not everything and not where you start."

Kinkor felt differently from Rushing, about both the pirates and the meaning of what they did.

"Many would see the pirates as scoundrels, pure and simple," said Kinkor. "I take a different approach. If we look at the pattern of European society of the period, we are compelled to conclude that these men were not simple robbers, rather they were acting against social grievances."

This would not be the last word on race and the *Whydah,* especially from Rushing, who would later lead a successful fight against establishing a pirate museum in Boston.

It would also not be the last word from Kinkor, who published a major paper in *American Visions* magazine entitled "Black Men Under the Black Flag." By studying the historical record, he found that as much as 25 percent of Bellamy's crew was black. Further research revealed that as many as 30 percent of all pirates during the years 1715 to 1725 were of African descent. The reason, he felt, was that escaped slaves could be counted on to fight to keep their freedom. He even found two entirely black crews, with the exception of a single white man apiece.

"Piratical racial tolerance did not proceed from an idealistic vision of the fundamental brotherhood of man," wrote Kinkor. "Instead, it sprang from a spirit of revolt against common political, economic, and social oppression. The shared experience of oppression was thus a solvent that broke down social barriers within a pirate crew. Shared feelings of marginality meant that the primary allegiance of pirates was given to their brethren. It is hardly surprising that so many blacks—confronted with far worse prospects by staying put within the European or American social order—chose piracy."

With a great devotion to detail, Kinkor began to research every aspect of the *Whydah* and her crew. He searched birth records in England for the birthplace of Bellamy and death records on the Cape to find the true identity of Maria Hallett. He found records of Bellamy's crew in Boston and plowed through obscure depositions of captains and crew members who had been captured by Bellamy and his men throughout the Caribbean and up the Eastern seaboard. Eventually he was able to trace Bellamy's entire route from England to Cape Cod, to the Caribbean, and back to the shore where he met his end.

Despite his interest in pirates, Kinkor has no interest in visiting the site. Boats make him queasy and mechanical abilities elude him, making him virtually worthless on a working boat like the *Vast*. One time I asked him if he wanted to strap on a scuba tank and see some of the pits where we worked. The look I got back was deadpan and strange. "Barry," he said, "I want to study dead pirates, I don't want to visit them."

Without Kinkor, we might never have known what happened to Bellamy after he stole Jennings's booty from the French ship *St. Marie.*

Whether by accident or intention, somewhere near Cuba, Bellamy and his men met up with Benjamin Hornigold, the famed buccaneer. He operated out of New Providence, in the Bahamas, and trained many pirates from this base. Hornigold developed pirates because he needed as many able-bodied seamen as he could get to pounce on a profusion of targets. The seas of the Caribbean teemed with merchant ships traveling to the Americas—easy pickings for pirates who knew how to strike quickly and escape using their knowledge of the locations of reefs and shallows, easily evading the frigates that formed the inadequate coast guard of the British navy.

Perhaps Hornigold's best-known pupil was Edward "Blackbeard" Teach, known for boarding prize merchant ships with sizzling matches in his hair and beard to appear especially fierce to the prospective targets. A heavy drinker, Blackbeard impressed patrons in the New Providence bars by floating gunpowder on his rum, setting it on fire, and drinking the flaming mixture. It is not known if Blackbeard learned these tricks from Hornigold, but the pupil certainly absorbed other lessons. Hornigold promoted this prize pupil as quickly as he could, putting him in charge of a sloop that had been captured in a savage battle. Teach equipped the sloop with a half-dozen cannons and seventy men and sailed as a member of the Hornigold flotilla.

Hornigold was still searching for pirate talent when he met Sam Bellamy. Hornigold listened as Bellamy told him of his double-cross of Jennings. Not being fond of Jennings, Hornigold laughed. Hornigold liked this enterprising young upstart and the crew that loyally followed him. Hornigold increased his flotilla by giving Bellamy's company the *Marianne,* a New England–built sloop that was capable of carrying about forty tons of booty. The crew gathered on the deck and unanimously reelected Bellamy as their captain.

EDWARD "BLACKBEARD" TEACH

With Hornigold and Blackbeard to back him up from the sea, Bellamy took the *Marianne* on a successful raid into Cuba's Portobello Harbor. Returning to the Hornigold flotilla, Bellamy found that his fellow pirates had stopped a ship loaded with logwood and were arguing over whether the ship should be plundered or not. Although the wood carrier was Dutch-owned, her captain was English, which raised an interesting issue, since Hornigold would never attack an English ship.

Finally, the pirates agreed that the ship's nationality mattered more than the captain's, and the ship was plundered. When the crew of the captured ship was offered the chance to turn pirate, a young man named John Brown, who was possibly black, stepped forward and was taken on by Bellamy's crew.

A few days later, two cocoa-carrying brigantines were stopped by Bellamy on their way to Vera Cruz, Mexico. After the pirates looted the ships, their crews were offered a chance to "go on the account." Hendrick Quintor, a seaman of African ancestry who had been born in Amsterdam, joined Bellamy's crew.

BELLAMY'S FIRST PIRATE SHIP

Bellamy's first real pirate command was the *Marianne,* a single-decked New England sloop built for speed.

The Bellamy gang continued a life of easy plunder. In June 1716, they captured an English ship captained by John Brett. Since the ship was English, Hornigold wouldn't allow her cargo to be taken, but the pirates did plunder the liquor before setting the ship free. After that interlude, the pirates stopped some slow cargo haulers called "pinks" off the coast of Cuba and robbed them. Four of their crewmen joined the pirates. Then Bellamy sailed to Samana Bay, on the coast of Cuba, where the pirates careened their ships—beaching the vessels and turning them on their sides so they could scrape the marine life off the hulls and cover them with a protective layer of tar.

While the ships were being careened, a serious dispute broke out among the pirates. Some of the men were angry at Hornigold over his refusal to plunder British ships. He did have defenders, especially among those pirates who knew his history as a privateer for the king. Some English-born pirates sympathized with Hornigold's loyalty to England. Many of the pirates were not English, and they saw no reason to spare His Majesty's ships over those of Spain and France. Business is business, they argued, and the business of piracy sees no flag as a barrier to plunder.

It is clear that Bellamy was a strong proponent of free plunder and that Blackbeard also leaned in that direction. Hornigold and Bellamy heatedly debated the issue for several days while the seamen acted as active spectators, offering their opinions at every opportunity. In keeping with the Articles that governed them, the crew took a vote and chose Bellamy to replace Hornigold as captain of the pirate fleet.

Hornigold was allowed to keep his share of the booty, as were the men who decided to join him. Among that group of about two dozen men was Blackbeard. Although he sympathized with the men who left Hornigold, Blackbeard had decided to stay with his captain out of loyalty. The Hornigold gang was given a sloop and all the provisions needed to reach safe harbor. Then they were sent away, never to be seen again by Bellamy.

Continuing to plunder with their sloop in the months that followed, Hornigold and Blackbeard captured the *Concord,* a French Guineaman bound for Martinique. Blackbeard took command of the ship and outfitted her with forty guns. He renamed her *The Queen Anne's Revenge* as a sort of living memorial to the War of the Spanish Succession, also known as Queen Anne's War, in which he had learned many of his nautical skills.

With a crew of three hundred men, Blackbeard terrorized the American coastline. He continued growing the facial hair that gave him his name, creating a beard and mane so monstrous that an early writer compared it to a

CAREENING THE HULL IN
SAMANA BAY

"frightful meteor [that] covered his whole face and frightened America more than any comet that has appeared there in a long time."

Blackbeard was killed in November 1718 in a bloody assault by the British navy. His head was severed and hung from the bowsprit of a navy frigate by the lieutenant who led the attack.

Some of the entries found in Blackbeard's journal read like free verse and summarize the travails of the pirate captain. Take this one, for instance:

—Such a day, rum all out;
    —Our company somewhat sober;
    —a damned confusion among us!
    —Rogues a plotting; great talk of separation. So I look for a prize;
    —such a day took one, with a great deal of liquor on board; so kept the
company hot, damned hot, then all things went well again.

Gold coins.

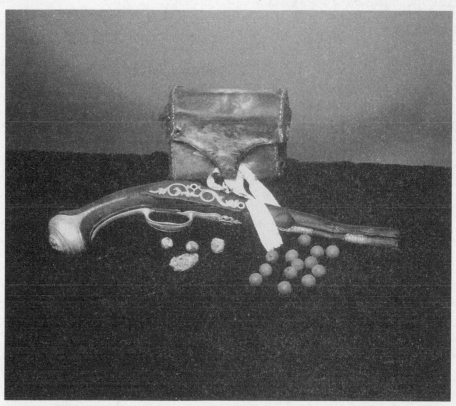

Pistol with powder and ball carrier.

Hornigold left piracy shortly after his overthrow by Bellamy. The new governor in chief of the Bahamas, himself a former pirate, offered a king's pardon to all pirates if they surrendered before September 5, 1718, and promised not to return to their former occupation. Hornigold took early retirement. In an elaborate ceremony that involved a three-hundred-gun salute by the veteran pirate's crew, Hornigold and the more than one thousand pirates on the island received their pardons.

The dean of pirates never terrorized the high seas again—as a pirate, that is. He did become a pirate hunter, and met his demise in a shipwreck while pursuing pirates for the king.

Bellamy's democratic election to the office of captain was a leap forward for his career. At the same time, new officers were elected for his ship, the *Marianne*—including newcomer John Fletcher as quartermaster, William Main as sailing master, and Jeremiah Burke as boatswain.

A second sloop joined them as well, *La Postillion*. Captained by French pirate Oliver Levasseur, also known as "la Buze" (the Vulture), this ship and its captain had served under Hornigold for several months.

Like-minded in their desire to ravage shipping, the tiny flotilla sailed into the blue Caribbean, its men the masters of their universe.

21

Name Unknown

Staff archaeologist Rob Reedy, right, and John Beyer hoist an encrusted artifact on board the *Vast*.

✺ "Look at this!" said Rob Reedy, our latest field archaeologist.

I held up the concretion and looked at the nub of metal that was protruding from one side. It was black and looked like a short pan handle.

"What is it?" I asked.

"Take a close look and let your mind run free," said Kinkor.

I took Ken's advice and tried not to think about everything else that was on my mind. Objects that are concreted change shape so much that it is difficult to tell what they are. Even everyday objects, like plates or pots, can become so encrusted that they look like cannonballs or door handles. I cleared my mind and looked at the object again. This time the face of the devil was staring back at me.

"It's the butt of a pistol!" I shouted, as I carefully cradled the concretion to take a closer look. Toward the top, where the gun disappeared into the

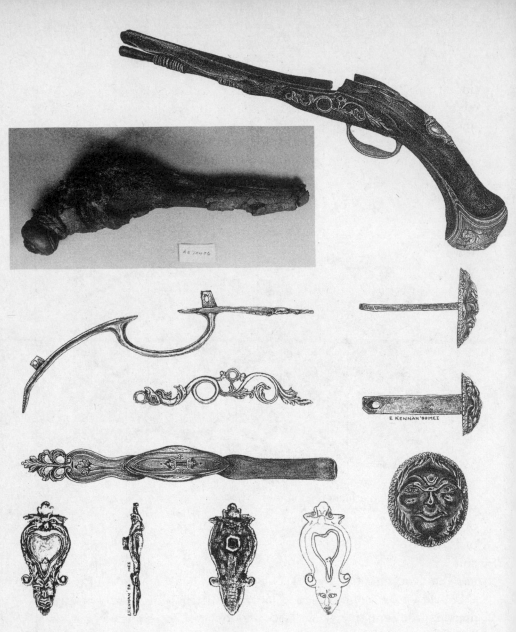

Fine Weaponry

Finely made pistols were so prized that a pirate might bid almost two years' worth of seaman's wages for a particularly fancy pair. This pistol is just such a weapon. Note the brass serpentine sideplate, the devil mask on the escutcheon (detail, bottom left), and the gargoyle design on the butt cap (detail, bottom right). This solar deity may commemorate Louis XIV, the "Sun King" of France. On the other hand, certain features suggest a Scottish manufacturer. The design may therefore likewise commemorate William III, the lifelong enemy of King Louis, as a "sun king."

This weapon—together with the hemp holster in the photograph above—was found buried in the encrustation surrounding a cannon. Its handle was wrapped with a silk ribbon with a floral design.

incrustation, I could see what looked like a decorative plate that would run above the trigger. At the very end of the handle was engraved a devilish face framed by rays of fire.

"The face is very unusual," said Kinkor. "I'll have to do a great deal of research, but I think it depicts a Roman god. I'm not sure which one."

The pistol, said Reedy, had been found by some of the conservators, including my father, who was now working with great zeal in the conservation lab.

"It may be intact," said Reedy, proud that the lab had made such an unusual find. "If we're real careful it might be virtually complete. That means we'll have the first intact weapon to come off the *Whydah*."

I looked around the room at the water tanks filled with cannons. They did not have the wooden carriages that supported them in 1717 and were therefore not technically intact.

The cannons were such a presence in the conservation lab that the conservators had named each for one of the pirates who had been on the *Whydah*. Hence, Paulsgrave Williams was there, as were Richard Nolan, the quartermaster from England; William Osborn, who aimed the cannons; Ferguson, the ship's surgeon; and Lambert, the sailmaster in charge of navigation.

"Which cannon did you find this pistol on?" I asked Reedy.

"We discovered it on the one named Captain Bellamy," said Reedy.

If quality artifacts are a measure of success in an archaeological dig, then we were wildly successful. As I looked around the lab, I could see the fruits of our labor piling up. Already we had more than three thousand silver coins of the Spanish empire, including 2,019 Mexican coins and 996 Peruvian coins. Gold coins and bars needed no conservation and were being stored in a vault at a local bank.

Soaking in electrified tanks were an anchor eight feet long and the cannons just mentioned. Also soaking were smaller items, including cannonballs, hundreds of musket balls, four trigger guards, brass shoe buckles, cuff links, a sword hilt, samples of cloth, a mortar jar with the letter *W* etched into the bottom, pewter plates stamped with assorted seals, and a gold ring with a mysterious inscription.

Some of the objects in the lab were chilling. When we opened one concretion, we were shocked to find a small leather shoe with a leg bone and stocking still inside. The materials were in such good shape and the bone so clean that it looked almost as though the occupant had vaporized, leaving this remnant behind.

"What do you think happened to this one?" asked one of the conservators.

The question spurred everyone in the laboratory to speculate about the events of that last horrible night, when the person who wore this shoe had been pinned to the bottom of the ocean with no chance of survival.

On another occasion, we broke apart a concreted pile of cannons and found a human shoulder bone. It was obvious what had happened to this poor seaman. As the ship struck shore and began its fatal roll, the cannons shifted like logs rolling down a mountain. The pirate was crushed by cannons weighing hundreds of pounds. Over the years, the rest of his body had been eaten away by sea creatures or dissolved by seawater, but somehow his shoulder bone had lasted long enough to become part of a massive concretion.

"This is like a time machine," said one of the conservators. "When the artifacts emerge, it is like traveling backwards, like touching colonial America."

Despite the fact that we hauled up eighteenth-century artifacts every time we dug on the site, the Massachusetts Board of Underwater Archaeological Resources refused to identify the find as the *Whydah*.

FOR FLASHY FINERY

As Sam Bellamy grew up on the streets of Plymouth, he may have seen former pirates strolling local docksides. In deliberate defiance of their humble origins, many pirates liked to dress well, often bedecking themselves in stolen finery. Clean white shirts and expensive embroidered vests were popular.

This is shown by the stylishness of some of the brass buttons and silver collar studs recovered from the *Whydah* wreck site. Wearer beware: Any sailor wearing fine clothes ashore risked drawing unwanted attention from the authorities.

MIXING MEDICINE

A *W* (not shown) is etched into the bottom of this brass apothecary's mortar, possibly indicating that it may have belonged to the *Why-dah* during her incarnation as a slave trader. After the *Whydah* was converted to a pirate vessel, Dr. James Ferguson may have used this mortar to compound remedies for sick crewmen.

Most frequently prescribed were tonics intended to strengthen a body that had been weakened by disease, particularly fever. The most popular such tonic was chinchona (also known as Jesuit's bark), which was effective in the treatment of malaria owing to its quinine content.

Next most often used were cathartics that were thought to flush out unbalanced physical "humours" with the feces. Examples included castor oil, calomel, rhubarb, and sodium potassium tartrate. Likewise used to remove foul humours were vomit-inducing emetics such as ipecac and antimony potassium nitrate.

CRYPTIC RING

This crudely engraved gold ring has been the subject of much conjecture. One story has it that this may once have been the ring of a Royal Navy seaman named Teye who later turned pirate.

Teye is a fairly common surname in the north of England. *BA* not only means "Bachelor of Arts," but might also stand for the able-bodied seaman's certification—an important milestone in a sailor's career. The most telling clue, however, is the *WFS* initials. These probably stand for "Western Fleet Station," a base for the Royal Navy located at Kingston, Jamaica.

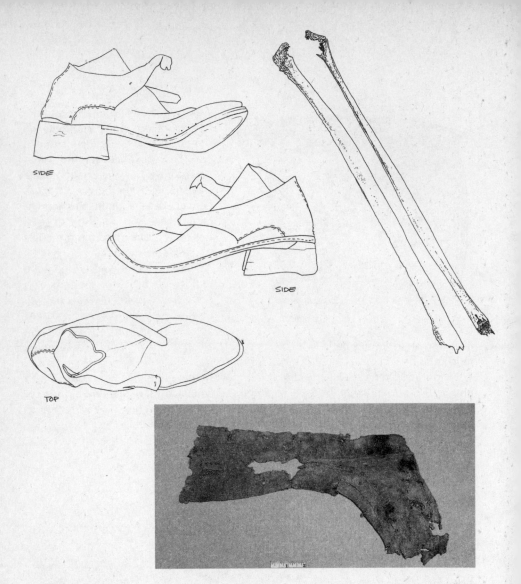

All That Remains

In the days after the wreck, more than one hundred bodies washed ashore. These objects are from one that didn't. The shoe, stocking, and leg bone were found together in the same incrustation. They were protected from decay by concretion from a cannon that pinned this man's leg to the seabed.

Shoes were seldom worn aboard ship; they were reserved for special occasions ashore. This leather shoe, fastened with a buckle, was made with a centered toe so it could fit either the right or the left foot. Of an upper-class style, it is approximately a man's size five.

While some might be surprised by the small size, it's a common mistake to think of pirates as tall and burly men. The average height of upper-class males during the eighteenth century was five feet, nine inches, while lower-class males appear to have averaged only about five feet, four inches. This difference was almost completely due to nutrition.

LOVE, DEATH, AND HONOR

Sailors joined pirate companies by signing the Articles and swearing an oath to obey them and to be true to their shipmates. They thereby gave their consent to be governed by the rules of their "floating commonwealth." This "pledge of allegiance," as an affirmation of citizenship, was important enough that even a sailor who could not write his own name would nonetheless make his mark with a scrawled sign or the imprint of a wax seal in order to be considered a full-fledged member of the company. A celebration, complete with cannon salutes, was often held when a new recruit signed the Articles.

This silver seal was not only for signing documents, but was also a good-luck charm and love token. It features two turtledoves—a traditional sign for a pair of lovers—facing each other over the ocean, which represents an impending hazardous journey. Above them hover the balance scales of Fate, which, in turn, are contained by the laurel wreath of Victory. The inscription is an abbreviated version of the French phrase "Death, if I lose thee."

"The evidence is extraordinarily suggestive," said one of the board members. "There is a high probability that it is the *Whydah*, but it is our responsibility to be cautious and keep questions open."

I knew I had the *Whydah*, and I continued to argue the point with the board.

"There is no record of any other ship sinking with such a treasure," I told the board. "The historical record points clearly to what happened. If another ship like the *Whydah* had gone down, it would have been known."

One night I brought artifacts and a slide show to the state board meeting. The board, press, and spectators all gathered like eager children around the table where I was displaying a brass-barreled sawed-off shotgun, a silver shield, silver pieces of eight, and gold doubloons.

As our archaeologist, Rob Reedy, described each object, I started the slide show, flashing pictures of the laboratory, the site, and divers bringing artifacts onto the *Vast Explorer*. I clicked through each of these photos until I reached the last one, which was a prank photo of me kneeling on the beach before a treasure chest full of shiny gold coins.

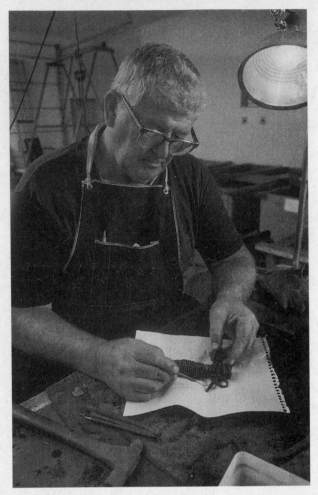

Artifact conservation
became a family business
when my father, Bob,
went to work at the lab.

There was silence in the room until I started to laugh. Then people realized that it was a mock photo and they began to laugh, too.

"Who's the pirate?" asked one of the reporters.

"The only man determined enough in two hundred fifty years to actually find the ship," said our archaeologist.

At least I am getting credit for having found a ship, I thought. That they
can't deny.

Later that evening, a reporter pulled me aside and asked what it would
take for the board to recognize all the artifacts as having come from the
Whydah.

"I don't know for sure," I said. "One of the archaeologists on the board
said that he wouldn't believe it unless we brought up the quarterboard with

'*Whidah*' (how we spelled it then) written on it. Short of that happening, I don't know what it will take. There should be a bell down there somewhere. If I'm lucky, maybe it'll have the ship's name on it. Until then, I'll just keep excavating the pirate ship I'm on, name unknown."

My job had broadened, so much so that I was not able to oversee the search operations as much as I would have liked. Much of my time was spent telephoning investors, dealing with suppliers, talking to the various regulatory boards, and fielding calls from people who wanted Maritime Underwater Surveys to help them excavate wrecks they had found. In short, I was becoming a bureaucrat. I had also been told to curtail my diving activities by an ear doctor who had become increasingly concerned about the damage it was doing to my hearing.

To fill in for me at the site, I let McClung function as director of operations. The result was a tension headache for the project, as McClung began to exert authority in ways that were grating to the veteran crew.

One night, for instance, Grey and Beyer offered to stay at the site so they could get an early start excavating a particular spot that interested them. In

PAGAN SEAL

This handcrafted brass seal features a number of non-Christian motifs unusual for the eighteenth century. The central heart pierced with two arrows is an old pagan symbol for a wounded heart, or suffering, which is sometimes also recorded on pirate flags. The twin crescents are waxing and waning quarter-moons, which represent the lunar cycles of nature and fertility, while the flaming star is probably the sun, or possibly a hermetic symbol for divine guidance. Some have interpreted the delicate trefoil post as a symbol of the Celtic "Triple Goddess" of Ireland, Wales, and northwestern France. In any case, the design of the post indicates that the seal was probably intended to hang from a necklace.

the morning they awoke before sunrise and blew a hole with the mailboxes. Much to their delight, they had uncovered a cache of silver coins.

They scooped coins by the handful, depositing them in dive bags that they emptied on the decks, then went back down for more. In less than three hours, the two divers had brought up more than eight hundred coins.

When the *Crumpstey* arrived at 3 P.M., with McClung at the helm, both Grey and Beyer were laughing like children as they lined the railing with the imperfectly shaped coins.

"Look at *this* booty!" shouted Grey.

McClung jumped angrily onto the deck of the *Vast* and pointed his beefy arm at Grey, ordering the others with him, "Search them for stolen coins!"

Beyer, myself, and McClung pose with a table full of artifacts.

It was only the intervention of the other crewmen that separated Grey and McClung and kept them from engaging in a monumental fistfight.

That McClung was taking the fun out of the job seemed to be a general complaint of the crew. One by one, crew members complained to me about McClung's heavy-handedness in handling almost all matters. He would usually show up late on the boat, sometimes not until mid-afternoon. Then he would start shouting orders, generally orders to do things that had already been done.

"He's pushing everyone around like he's a cop," complained Murphy.

"That's because he *was* a cop," Stretch said. "There are some things you just can't take out of a person, and being a cop is one of them."

I knew I would have to deal with this situation someday, but I had other problems that needed attention first.

Once again, we were almost out of money. Our second financing had given us about $300,000 to work with, and that money was nearly gone. We had built an expensive conservatory, but we were still years away from having the artifacts in good enough shape to stock a museum. Again, I had to find financial backing.

As fate would have it, I made my next financial connections at the home of William Styron. I had gone there one day in June to visit the writer's son, Tom, who was home for the weekend. To show the Styron family what I had accomplished during the last three years, I brought a bag of coins and some gold and silver bars. I thought they would like to see the fruits of the search that started in their living room when I told them the story of the *Whydah*. I poured the coins out on the dining room table and told them about the bumpy road I'd followed my last three years. As they listened and asked questions, they examined the coins, noting that the experience made them feel a visceral link with history.

"You need to do a book about this," said Styron, rubbing a piece of eight between his thumb and forefinger. "I have a friend coming to town for a vacation. Let me see if you can meet him."

A few days later, I was sitting on a sun-drenched porch next to Bob Bernstein, then CEO of Random House. He was renting a Martha's Vineyard cottage for a few weeks and agreed to talk to me for a few minutes about the possibility of a book on the *Whydah*. I ended up talking to him for a lot longer than that.

I arrived with a plastic battery box full of coins and other objects from our recent digs. Bernstein was a little stiff when we first started talking, but when I emptied the content of the box onto the table in front of him, his defenses vaporized.

"What is this?" he said joyfully, holding up a bent and uneven piece of eight stamped across its face with a Spanish cross.

The treasure cast a spell on the publishing executive, and soon he was hunched over, examining each piece with an interest usually reserved for small boys examining colorful bugs.

Since the house he was renting was perched on one of the highest points in Martha's Vineyard, I was able to point out the general direction of the shipwreck site. As we both stood straining our eyes to the north, Bob's son, Tom, walked into the room. A young lawyer with red hair set off by a spray of freckles, young Bernstein began squinting into the distance, too.

"What are we looking at?" he asked.

"Where that came from," said Bob, pointing at the pile of coins on the table.

Within seconds we were all bent over the coins again, talking about every aspect of the *Whydah*.

By the end of our conversation, it was Tom and not his father who was most interested in the *Whydah*. He and his partner, Roland Betts, had recently started Silver Screen Management, Inc., a New York company that raised money to finance motion pictures. They initially raised $80 million to produce films for Home Box Office. That deal soured when HBO stopped making movies, and now their company was doing business with the Walt Disney Company, financing their newly formed production company, Touchstone Films.

What appeared to interest Tom Bernstein most was the notion of a pirate museum. As an entertainment lawyer with an inside view of Disney, he had been exposed to the income possibilities of theme and amusement parks. Bernstein, like everyone else who has come into contact with the *Whydah* project, was infected with treasure fever.

A few days later, Bernstein called his partner and recounted the story of the *Whydah,* right up to the pile of coins I had poured on their table in Martha's Vineyard. It was Bernstein's idea to finance the project and turn the whole thing into a major, Disney-style attraction their company could finance and eventually manage for a hefty fee.

Betts was less enthusiastic.

"Sure, Tom," he said on the phone. "I think you need some rest."

Still, young Bernstein convinced his partner at least to meet me and hear the story of the *Whydah*. Within a few days I was in New York City with Bob Bernstein, carrying a sack full of coins into a swank East Side restaurant.

"Excuse me, sir," said the maître d', blocking my path to Betts's table. "You have to wear a tie to dine here."

Since I didn't have one, the maître d' provided one from a rack of ties kept for the chronically underdressed. Knotting the tie over my T-shirt and refusing to remove my baseball cap, I strode into the restaurant for my first meeting with Roland Betts.

He, too, was impressed by the coins and the story of the *Whydah*. I told him about the two financings that had supported the project thus far, and leveled with him about the fact that we were nearly out of money and needed more funding to continue the search for the artifacts of the legendary pirate ship.

"Just think what an amazing museum all of this stuff will make," I said. "The only pirate ship in the world. People would come from all over the world just to see it."

I thought my lunchtime pitch was a convincing one. Frankly, I was certain that the other half of Silver Screen Management was ready to propose a deal that would involve a museum and continued excavation. It's amazing how quickly business can turn around, I thought, certain of a successful merger of our respective talents. The *Whydah* museum is going to happen!

Within a few days my bubble burst. Tom Bernstein called to tell me that his partner was not interested in providing any money for the *Whydah* project. They had too many irons in the fire with all the complicated deals they were managing for Disney.

"And besides that, there's another problem," said Bernstein.

"What's that?" I asked.

"You still haven't proven that this ship is actually the *Whydah*."

22

Cast-Iron Proof

Finding the *Whydah*'s bell, shown here on the ocean floor moments after it was uncovered, proved once and for all that we had found the pirate ship.

✳ Toward the end of summer in 1985, we blew a pit about forty feet south of where we found the first cannons. A large hit had been registered in this spot by the magnetometer and we wanted to check it out before fall weather put an end to our season.

McClung went down wearing the Aga so we could hear him over the communications system as he waited for the sand to settle and the pit to clear.

"There's something huge down here, but I can't tell what it is," said McClung.

"Maybe it's a rock and you just don't recognize it," quipped Stretch Grey.

"I don't think so," insisted McClung. "I think it's a bell."

McClung had a penchant for melodrama, so none of us got too excited. "I still can't tell what it is," said McClung.

I told him to come back up, and when he did, Grey started the engine and blew more prop wash down on the site. By the time he was finished, I had suited up and was in the water with McClung.

We dropped down to the pit and waited for the sand to settle. When it did, I could see it clearly: a bell was sitting in the bottom of the pit. My heart began to trip. I kicked down and tried to rub the side of it clean to see if there was a name etched in its cast-bronze sides. The metal was heavily concreted, and I couldn't tell what ship it was from.

"It's a bell, all right," I said when I got back to the surface.

Bob Cembrola, a visiting archaeologist, quickly put on his dive gear and went down to measure the artifact and map the site. A few days later, on October 7, we wrapped the bell in straps and pulled it up from the bottom of the ocean.

When the bell was brought up, we all posed with our greatest of finds.

"It looks like the right bell," said Cembrola, who is now an archaeologist with the Naval War College in Rhode Island. "It is definitely eighteenth century. I can tell that from its shape. But I don't know if it's from the *Whydah*."

We took the heavily concreted bell back to the lab and submerged it in a water tank. Then we turned on the electrical current and waited for the incrustation to break free.

I tried not to think about the bell after that. For one thing, it might not have been the *Whydah*'s, or it might have been a bell from one of the ships that the pirates robbed. Another reason not to think about the bell was the incrustation that covered it. Sometimes it takes months or even years for the incrustations to fall away. You can hurry them a little, especially if they are loose, but usually you want to wait until they are ready to fall off before doing any kind of chipping. That way you avoid damaging an artifact.

The day before Halloween, a big chunk fell off to reveal the word *Gally*. "What does that mean?" I asked Carl Becker, one of the lab conservators.

"It's probably 'galley' without the 'e'," he said. "Someone spelled it different than we do now."

By now a crowd had gathered, including McClung, Murphy, and Tuck Whitaker, an investor.

Becker and some of the other conservators scraped away at the concretion using dental picks. After twenty minutes they had uncovered a Maltese cross and the date *1716*. Suddenly, a lump of concreted material fell away and the blessed words we had been looking for were exposed:

THE † WHYDAH † GALLY † 1716

We went wild with elation. Up until now, everyone had assumed that the ship's name was spelled *Whidah*. But now we knew the true spelling, which in a way was like being reborn. I felt like a company that was changing its name to get across a new image.

"I guess I'll have to change all of the stationery," said Murphy glibly.

"Not to mention all of the T-shirts and caps," I said.

"Forget that stuff," said Whitaker, smacking his chest. "I have to change my tattoo."

We contacted everyone we could think of with the news, and virtually everyone came to see and record the discovery. The MBUAR came along to see the bell. Even archaeologist Paul Johnston, the one who had declared the *Whydah* a myth when I first applied to look for it, grudgingly had to admit that we had found the *Whydah*, right where we thought we would

THE SOUL OF THE SHIP

The ship's bell, still undergoing conservation, conclusively authenticated Barry Clifford's discovery of the *Whydah*. It may have been manufactured at the foundry of Evan Evans at Chepstow, in Monmouthshire. The bell appears to have hung stationary on a bracket frame. A lanyard was probably attached to a ring on the end of an iron bar behind the clapper ball. The bell was run by pulling the lanyard so that the clapper would strike the inside of the bell.

find her. Even some of the people who were fighting to get adjacent claims to ours showed up to admire the find.

Then, of course, there was the media. All the networks sent camera crews, and newspapers sent their reporters. On November 1, 1985, the *New York Times* ran a front-page article that showed the bell being brought on board the *Vast* from the ocean's bottom. The headline read: BELL CONFIRMS THAT SALVORS FOUND PIRATE SHIP OF LEGEND.

The article proclaimed the *Whydah* the "object of debate, search and wonder" for 268 years, and declared the bell to be the "first identification in history" of a pirate ship. They quoted Mendel Peterson, the retired direc-

With my son, Brandon, we pose in the conservation lab with the bell and a handful of *Whydah* treasure.

Cast-iron proof of the historic find.

tor of underwater exploration projects at the Smithsonian Institution, who called the now-verified *Whydah* "a significant find. One of the outstanding ones known in the record."

The article in the *Times* lit a fire under Tom Bernstein. Silver Screen's business was progressing nicely, as they raised millions of dollars for a number of Disney movies that would eventually include such hits as *Good Morning, Vietnam; Honey, I Shrunk the Kids;* and *Who Framed Roger Rabbit?*

Always on the prowl for a financial venture that was also fun, Bernstein said that he had never quite gotten the *Whydah* project out of his mind. Now that we could prove beyond a shadow of a doubt that this was the *Whydah,* Bernstein would try once again to interest his partner in some kind of venture.

"You are excavating the only pirate ship in the world," said Bernstein. "That means a *Whydah* museum would be the only place in the world that people could see authentic pirate artifacts."

This was the year I call "the year of the bell." I seemed to hear cash register bells ringing to record the onslaught of people who would eventually

visit the proposed museum. And the finding of the bell as well as the revelation of what we had accomplished in finding and restoring artifacts was
like a clarion call for the press.

The national media camped at our door. It was not uncommon to see
the *Vast Explorer* or members of the crew on the evening news. Sometimes
camera crews would be on the dock as we returned from several days of
digging, their film recording the uneventful act of docking the boat.

"This is worse than the days when JFK Jr. was on board," said Stretch
Grey, who had become progressively fed up with McClung and was close
to leaving the project. "Then you could yell at the press and tell them to get
the hell out. Now they are filming us instead of a president's son, so you
have to be nice or you'll come off looking bad."

But the media experiences certainly weren't all obnoxious. *Parade* magazine ran me on its cover, an open box of treasure in front of me and a cover
line that read: THE MAN WHO DISCOVERED A $400 MILLION PIRATE TREA-
SURE, an estimate given to the *New York Times* by Robert Cahill, president
of MBUAR. The article, written by David Fairbank White, son of famed
journalist Theodore White, caused a frenzy of queries from Cape Codders
who wanted to know how they could invest in the *Whydah* project.

To my horror, a number of my crew members helped them do just that.
Some of them had taken stock as part of their payment for excavating the
wreck site. Now, when approached by people who wanted a piece of the

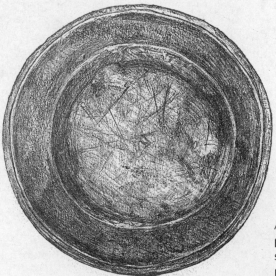

As knife marks on recovered
pewter plates suggest, the
salted meat eaten by the
pirates was very tough.

My children spent many days working on the wreck site. Above, Barry Jr. is with us on a cold October day. Right, daughter Jenny carefully draws an artifact.

action, they gladly sold them their shares. It became commonplace for me to be approached by a stranger holding a stock certificate and asking where he or she could cash in the shares or pick up more.

Walter Cronkite boarded the *Vast Explorer* to showcase our efforts for his television show, *Cronkite at Large*. Because he was considered the most respected man in America based on a number of national polls, I was concerned that Cronkite would expect regal treatment everywhere he went. Before he arrived on the boat, I told the entire crew only to speak when spoken to and to always call him "Mr. Cronkite."

The crew was extremely well-behaved that day. No one yelled, no one swore, no one even took his shirt off. For the first half of the day the *Whydah* excavation looked like a military operation. Then at lunch, our cook,

Newsman Walter Cronkite was excited by the discovery of the *Whydah* and produced an enthusiastic documentary for CBS.

the irreverent Mike Anderson, stuck his head out the engine room door and shouted, "Hey Wally, how do you want your burger?"

From that point on, Mike and Walter Cronkite were inseparable. I realized that despite his extraordinary talents, he was an ordinary guy who wanted to be treated as such.

He interviewed critics of the operation, namely a few archaeologists who had never visited the site but said we were not paying attention to archaeology. In a short time, however, the shipboard operations won him over.

"See those bubbles?" he intoned, pressing his face against a wooden barrel that the crew had just brought to the surface. "That's air coming out of the barrel. That was the air those pirates were breathing the last moments of their lives."

With his cameras rolling, we toured the lab so I could show him the efforts being made at conservation. I told him our goal was to do good archaeology with an eye on the bottom line.

"We're in this to make money, and we're in this to make our investors money," I told Cronkite.

A few months later the program was beamed across the nation as part of a Cronkite special. Before that happened, Bernstein and Betts had formed the *Whydah* Partners Limited Partnership with E. F. Hutton, the now-defunct stock brokerage house. Their goal was to raise $6 million for the continued discovery and conservation of the *Whydah* artifacts. They also contacted Sotheby's auction house about selling the artifacts if the limited partnership decided to break up the collection.

Breaking up the collection was likely if the state owned 25 percent of the *Whydah* artifacts, as it claimed. So far, Allan Tufankjian had won in superior court against the state, successfully laying claim to everything we found from the *Whydah*. When the state appealed to a higher court, the general feeling among everyone except Tufankjian was that we would lose the case and have to give the state its share. If that were true, we would almost certainly be forced to sell the treasure, an irony since many of the archaeologists opposed to the sale of artifacts were supported by the state.

The E. F. Hutton prospectus had Maritime Explorations, the company I had formed to search for the *Whydah,* transferring the rights to the shipwreck to *Whydah* Partners in exchange for $150,000 and several million shares valued at ten cents per share. My company was then contracted by *Whydah* Partners to excavate and salvage the *Whydah.* Together, *Whydah* Partners and Maritime Explorations were known as the *Whydah* Joint Venture. *Whydah* Management Co. Inc. was then established by Bernstein and Betts to manage the $6 million they hoped to raise from about three hundred shareholders at $20,000 per person.

In exchange, the investors had a chance at high profits. They would receive 80 percent of the first $6 million made by the *Whydah* Joint Venture and then, on a sliding scale, a smaller and smaller percentage of whatever was made through exhibit or sale of the loot down to 20 percent of all cash received in excess of $55 million.

On the surface this seemed an excellent deal, but it was full of risks. That is why it was only offered to high-end customers of the brokerage house who were aware that they might never see their investment again.

The prospectus that E. F. Hutton prepared and sent out was filled with disclaimers and caveats. I counted twenty-six "risk factors," ominous red flags like: "The Ship May Not Be the *Whydah*," "There Is No Guarantee As to How Many Artifacts Will Be Salvaged," "Uncertain Market Value for Salvaged Items," "Sale or Disposition of Recovered Objects May Take Five Years or More," "Role of Commonwealth; Possible Claim of Key Artifacts," "Risk of Total Loss," and "Quantity and Value of Recovered Objects . . . May Be Highly Speculative and Exaggerated."

With advance billing like that, I had my doubts about the success of this money-raising venture. Were people interested enough in history to risk this kind of money? Despite the warnings, did they really know how iffy and heartbreaking treasure hunting could be?

"I don't think people are going to go for this," I said to Bernstein in a fit of doubt.

"They love it already," he said. "I just attended a meeting of brokers who said they can sell this in a couple of months."

"But they're going to look at this and say, 'If this thing is worth so much, then why isn't Barry Clifford rich?'" I said.

"What are you talking about?" asked Bernstein.

"They'll want to know why I don't just sell this stuff and get rich on my own," I said.

"They'll understand why," said Bernstein. "Most investors are dreamers, and they don't just dream about money. They understand the search for the unknown. A lot of these guys would fund a treasure hunt in the Amazon just to be the first to hear the stories that came back."

"They're that interested in this story?" I asked.

"Barry, they'll be able to dine out on this story for years to come."

As it turned out, Bernstein was right. The private offering went on sale March 13, 1986, and was sold out by May 14. Sixty percent of the sale went to the high-end investors Bernstein told me about. The other 40 percent, however, went to the employees of E. F. Hutton itself.

"I thought the people who sold these projects were immune to treasure fever," I said to McClung when it was all over.

"My friend," he said, "nobody is immune to treasure fever."

In succeeding months, Allan Tufankjian won an astounding legal victory that gave us complete control of the *Whydah,* from site management to ownership of all the artifacts. Not only did this ruling by the Supreme Court of Massachusetts take us out from under the thumb of MBUAR, it also meant that we did not have to give 25 percent of our find to the state of Massachusetts. In effect, this meant that we as investors owned every piece of eight, coin, cannon, pistol, and fork that the ghosts of Bellamy and his crew would give us.

Tufankjian had doubted the state's claim of ownership from the beginning. Based on the ancient admiralty law of "finds," a ship that has lain abandoned on the ocean floor for many years and has no rightful owner becomes the property of the person who finds it.

The state, on the other hand, claimed ownership of the *Whydah* based upon the 1953 Submerged Lands Act, a federal statute that gives states control over the natural resources (oil, gas, and minerals) found within three miles of their shores. The state claimed that because the *Whydah* was within the three-mile boundary, it was theirs and they were entitled to a percentage of our find.

Tufankjian fought the state's claim from the beginning. He said that federal law was very specific in its definition of natural resources. "If they had meant to include shipwrecks, they would have included them in writing," he declared.

The superior court agreed with Tufankjian in 1986, but the Common-wealth of Massachusetts appealed the case to a higher court. We all thought it was unlikely that we would beat the state. I remember Tufankjian ex-plaining the case to Frank Wells, the late president of Disney and an investor, who just shook his head at the futility of fighting the state. "You can't beat the state on a case where money is involved," he said. "Least of all a state nicknamed 'Taxachusetts.'"

But Tufankjian persisted, this time with additional help from the federal government. In 1987, Congress passed the Abandoned Shipwreck Act, which gave title to all submerged shipwrecks to the federal government and transferred title to the state where the shipwreck is located.

This was good news for anyone contesting a claim that they had made on a shipwreck before 1987, according to Tufankjian. The new law proved that the Submerged Lands Act did not apply to shipwrecks, only to natural resources, as he had argued. Since our claim was entered before 1987, the Abandoned Shipwreck Act did not apply to us.

Tufankjian also argued that because we had filed a claim on the *Whydah,* we were entitled to that ship, wherever it was found, even in an adjacent claim site. Winning this point would nullify all the claims around us, since they seemed to have been made just to find the parts of the *Whydah* that may have scattered from the original wreck site.

He argued our case before the Supreme Court of Massachusetts and then waited impatiently for six months for their written opinion. In May 1988 the judge made his ruling in a beautifully written opinion made even more beautiful by the fact that it ruled in our favor. The judges agreed with Tufankjian's argument that the Submerged Lands Act did not include ship-wrecks, declaring "the Act did not contemplate a transfer of rights in under-water archeological treasures or artifacts."

They also gave us sole title to the *Whydah* wherever she might be found. This was the sweetest victory of all.

The judges wrote:

"The ill-fated *Whydah,* nearly three centuries [after crashing], has sailed into this court's jurisdiction as the subject of a dispute between contempo-rary treasure seekers and the would-be modern sovereign of the coastal waters—a conflict mired in competing claims of title to the shipwreck and its cargo, involving issues of Federal maritime and admiralty law, and dis-puted dominion over submerged lands in the marginal sea. . . .

"[T]he claim of the Commonwealth founders on the shoals of Federal sovereignty as surely as the *Whydah* foundered on the shoals off Wellfleet, ironically suffering the same fate as the 1717 proclamation of the Colony's Royal Governor Samuel Shute, which claimed the wreck for the Crown."

We were happily stunned by the victory. Tufankjian told the *New York Times,* "It's great. This means millions of dollars for the company, because Mr. Clifford will not give the state 25 percent of the treasure." I told the *Boston Globe,* "I think I've got a great lawyer." Frank Wells from Disney called to congratulate us, saying, "Victories like this only take place in the movies."

Life couldn't have been better. We had money, freedom, and future. Nothing could stop us now.

23

Boom and Bust

✸ Overnight, the *Whydah* expedition became a bureaucracy, complete with high overhead and impressively titled executives.

Executive offices were opened, complete with a controller, office manager, several secretaries, and Dana Thayer, an executive from Silver Screen who oversaw operations by analyzing every expenditure closely before approving it. Some of us called her "No More Thayer" because to almost every request for money she would reply, "No more."

Corporate office expenses cost more than $348,000 per year, 23 percent of the annual budget.

Christopher Hamilton joined the project as chief archaeologist. As a member in good standing of the Society of Professional Archaeologists, Hamilton told the newspapers that good archaeology, even when privately funded, is good business. He then set out to do good archaeology, hiring more than a dozen conservators and lab workers to restore the artifacts to pristine condition. Rob Reedy became field director for archaeology, overseeing the handling of artifacts that were brought onto the boat. The combined work of Hamilton and Reedy won us accolades from the MBUAR, who now called the *Whydah* excavation "a model project in private archaeology."

Good archaeology doesn't come cheap, though. Preservation expenses ran $306,000 a year, eating up another 20 percent of the budget. And a new search vessel accounted for another big chunk of cash.

We purchased a large boat from a Louisiana oil company at a cost of $400,000. Three times larger than the *Vast Explorer*, the *Maritime Explorer* was 166 feet long and came equipped with a recompression chamber, a propwash diverter similar to our mailboxes that dropped into place with the push of a button, and very powerful cranes to lift large artifacts easily. We immediately tested the lifting capacity of the cranes by pulling up a heavy mass of cannons, barrels of nails, a couple of muskets, and ship's rigging that had concreted together in an encrusted boulder that was too heavy for us to lift with the *Vast*. Effortlessly, the *Maritime*'s machinery pulled the artifacts up and deposited them on its deck.

For the *Maritime*, we hired a captain and crew of six, including a chef who cooked gourmet meals for the divers and their support workers. The toilet even flushed in the regular way, instead of the pump handle method used on the *Vast*. And there were eight staterooms for sleeping.

The added luxury and convenience of the new boat came with a price, nearly $600,000 per year for crew, fuel, dock space, and maintenance, or 38 percent of the annual budget. Another 16 percent went to salvage operations carried out from the *Vast Explorer*. Although the new boat performed many operations better than the *Vast,* we still needed a small-draft boat to operate closer to shore and to work in certain areas at low tide. Operations from the *Vast* were figured in at almost $250,000 per year, more than our first year's entire operating budget, largely due to increased crew costs.

So large were the decks of our new boat, the *Maritime Explorer,* that we never worried about running out of room, as we did on the much smaller *Vast* in the background.

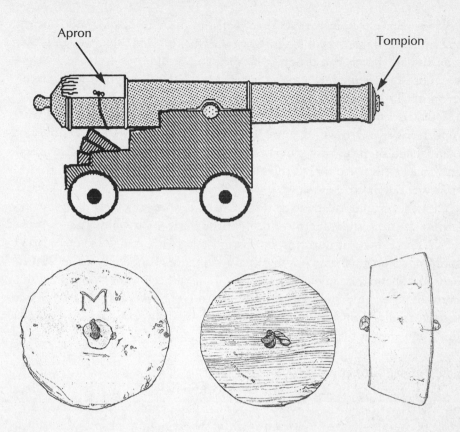

Apron

Tompion

READY TO FIRE

Cannons were kept loaded and ready to fire at all times aboard a pirate ship. To keep salt spray from spoiling the powder charge, wooden plugs called tompions plugged their muzzles.

A sheepskin was laid over the touch hole at the breech, and a thin lead apron was tied down over that.

Cannons could be quickly readied for firing with just a few quick tugs on the apron ties and a hard yank on the tompion's lanyard. With such a head start, a well-drilled gun crew could get off two shots in three minutes with a six-pounder—perhaps four minutes with an eight-pounder.

The letter M on this tompion may stand for the Marianne, Bellamy's first command, or it could in fact be a stylized letter W, standing for Whydah.

I was making about $70,000 per year, a livable amount for sure, but not the millions so many people thought I was making. Since finding the *Whydah,* my net worth had dropped more than a million dollars. Finally, after years of negative income and red ink, I could breathe a sigh of relief at taking a small step back into the black.

But was I happy? That question was put to me one day by a newspaper reporter as I sat at my desk in our Chatham offices. Surrounded by baskets of mail and memos, answering telephone calls from lawyers and investors and faced with personnel problems, I realized that the answer to that question was a definite "No."

"I'm not having nearly as good a time as I once was," I confessed. "I'm sitting at a desk, spending most of my time on really nebulous issues.

"When I first got into this, I'd just go off with a couple of friends, get into a little boat, take a couple of days' supplies, go out and survey a little area, and spend a couple of days diving. Today I have a 166-foot ship and a crew of people living on the ship twenty-four hours a day; it's like an extended family with all its problems. I just get up to my office here, sit at my desk, and answer the telephone all day. I never leave.

"Anybody with any sense wouldn't want to have me in the office. You can get a business guy better than me. I'd really like to get back in the field."

That interview, which ran in a Cape Cod newspaper, angered Bernstein and Betts, who felt that I was being ungrateful. But I wasn't. I was being realistic. Suddenly, the *Whydah* project had become big business and I, the founder, had been kicked upstairs. I was no longer a part of many of the key decision meetings. When investors visited the site I was brought out to entertain them, a job I genuinely liked. The rest of the time, I was becoming more of a bureaucrat.

Some of the original crew members felt the same way I did. John Beyer, no longer able to cope with the big-business aspects of treasure hunting, left the crew and returned to his home-insulation business in Martha's Vineyard. Stretch Grey, too, was having difficulty with the spit-and-polish transformation that had now swept the company. And, of course, he still simmered at Rob McClung for accusing him of stealing artifacts. Grey and McClung had clashed several times since that day McClung had accused him of stealing artifacts. By the time the *Whydah* Joint Venture became a reality, it was obvious to me that the fun of treasure hunting was gone for Stretch. Finally, at the beginning of the 1988 season, he resigned.

"I don't have it here anymore," he said patting his heart with his massive palm. "All this business stuff isn't me and I'm afraid that something really bad is going to happen between McClung and me."

For a while, we talked about the early days, which suddenly seemed as if they had taken place a hundred years ago. The best time of all, said Stretch, was the day we went out with Mel Fisher and got the first hits on the magnetometer.

"That was an eye-opening event for me," said my favorite captain. "All of a sudden I realized that there was a field of treasure right where I had been fishing all those years for lobster. That was when I caught treasure fever."

"Once you catch treasure fever you can never lose it," I said. "It's always in your blood."

"Maybe so," he said. "If that's true, then I'll be back. But until then I'm going back to being a lobsterman."

Since the dive operations on the *Whydah* were running generally well, I decided to accept some of the offers I had received to have Maritime Explorations salvage other wrecks. My agreement with the *Whydah* Joint Venture allowed me the freedom to work on other projects. Although Bernstein and Betts wanted me to devote full time to the *Whydah,* I wanted to grow my company beyond a "one wreck" salvage operation.

I did that very successfully, pursuing shipwrecks in New York City's East River, Central America, and eventually in Scotland, where I searched with Prince Andrew of England for the personal ship of King Charles I, which had sunk in the Firth of Forth that runs through Edinburgh.

The side activity of mine that upset the archaeological community the most was my effort to excavate the site of the Boston Tea Party in Boston Harbor.

On December 16, 1773, enraged by repressive taxation, Boston colonists dressed like Indians and dumped 342 tea chests into Fort Point Channel. The destruction of this tea sent a message to England that the colonists felt they were overtaxed and weren't going to take it any more. The chests were smashed to pieces, according to one participant, "[split open] with our tomahawks, so as to thoroughly expose them to the effects of the water."

A little over two years later, during the evacuation of Boston, vast quantities of British war materiel were jettisoned here as well, as the British left Boston in haste ahead of an angry crowd and the Continental army.

There was good reason to think that much of this material and possibly even some of the tea chests themselves had sunk into the harbor mud and could now be found. No one had ever looked for these chests, and it seemed

I received the royal treatment in Scotland, working with Prince Andrew, top, second from left, in the search for the personal ship of King Charles I. Although not knighted, the search crew got "kilted" for this group photograph.

like a worthy venture into the past. After all, the Boston Tea Party was one of the sparks that led to American independence. Relics from that event would be living reminders of our own history.

One problem existed, however. The state was now planning to build a train tunnel through this very area. Although the site had been surveyed for artifacts by Dr. Ricardo Elia, director of Boston University's Office of Public Archaeology, no underwater searching had been done. I was surprised that the state would allow a tunnel to be put through such an important site as this with scant proof that artifacts did not exist. I felt that a full-range site analysis should be conducted, including excavation into the cool, anaerobic mud of the harbor where the artifacts might still be preserved.

So I petitioned the Massachusetts Board of Underwater Archaeology, explaining my point of view in person and in letters. Ken Kinkor found an inventory of supplies and armaments that the colonial army had already seized from the thirteen ships that had been scuttled by the British navy and was able to determine from the quantitites that there was much more on the harbor floor. I presented this list and told them that I was targeting three of the scuttled ships and a large quantity of material that was on thcm.

I was accused by archaeologists of once again launching a hunt for treasure. When a newspaper reporter asked if I minded being called a "treasure hunter," I said no, as long as he defined what the term meant when applied to my operation.

"I don't mind being called a treasure hunter, but in the modern sense of the word," I said. "Sure, we're looking for treasure, but treasure is a number of things, whether it's lost knowledge or lost gold. What we are after in Boston Harbor is boats that were scuttled by the British and a hundred fifty cannons thrown from the docks that were fired at the Americans on Bunker Hill. Treasure hunter? Sure, but you have to include history as a treasure."

Despite Elia's objection and those of other archaeologists, MBUAR granted my company a permit to survey the area off Long Wharf. The only board member to vote against us was the state's archaeologist.

As with the *Whydah* artifacts, I felt that any historically significant objects found in the harbor should be displayed in a museum. The academic archaeology community ignored my intent, choosing instead to vent about commercial salvors being granted state contracts to excavate archaeological resources. The Society for Historical Archaeology went so far as to link Maritime Explorations with "looters" and declared MBUAR's action "a remarkable and utterly incomprehensiblc move."

It was not incomprehensible to me or any of the people who worked

A

E

B

D

C

THE GOLD OF AFRICA

West Africa was a major gold-producing area in the early eighteenth century, and European ships were usually able to obtain substantial consignments of gold dust, nuggets, and native gold jewelry in the course of trade with African tribes on the coast. One such group of related tribes were the Akan peoples in the area of modern-day Ghana and Benin. Gold ornaments found on the site of the Whydah wreck have been identified as the oldest reliably dated collection of Akan gold jewelry in the world.

Artifact A is half of a gold bead probably from the Baule tribe.

Artifact B was often seen on strings of gold beads worn by Ashanti royalty. The symbolism is associated with wealth or luck.

Artifact C is also probably of Ashanti origin and depicts an *apupuo* (a type of water snail), which, in turn, symbolizes defiance, steadfastness, or resolution.

F

G

H

Artifact D is a type of Akan bead often found on Ashanti charm (*suman*) bracelets. Its cocoonlike form suggests power, adaptability, and transformation.

Artifacts E and F are actually examples of Akan currency. The holes indicate that the pieces could be strung in a necklace.

Possibly from the Baule tribe, the type of bead represented by Artifact G was also frequently found on Ashanti bracelets and necklaces.

Probably Ashanti in origin, Artifact H is believed to be a charm for unity, balance, and harmony.

on the *Whydah* project. Elia and his office of public archaeology had as-
sured the state that there was no cultural material in the Fort Point Channel where the Boston Tea Party took place without going underwater or
doing any kind of remote sensing, all at a cost to the public of almost
$700,000. Until you actually go underwater and get your hands dirty, there
is no way to know what is in the sand. We knew that from our work on
the *Whydah*. As far as I was concerned, the professional archaeologists
should know that as well.

Ultimately, we did not attempt an excavation of the Boston Tea Party
site. The investor who was going to fund the project encountered financial problems, and rather than pursue other financing, I decided to devote
more time to the *Whydah* excavation. Still, the academic archaelogists continued to blackball us at every archaeological or historical conference that
they could. Chris Hamilton, for instance, who had planned to speak at a
conference of the Society for Historical Archaeology, was refused the
opportunity to present his findings about the *Whydah,* because it was a
"for profit" operation. Ken Kinkor was denied the chance to present new
historical findings about pirates for the same reason, as was Martha Ehrich,
Ph.D., an art historian from Southern Illinois University, who studied
more than four hundred pieces of rare Akan gold jewelry that we had
retrieved from the *Whydah*.

Ultimately, these rebuffs from professional archaeological associations became frustrating to the government organizations that regulated us. Some
even wrote letters on our behalf, protesting the decision of these academic
archaeologists not to allow the presentation of our findings about the *Whydah*. One of these letters, the one from MBUAR, said that the refusal to
hear our presentations "wrongly penalizes" a government-supervised project, inhibits the "free flow of information" and fosters an "elitist image" of
archaeology.

The response to this letter came from Dr. Paul Johnston, then the curator of Maritime History at the Peabody Museum in Salem, Massachusetts,
and a longtime critic of the *Whydah* project.

"When work is done for profit it is not in the investors' best interest to
excavate slowly and scientifically," he said.

His cryptic response struck a chord of black humor with all of us on the
Whydah project. We were, after all, spending more than $300,000 a year on
careful archaeology. In fact, had we not been so concerned with good
archaeology and just excavated the site like treasure hunters who didn't care,
the outcome would have been very different.

Despite our best efforts, the mother lode did not materialize. Although

SIDE

SIDE

TOP

LIGHT AND A LITTLE HEAT

Time spent below was endured in dim twilight at best. Coupled with the cold of the ocean, the constant dampness of the leaking hull, and the vile odor of the ship's bilge water, this made the area belowdecks unpleasant.

Still, when the pirates did spend time belowdecks, they used candles for light and even a little heat. This candlestick is in the rare Jacobean style, dating from the 1680s. It is shown here with a portion of the candle-snuffer holder.

we found thousands of coins, we did not find the hundreds of thousands of coins the historical record showed was down there. As we searched, the money bled out of the *Whydah* Partners. In 1987 we spent $1.5 million, with 40 percent of that going to the salvage operation and 20 percent to preservation expenses, including salaries for the sixteen archaeologists and conservators we had employed at the lab in Chatham.

In 1988 we spent an even greater amount of money, and still the search was not yielding the quantity of coins and gold artifacts Bernstein and Betts wanted. Though they intended to keep most of the collection together, they weren't ruling out the option of auctioning some of the coins.

"Why have all seven thousand coins in a museum?" said Bernstein when asked for his plans by a newspaper reporter. "We can auction some, we have the right to do that."

They prepared for this auction by signing an agreement with Sotheby's. The agreement said that the New York auction house would identify, appraise, and market the objects at no cost to us. If there were to be an auction, they would receive a percentage negotiated before the bidding began.

I thought it was fine to have the collection appraised by the venerable auction house. Since the beginning of the project, I had heard a variety of estimates on the *Whydah*'s value, ranging from $200,000 to $400 million. I knew this wide range in value was typical of appraisals of shipwreck artifacts. One collection, from the recently salvaged *deBraak*, was originally estimated to be worth $5 million to $500 million. When appraisers from Christie's auction house finally examined its booty, they established an anemic worth of $289,000.

Although the *deBraak* collection was largely bottles, barrels, and similar artifacts, it was sobering to think that a half-billion-dollar dream could turn into a quarter-million-dollar one at the flick of an appraiser's pen.

As usual, though, no one agreed on much of anything. One coin appraiser called the coins a "collector's dream" and said, "There will be buyers lined up the minute the coins go on the market. It will be a bidding war. The demand is going to be astronomical."

Another said that the bell itself could fetch millions: "Because it is from the only verified pirate ship ever found, it is something every collector wants. I see that bell as being priceless."

Still another said that there was a danger in pricing the artifacts too high: "If artifacts are put on the market at inflated prices, they become almost worthless."

One appraiser said the pieces of eight alone were worth as much as $2,000 apiece, while another said they were worth $500 apiece.

When it was all over, appraisals ranged from under $20 million to over $40 million. One appraiser, accustomed to a different style of business, asked us what we *wanted* the collection to be worth.

Gradually, though, as the project's money continued to drain away with no big find in sight, Bernstein and Betts lost their treasure fever.

I tried to revive their interest by pulling out the historical record that proved from a variety of sources that the *Whydah* was carrying as much as £30,000 when it was taken by fate. I was still convinced that the treasure they wanted was down there. I consulted the search maps, showed them how we had excavated only 15 to 20 percent of the site, and did the math for them.

"We have fifteen thousand coins right now," I said. "If we find an equal amount to what we've found so far after excavating the entire site, we'll have at least one hundred thousand coins."

It was simple extrapolation, perhaps too simple for the occasion. Bernstein and Betts were adding and subtracting the money that still remained in the *Whydah* partnership and were concluding that they should direct the search for treasure in another direction—amusement parks.

Their time spent with Disney executives had sold them on the idea of amusement parks and commercial exhibits as a source of continuous revenue. Disneyland, Knott's Berry Farm, the Smithsonian, and the Metropolitan Museum of Art in New York City were going concerns. Now the Silver Screen partners were considering the prospect of a pirate museum with many of the features of an amusement park.

A museum is what I had wanted all along, but the notion that we would stop digging on the site so all of our remaining resources could be directed toward designing and locating a facility held no appeal for me.

"The mother lode is out there," I insisted. "One more season and we'll find it."

"One more season and we'll be broke," said Bernstein. "This is what you've always wanted anyway. Why complain?"

Chris Hamilton was informed of the plan by Bernstein and Betts and told to prepare a final report declaring that the *Whydah* site had been fully excavated.

I argued that 85 percent of the treasure was still down there, but Bernstein and Betts were determined to close down the site and direct the remaining money to creating plans for a *Whydah* museum.

I realized that my arguments were in vain. I may have been the man who found the *Whydah,* but others controlled her now, and they were taking her destiny in a different direction.

Salvage on the *Whydah* site was stopped. Most of the crew members stayed on with me as employees of Maritime Explorations. We were already working on other projects and tried to take the end of the *Whydah* excavation as gamely as possible. The one exception to the rule was McClung. He let it be known among the crew that he was going to start his own salvage company in Florida and had already mapped out a few wrecks that were "sure things" down in the Bahamas. One by one, he asked crew members if they wanted to join him at his new company, and one by one they refused. Finally he left, with a whimper instead of a bang.

The *Maritime Explorer* was sold to an oil company whose owner was an investor in Maritime Explorations, Inc. He listened to McClung's ideas for a new company and thought he might be interested in excavating some of McClung's ships. The two of them sailed with the *Maritime* down to Florida. Shortly thereafter, the oil company went broke.

I have not seen Rob McClung since.

The search for the rest of the *Whydah* treasure was over.

Or so some people thought.

24

Banned in Boston

An artist's rendering of the *Whydah* Pirate Complex, which would be killed by racial politics.

✳ Ultimately there would be no *Whydah* Pirate Complex established by the *Whydah* Partners. History and politics conspired to stop the proposed $70 million project, first in Boston and then in Tampa, Florida. Less than two years after the announcement that *Whydah* Partners, led by Bernstein and Betts, would build a theme park using state-of-the-art entertainment technologies to tell the pirates' story, the project was dead.

The project started with the best of intentions. Bernstein and Betts met with staffers from lieutenant governor Tom O'Neil's office and explained their goal of building a 170,000-square-foot theme complex that would explore the life and times of Black Sam Bellamy and his crew. The facility would contain a full-scale replica of the *Whydah* and would even feature a holographic image of Bellamy that would materialize before the dazzled guests and tell them what the life of a pirate was like. Among other things, we would exhibit the piles of gold and silver we had brought to the surface, show conservators working meticulously on the concretions, and act out the hangings of the pirates several times per day.

The *Whydah*'s brief history as a slave ship would also be explored, and through it the dark history of slavery itself. There would be exhibits showing the horrors of being captured by slavers in Africa and then the agony of enduring the crossing, or "middle passage," of the Atlantic to Jamaica, where the survivors were sold into a life of bondage.

Bernstein and Betts estimated that the facility would employ three hundred people and host 1.5 million visitors per year. It would be a wonderful, high-tech educational opportunity that would be fun for the entire family. To complete the experience, the facility would have a gift shop and a Black Sam's Tavern.

The pirate complex sounded good to O'Neil, who introduced the developers to Paul Barrett of the Boston Redevelopment Authority (BRA). He liked what he heard and the project moved forward. Different sites were explored, including one at the World Trade Center, another at the site of the Boston Aquarium, which planned to move very soon, and a third at the historic Charlestown Navy Yard.

By December 1991, it was decided by the BRA that the ideal site was the one in Charlestown. Bernstein and Betts took steps to develop five acres there.

Plans were drawn up and a scale model of the museum was constructed. The group that had raised $1 billion to finance seventy-five Disney movies was about to go into the business of building and managing a historical theme park.

The plans hit a rough spot on June 3, 1992, when the *Boston Globe*'s business section ran a long and laudatory piece about Bernstein and Betts and the *Whydah* Pirate Museum. Leisurely reading this piece was Boston's state representative Byron Rushing. Our paths had crossed before when he had expressed anger that we would link the issue of slavery with pirates, whom he regarded as "gangsters."

What shocked him now, though, was the notion that a "theme park" was being centered on a converted slave ship. Later, he summed his feelings up sardonically, when he asked Bernstein and Betts to give him "an example of a theme park based on a concentration camp."

He called the reporter at the *Globe* who had written the story and told him what he thought about the proposed pirate complex. Rushing was a power to be dealt with in the African-American community, and remains so today. Moving from New York in the 1960s to attend Harvard, he ended up organizing rent strikes, voter registration drives, and other events that gave him a reputation as a successful and respected street politician. He ran the Museum of African American History for ten years before running for the State House and winning in 1982.

The public relations people representing *Whydah* Partners had forgotten to bring Rushing into the loop.

I was offended at the way my pirate ship was being represented. The *Globe* had described it as a "pirate motif tourist attraction" and made it look like a theme park that could trivialize both black *and* white history. Some of the early renderings of the exhibits showed slaves being transported from Africa in comfortable little beds that were lined up in rows below the *Whydah*'s decks. The truth was that the slaves were shackled to the deck and forced to live in their own filth for the several months it took to cross the rough ocean.

Given the cruel nature of slavery, a "theme park" motif was not appropriate. I wanted this portion of the exhibit to resemble the Holocaust Museum in Washington, D.C., which has preserved the horror of the holocaust of World War II for all to see. I felt that the facility should maintain its historic and archaeological integrity and not become a Disney-esque display. I think Bernstein and Betts had come to feel the same way and were making moves to reintroduce the hard, cold facts to the exhibit.

I voiced my opinions to the newspapers, saying that the publicists who had provided the newspaper with its information had been mistaken.

"Though it may appear to be a theme park, part of it is unquestionably a museum," I said for print. "What we have here in Provincetown is an excellent example of what it will be. It will be a working museum, where the public can watch scientists working and studying history, sociology, and archaeology."

At that time, Rushing didn't care much about my opinion or that of anyone else associated with the project. Even Roland Betts, who is married to a black woman, taught school in Harlem for seven years, and was a member of the Lawyers Committee on Human Rights, could not convince Rushing of the good intentions of *Whydah* Partners.

"This project is a disaster," Rushing declared. He would not even meet in person with the partners he chastised. When invited to do so, he declined, declaring that he was "not going to be a notch on your gun."

Instead, Rushing made three demands:

- A statement from Silver Screen expressing sensitivity to slavery.
- A forum where the developers could meet with historians knowledgeable about the slave trade.
- Annual archaeological reports from the *Whydah* salvage operation.

Bernstein and Betts were perplexed. They were card-carrying liberals with a long history of support for African-American causes. Plus, in their meetings with Charlestown residents, they had discussed the issue of slavery and promised that it would be handled with sensitivity in the pirate complex. The residents, who were predominately African-American, never voiced concern about slavery; what they were interested in was the three hundred jobs and tourist income the facility would create in their neighborhood. To Bernstein and Betts, this was a purely political issue, and neither could believe politics would prevail.

"I can't believe that this issue might kill our idea," Betts said to me one day before attending one of the frequent meetings they had to attend. "Doesn't anyone think this can be worked out?"

The answer was no. On July 14, 1992, the two developers appeared before the Boston Redevelopment Authority to discuss the content and design of the complex and were met with a barrage of angry questions from board members who were aligned with Rushing. After fifteen minutes during which their sensitivity was heatedly questioned, the investors closed their briefcases and left.

"It wasn't fun anymore," Bernstein told me later. "No matter what we did, things just got worse and worse. After that, it didn't seem worth it anymore."

City government tried hard to woo the *Whydah* project back to Boston. On a return trip, Bernstein and Betts were picked up from the Bostonian Hotel by a limousine and taken to a meeting at which Mayor Flynn's representatives promised to cut through the lengthy approval process that city-aided businesses usually have to undergo. A mock copy of the *Boston Globe* was delivered to their hotel rooms, carrying a story announcing the arrival of the *Whydah* complex. African-Americans who had been so angry at the July meeting now encouraged the puzzled investors to keep the project in Boston for the jobs it would bring to their community.

Despite the apparent change of heart, the developers remained uneasy about Boston's political schizophrenia. Although they preferred Boston for its lifestyle and ambience, Bernstein and Betts now saw Tampa as a mecca for the *Whydah* project. Its year-round good weather and emphasis on tourism would make it ideal. They estimated that twice as many people would go through the museum in Tampa as in Boston.

"If this was a decision about where to live, we'd probably choose Boston," Betts told the press. "If it's where to place a business, Boston wasn't the right place. Boston has a racial history that had been very strained and very tense, and you need government out in front of you, given that. We were a political football."

Unfortunately for Silver Screen Partners, the football game didn't end when they left Boston. Word of their travails in the north reached the black community of Tampa just as the meetings with Tampa port and city officials were getting under way. Tampa officials were offering city land for the privately financed project, as Boston officials had. Although the officials knew what had happened in Boston, they fell into the same racially explosive trap by courting Silver Screen Partners and their Japanese investors with an all-white group of political and business leaders.

The luster left the project almost immediately, as black leaders began organizing against the *Whydah* Pirate Complex. One of those leaders, civil rights activist Warren Dawson, was told of the events in Boston by a law school friend and immediately contacted the office of Byron Rushing. Before long a diverse array of African-American leaders came together. Ironically, the last time they had joined in a common cause had been during the 1991 Super Bowl, when they sought to integrate Ye Mystic Krewe, a private club of white New Orleans businessmen who dress in pirate garb. Now, calling itself the Coalition of African-American Organizations, the group called a press conference in Dawson's office to fight the *Whydah* Pirate Complex.

There, with the undivided attention of the media, they declared that the city of Tampa had "once again" ignored the sensitivities of blacks in pursuit of development dollars.

Dawson declared that Silver Screen Partners had tried to keep African-Americans in Boston from having any say in the zoning process, but Representative Rushing had run them out of town. Now, the New York investors were trying to pull the same trick in Tampa.

Dawson demanded to meet with Bernstein and Betts, who soon found themselves facing the same charges of racism and insensitivity they had faced in Boston. In a meeting of the coalition, the beleaguered partners recounted their personal stories of teaching in Harlem and doing free legal work for minorities. They also told the story of the *Whydah,* from slaver to pirate ship.

Dawson was unimpressed.

"The African-American communities in the Tampa Bay area are not nec-
essarily looking for a standing reminder of the darkest hour of Africans' existence," he told the newspapers. "We're not interested in having a
carnival-like sideshow where people pay fifteen dollars a pop."

A public meeting was organized by the coalition at the St. Paul AME
church, a 122-year-old church with wooden pews and an arching ceiling.
The two developers sat in the front row. They had been told that they would
have a chance to speak, but when the choir stopped singing, they were lam-
basted by angry people who felt disenfranchised by the climate of racial
hatred in Tampa and were more than ready to vent.

The developers agreed to follow strict guidelines to ensure that the story
of slavery would be told with sensitivity and not become a "sideshow attraction." They also agreed to hire an African-American curator and, if need be,
to build a separate wing to house an exhibit on slavery. They would even
pay $25,000 for a study to be done by academicians on how the *Whydah*
Pirate Complex could deal with slavery. Art Jones, pastor of the Bible-Based
Fellowship Church, led a group of slavery scholars to New York to learn
about the history of the *Whydah* and of the archaeological dig I had started
ten years earlier.

Despite all the best efforts of the developers, the *Whydah* Pirate Complex
continued to be assaulted by Tampa's African-American community. At a
public forum, member after member of special-interest groups, including
the coalition, the American Indian Movement, and the National Organization for Women blistered the *Whydah* project, Bernstein and Betts, and city
politicians, who, in their eyes, had created a racially divided city. What they
said at the meeting, as quoted in area newspapers, makes their feelings clear.

"Haven't the wealthy and powerful profited enough from the bestiality
of slavery?" asked Twyla Hoodah, a local radio personality.

"We have already paid for our fare with blood, sweat, and let us not forget, tears," declared Tampa resident Tim Griffin. "Haven't we been raped
enough?"

"It's not about sensitivity to African-Americans," said another resident
Helen Lacount. "It's not about jobs. We shouldn't have to sell our dignity to
provide for our families."

"You don't know us," insisted James Evans, a former football player with
the Tampa Bay Buccaneers. "You live in a world with different values."

And so it went. The process dragged on so long and so venomously that
the Japanese investors pulled out, afraid that they would be painted as racists.

The *Whydah* Pirate Complex, as perceived by Silver Screen Partners, was
dead.

In nearly three years of negotiating with two cities, I was never invited by my partners to speak even once on behalf of the project. Although I had found the ship and was ultimately responsible for bringing up the artifacts that would make any kind of complex possible, Bernstein and Betts chose to act alone in trying to sell it to all the concerns and special interests that make up the fabric of a city. I had been vocal in my belief that we had found only 15 to 20 percent of the artifacts and was quick to express that viewpoint to both of them. Maybe they didn't include me in the process because they thought I would be a loose cannon. Or maybe they decided to handle things the big-city way, with hired consultants who would navigate the dangerous shoals of politics for them, using connections and their knowledge of the process as navigational tools.

I still can't help thinking that I should have been involved, at least to explain the viewpoint of the pirates toward Africans, who sailed as equals with the French, Spanish, English, and members of other nationalities who sailed under Bellamy's black flag.

Out of frustration, I finally wrote an op-ed piece for the *Cape Cod Times* about black men under the black flag. It expressed my feelings about the whole mess from a historic perspective:

During the 18th century the deck of a pirate ship was the only place a black man could be empowered. In fact, thirty percent of all pirates were black. Blacks were elected as officers and captains of pirate crews.

The recent protest over the *Whydah* Museum proposed for Tampa, Fla., has been misguided and grossly inaccurate. The *Whydah,* though built in 1716 as a slave vessel, ironically became a lethal weapon in freeing slaves.

More than 50 of the *Whydah*'s crew of pirates were black, most former slaves, at least 25 of whom had been liberated from a Guinea slaver by the pirates. . . .

The *Whydah* was a free ship, and it is an injustice to the free men who liberated it out of the clutches of the slavers to have their efforts diminished and forever silenced. . . .

History has often been described to the masses by the winners of conflicts and the power elite, to their advantage.

Perhaps never before in this country's history has a time capsule come to us at a more critical moment.

The study of slavery and every aspect of the *Whydah*'s history should be told a million times, again and again, but to deprive the public its right to learn about the past, through exhibits and museums, is the same as burning books.

After Tampa, Bernstein and Betts were taking a pragmatic look at the *Whydah* Joint Venture and could see that it was eating up time they should be spending on their core business of financing films. Silver Screen Partners was devoted to the business of movies, not to the politics of a pirate museum. The more they thought about it, the less it made sense to own a pirate treasure, especially one they couldn't build a theme park around. They decided to sell the *Whydah* treasure.

Bob Lazier and I found out that Bernstein and Betts were planning to advertise the sale of the treasure and the rights to the site. If such a sale took place, there was a good chance that I would never again be able to explore the waters of Cape Cod for more of the *Whydah* treasure. Lazier and I took immediate action. First we contacted Bernstein and Betts and made a preemptive bid. I won't tell what we offered, but I will say that it was less than the $6 million the *Whydah* Joint Venture had already invested in the project and far more than we had.

When the offer was accepted, Lazier gave Bernstein and Betts $50,000 earnest money that he would lose in three months if the rest of the money could not be raised. Our plan was to raise money in $25,000 increments through a limited partnership much like the one we had put together in 1983 with the initial offering. After the three months, however, we had accumulated less than $50,000.

Lazier lost his $50,000, and we started all over again. We contacted Phil Crane, the owner of an aquarium in Scotland, and asked if he was interested in becoming a partner with Lazier and me. I had met Crane while in Edinburgh searching for the royal barge of King Charles I, and we had become fast friends. He jumped at the chance to join us in our new venture. Somehow, Lazier raised his third of the asking price and I sold my only remaining asset, a beautiful house in Orleans that I had managed to hang on to from my days as a developer.

In early 1994, we transferred the money and signed the papers that made us the sole owners of the *Whydah* site and treasure. All three of us were tapped out from the transaction. And Lazier and I were dazed from the roller-coaster ride of the last ten years.

Even so, we happily slapped each other on the back and applauded ourselves for gaining full ownership of the *Whydah* treasure. We both knew the truth, though. The *Whydah* owned us.

25

Bellamy's Shopping List

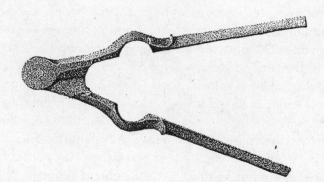

Navigation was less a science than it was an art, and less an art than a matter of more or less educated guesswork. Bellamy was able to chart his location through the use of a number of tools, among them the charting compass, one of which was found on the site.

✳ Ravaging the Caribbean netted Bellamy and crew the booty from fifty-two ships for sure, and possibly more.

He began his campaign of unrestricted warfare on ships of all nations with a bold attack on a French man-of-war off the coast of Puerto Rico. Despite being armed with only eight small cannons, Bellamy and his crew of approximately ninety positioned the *Marianne* off the stern of the cruiser, to avoid a broadside from the forty-gun ship.

For more than an hour, they maneuvered their small ship closer, hoping perhaps to board the heavily armed ship and engage her sailors in hand-to-hand combat.

Perhaps Bellamy got tired of being the underdog, or he could not get close enough to attempt a boarding. Whatever the case, the *Marianne* sailed away after the short standoff, with only one pirate dead and three wounded in the small-arms fire that had been exchanged.

This intrepid face-off against the French established Bellamy as one of the most courageous pirates of the Caribbean. The next months established him as the most successful pirate of this phase of the golden age. He robbed ships in rapid succession until the day he died.

Here is a partial list of the ships he claimed as his prizes:

Unnamed Ship, October 1716: After battling with the French man-of-war, the *Marianne* next appears in the historical record on the north coast of the Dominican Republic, where the pirates captured a prison ship containing several men convicted of smuggling. Among the seven men welcomed into the pirate fraternity were Simon Van Vorst of New York and Thomas Baker, a Dutch tailor.

Besides seven men, the pirates appear to have taken nothing.

The *Bonetta*, November 1716: Between St. Thomas and St. Croix, the *Marianne* and *Postillion* unfurled their black flags "with a death's head and bones across," according to the *Bonetta*'s frightened captain, Abijah Savage, and robbed the ship of her goods.

Savage told his story of being robbed to the British governor of Antigua, who wrote a letter to the king's secretary in England asking for more navy ships to "disperse those vermin if possible."

Bellamy extended his customary offer to the crew and passengers of the *Bonetta* to join his crew of pirates. Passenger John King stepped forward

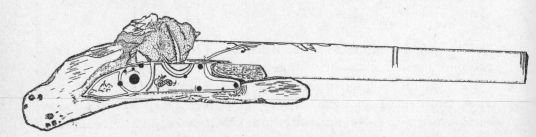

SAWED-OFF FOR SHORT RANGE

Short-barreled muskets, loaded with multiple slugs, were often used at short ranges as primitive, but deadly, shotguns. One very effective load during the eighteenth century was a "buck and ball" combination consisting of a musket ball and three heavy buckshot pellets.

The stock of the weapon depicted here was originally much longer, but was cut down by its owner to make it shorter and easier to handle.

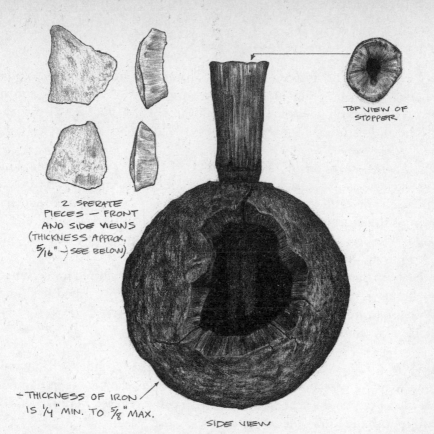

2 SPERATE
PIECES — FRONT
AND SIDE VIEWS
(THICKNESS APPROX.
5/16" — SEE BELOW)

TOP VIEW OF
STOPPER

←THICKNESS OF IRON
IS 1/4" MIN. TO 5/8" MAX.

SIDE VIEW

FROM SHRAPNEL TO STINKPOTS

Most eighteenth-century grenades were hollow cast-iron globes, generally about three inches in diameter, that were packed with gunpowder and ignited by a cloth fuse threaded through a wooden plug. Priming powder, moistened with alcohol, was pressed into the fuse-plug cupule to ensure a clean ignition.

Grenades could be thrown about twenty-five yards with a little practice. They were also sometimes fired from small mortars known as "coehorns." Sixteen grenades have been recovered from the *Whydah* site thus far.

Although they did little damage compared to modern grenades, they were devastating in the right circumstances. In a 1719 fight between a New York privateer and a Spanish privateer, the British crew, which consisted mostly of former pirates, "well accustomed to fighting . . . pelted the Spaniard thick with grenades." The Spanish ship soon blew up, and the remnant of her crew surrendered. Out of a complement of 133, ninety-one had been killed, with twenty-eight more severely wounded.

Not all grenades were of the exploding variety. Two of the *Whydah* grenades are most likely chemical grenades, or "stinkpots." One recorded compound includes pitch, saltpeter, tar, sulphur, coal dust, asafetida, "sagapanum," mercury, "spatula foetida," and ground-up hooves. Such weapons would have been particularly useful in literally "smoking out" defenders holed up belowdecks. The deck planking would simply be pried up and the shells dropped into these ill-ventilated areas, where the concentration of fumes might well reach a potentially lethal level.

and enthusiastically insisted that he be allowed to join. When his mother begged him not to join, he threatened to murder her if she stood in his way. There was no question that the most important thing in this boy's life was becoming a pirate.

The *Pearl* and the *Sultana*, December 1716: After capturing and looting a string of ships, Bellamy and La Buze spotted a pair of ships off the coast of Guadeloupe. After looting the *Pearl* and forcing some of her crewmen to join his band of pirates, which was only done when the specific skills of a sailor were needed, the remaining crewmen from the *Sultana* were put onto the *Pearl* and dismissed.

Bellamy then made the *Sultana* his flagship. He transferred his command to the newly acquired galley and lobbied to have his old friend Paulsgrave Williams made temporary captain of the *Marianne*.

Then he continued to plunder.

The *St. Michael*, December 1716: With luck on his side, Bellamy spotted the *St. Michael* about sixty miles from Saba on the very next day. With the *Sultana* under his feet, he seized the ship and relieved her of a cargo of prime Irish beef and other supplies.

He also forced four of her crewmen to join him, including Thomas Davis, a Welsh carpenter whose skills were needed on his ships. When he cried out that he didn't want to become a pirate, one of Bellamy's men shouted, "Damn him, he was a Presbyterian dog and should fight for King James." When he continued to put up a fuss, Bellamy promised to release him at a later date.

Laying over on the uninhabited island of Blanquilla, off the coast of Venezuela, the combined pirate gang of about 210 men decided to hold new elections to determine the captain and officers of the new vessel. These elections seemed a mere formality. Bellamy was elected captain of the *Sultana* and Williams replaced him as captain of the *Marianne*.

La Buze decided to leave Bellamy and, with the ninety men who had joined him, went to raid shipping off the coast of Curaçao.

Bellamy and Williams sailed for Spanish Town on Virgin Gorda, where Bellamy sold some of his booty to John Hamann, a former pirate who fenced stolen merchandise to the Dutch on St. Thomas.

While Bellamy was working a deal with Hamann, several of the men he had forced to become pirates tried to escape. It is reported that Bellamy threatened to burn the town to the ground if the runaways were not found and returned to his ships. The deserters were promptly returned.

Bellamy and Williams then sailed to St. Croix, where an ambush set for them by the British navy managed to trap five other pirate ships under the command of an Irish renegade named Kennedy.

The British Navy had been called to arms by Governor Walter Hamilton of Antigua, who was stung by Bellamy's visit to his waters. He sent Captain Francis Hume in HMS *Scarborough* to investigate. Hume found Kennedy's fleet at anchor in St. Croix. Despite being outgunned, Hume launched a fast attack; he sank two of the pirate ships and captured two more. One escaped. He was still searching for Bellamy.

Bellamy heard this story from the survivors of the sunken and captured ships. They had hidden on the island until Hume left and were now glad to see Bellamy and two boats full of their own kind.

They joined Bellamy's band of pirates, giving their new captain a reinforcement of well-seasoned hands.

By now, the ships under Bellamy's command were loaded with booty and manpower. He had approximately 180 men of all nationalities under his command and a cargo as varied as the men who had stolen it. By the end of this voyage, each of the men would have an equal share of booty that would make them all rich.

But the voyage was nowhere near its end. The pirates sailed westward, probably along the north shore of Hispaniola, toward the Windward Passage between Cuba and Haiti. They probably stopped briefly at Rio de la Plata, on the coast of what is now the Dominican Republic, before shoving off again to see what they could see in the heavily traveled Windward Passage.

It didn't take them long to find a prize. After a couple of days in the stiff wind, they saw the mother of all prizes, a three-hundred-ton galley, her sails filled with the wind that allowed her to ply her way northward.

"Give chase," was Bellamy's command.

The date was February 1717, and the chase would last three days. The ship they were chasing was the *Whydah*.

BOOK III

※

BACK TO BASICS

26

New Beginning

The Expedition Whydah Sea Lab and Learning Center in Provincetown.

❋ Provincetown is a shock, a relief, an escape, a trap, a new beginning, a rugged end, opportunity, a dead end. In the winter, it is a drinking town with a fishing problem. In the summer, it is a seething, simmering stew of humanity that contains nearly every human ingredient known to man. A walk down Commercial Street in front of the hook-shaped natural bay where our Pilgrim forefathers first landed in the Promised Land provides a vision of colonial American architecture that is populated by rugged Portuguese fishermen, wry New Englanders, transvestites hawking for nightclubs, and gays holding hands.

Orbiting around this scene like spaceships that can't quite punch through the atmosphere are hundreds of tourists, stunned, bewildered, and enlightened by what they see.

This human zoo exists at the topmost geographical part—the very head—of conservative Cape Cod and is the newest part of the Cape, having been created about eleven thousand years ago by an upheaval of inner earth and lashings of sand deposited by the pounding waves of the Atlantic.

The middle of town, the intersection of Commercial and Standish streets, is marked by an enormous anchor netted accidentally in 1963 by Richard Andrews, a fisherman. His boat, the *Cap'n Bill,* sank a few years later with him on board. Some of his bones were brought up in fishing nets and identified by his family doctor by examining X rays of old injuries. The anchor stands out in my mind because his son Michael served as our cook. He used to stand at the rail of the *Vast Explorer* and say nonchalantly, "I wonder if we'll find the rest of Dad today."

South of that anchor, jutting like a tongue into the sea, is MacMillan Pier. In 1995, Bob Lazier and I stood at the end of this pier admiring our new purchase, an eight-thousand-square-foot building that would become the new home of the Expedition Whydah Sea Lab and Learning Center and the first site of a museum dedicated solely to the display of *Whydah* artifacts.

Such a museum had been long in the coming. Until this point, we had been exhibiting *Whydah* artifacts at the Pilgrim and Provincetown Museum Monument in Provincetown.

Although the exhibit was professionally designed, it was not what I had in mind. It barely mentioned how we had found the *Whydah* and said nothing about how this difficult archaeological site had been excavated. There was not a word concerning the history of pirates. The focus of the exhibit was on conservation instead, particularly how the individual artifacts were "deconcreted" with dental tools. The conservators working on the deconcretion in public were not allowed to speak to the people coming through the exhibit.

"That's okay," said Ken Kinkor, only partially joking. "After someone has been working on concretion for three or four hours they are in no condition to talk to anyone, anyway."

Even though the display was not what I had hoped it would be, the staff of the Pilgrim Monument had been very supportive of us. The director, Clive Driver, had gone out on a limb to support the exhibit against the objections of our perennial nemesis, Ricardo Elia at Boston University. When Elia heard the museum was going to exhibit artifacts from the *Whydah,* he wrote a letter expressing his concern about the "ethical ramifications" of our "treasure hunting venture" and made clear his opposition to "the active collaboration of bona fide museums" with the *Whydah* project. Although displaying relics from the only excavated pirate ship in the world might seem worthwhile, Elia insisted a legitimate museum should have nothing to do with us.

"Although ostensibly a conservation exhibit may seem like a worthy exhibit for a museum," he wrote, "the fact that the *Whydah* project is undertaken for commercial reasons means that the conservation of the artifacts is being undertaken with a view to enhancing their market value and ultimate sale. Your museum's involvement in such a project would, in effect, be condoning and granting legitimacy to the mining of archaeological sites for profit."

He went on to ask Driver if the Provincetown Museum really wished to "become a pre-sale showcase for artifacts" that would eventually be sold to private collectors. "Is this the function of a museum?" he wrote pointedly. His suggestion was that we donate the artifacts to the Smithsonian Institution in Washington, D.C., where Paul Johnston, the archaeologist who had been vocal in his belief that the *Whydah* existed only in my mind, was now curator of the maritime collection.

Ken and I found dark humor in Elia's letter, especially the part about profiting from the sale of artifacts. In all the years we had worked the *Whydah* site, we had never sold a single artifact. Now, Ken was living close to the bone, making a meager living and driving a car so junky that no one would steal it if he left the keys in it. I was in a similar financial condition, and woke up many nights wondering how I was going to put my children through school and have enough money to live day-to-day.

All our financial problems could have been solved easily if we were selling artifacts, but the fact was that we could no more sell *Whydah* artifacts than we could body parts. Although the fame of the artifacts had made their value climb, a value that would rise even higher in the future, they were like precious family heirlooms and were no more subject to sale than my grandmother's wedding ring.

We were worried Elia's letter might cause the Pilgrim Monument to withdraw the *Whydah* exhibition. One thing most museum directors don't like to do is rock the boat. One sure way to do that is to buck the academic archaeologists, especially ones like Elia who have made their reputation by noisily criticizing those who disagree with their academic stance. We half-expected Driver to withdraw his support of the *Whydah* exhibition, but he did not do that. Instead, Driver wrote a letter that eloquently presented the other side of the story.

"Objects come to museums in a myriad of ways and often by circuitous routes," he wrote Elia. "Certain it is, however, that the majority of objects now in museums are there only because they were first found, identified, cared for, and preserved by private individuals. Moreover, few if any institutions can match the passion of the private collector, and to overlook the central role of the private individual in the building of museum collections is a grave mistake."

He went on to admonish Elia for arguing that museums are havens from commercialism, declaring that it is a "well-established principle" that museums routinely auction parts of their collection that are "redundant or duplicates."

"I am deeply disturbed by your insistence that none of the artifacts from the *Whydah* be exhibited in a reputable museum," he continued. "The clear consequence of this line of reasoning, it seems to me, would be to leave the principals with little option left except to sell off the material. Contrary to your apparent position, I certainly hope that this does not happen, and that, rather, the professional exhibitions planned for Provincetown . . . are able to generate enough revenue to enable the materials to be permanently housed in a professional museum setting."

With that one letter alone, Driver established himself as our friend and someone who understood the intent of the *Whydah* expedition. The exhibition at the Pilgrim Monument went on, thanks to the backbone exhibited by Clive Driver and his staff.

Now it was time for us to develop our own museum and tell the story as we saw fit. We began to redesign the space we had just purchased. The first thing we did was gut the building, which had been a restaurant, pulling out all the chairs and bar equipment and leaving nothing but a few walls and a gaping space overlooking the channel into the harbor.

With an empty building we set about designing an exhibit with one focus: to tell the story of the *Whydah* as we saw it. First we would recount the legend of Bellamy and my efforts to substantiate it. Then we would hit all of the high points: the recovery and conservation of this historic treasure and what we have learned from it, the history of pirates and piracy, their social structure, and, of course, the democratic precepts they lived under, including the fact that they were free to elect captains.

Then there was the history of the *Whydah* herself before being captured by Bellamy, and her intended purpose as a slaver. With that portion of the exhibit we would show how the ship was designed to hold six hundred captured Africans below her decks, shackled to the floor for weeks at a time on a rolling ship with no sanitation or methods of getting exercise. Artifacts from this sad period in history included shackles that we reproduced from concretion molds, replicas of a branding iron, and a "necklace," a cumbersome device that ringed the neck with iron bars to allow easy handling of

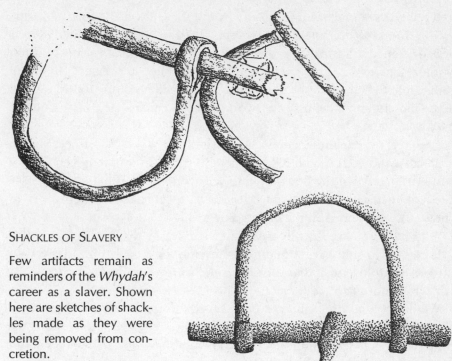

SHACKLES OF SLAVERY

Few artifacts remain as reminders of the *Whydah*'s career as a slaver. Shown here are sketches of shackles made as they were being removed from concretion.

While their small size would suggest that they were handcuffs, these restraints were actually leg irons that shackled together pairs of captives. Many believe that such shackles were not intended to forestall escape so much as they were to prevent captives from throwing themselves overboard. Nonetheless, it is recorded that as many as eighteen African captives at a time chose suicide rather than the horrors that awaited them on the infamous Middle Passage.

unruly slaves. To illustrate the artistic grandeur of these victimized people, we planned to display the golden Akan jewelry we had found, the oldest reliably dated examples of this type of jewelry.

It was our intent to tell this story in such a way that a person in a hurry could get through the museum in fifteen minutes with a whole new understanding of who and what a pirate was.

With our plans in place, we hired a designer and began designing the space and planning the exhibits themselves. Work like this never goes smoothly, and this was no exception. Contractors let us down, egos were bruised, friendships were forged and broken. The stress level steadily increased in direct proportion to the amount of progress that was not being made.

We didn't see much humor in this at the time, just hard work and frustration. In retrospect, some of the events that took place exhibited aspects of dark comedy. For instance, one of the women working for my Scottish partner came to the Cape after a long and draining trip overseas. Instead of going right to bed when she got there, she plunged headlong into the chaos of the museum remodeling. After working for a day or so, she passed out on the floor.

The dockmaster immediately called emergency medical services and an ambulance showed up with red lights flashing. At that moment Ken Kinkor came striding down the dock looking very concerned. When he didn't see me he immediately grabbed one of the EMS technicians and demanded to know if I was the person they had come to help.

"I thought the stress finally gave you a stroke," he declared.

It certainly could have. Building a museum for a collection that was so extensive and diverse and at the same time so close to my heart made this project extraordinarily difficult.

We had originally planned to open on Memorial Day, but by mid-May it was clear we wouldn't make it. The floor was covered with rubble, the contractors were slow, and Ken and I were arguing with the designer about the form and content of the exhibits.

We set our sights on a more reasonable deadline of July 4, Independence Day. As another month passed, work on the museum seemed to slow even more. When the Fourth of July fireworks were shot from their flaming mortars on the finger pier across the wharf from the museum, the light from their blazing spiderwebs showed a museum still closed and under construction.

We pressed on.

Catherine Harker, who had worked as an assistant archaeologist on a traveling exhibit of *Whydah* artifacts that we had mounted in Scotland, arrived just before July 4 and immediately became a construction worker, her wry Scottish humor offsetting the frequent outbursts of tension. She lived in a room above the museum, and every day she would come down early in the morning, beating most of the construction workers to work by a good half hour.

Finally, opening day arrived. The exhibits were on the walls, the floors were clean and clear of construction debris, and the lights were on. Exhausted from our efforts, none of us had any stomach for an official opening ceremony. Instead, on July 24, I simply opened the door and let the public in. The Expedition Whydah Sea Lab and Learning Center was now open for business. The first visitor was a little boy named Sam.

Ken Kinkor and I in front of the museum, where the public and the *Whydah* artifacts come together.

The reaction of the public was a tremendous reward for all of our effort. All summer long people streamed through the museum, in awe of the living history we had compiled. Children touched the cannons and looked at the pictures and maps, while their parents read the exhibit narration and examined the detail on the artifacts. It was virtually impossible for me to walk through the museum without being stopped by visitors who wanted to know more about various aspects of the expedition. It is like that even today, which proves that we have presented history in a way that piques the public's curiosity.

Not being ones to rest on our laurels, Ken and I began planning the Maritime Education and Research Center (MERC), an educational institution that would use the shipwrecks of the Cape as a means of studying underwater archaeology and other aspects of the marine environment. Included would be courses of study in shipwreck salvage and underwater archaeological excavation, with emphasis on laboratory conservation of artifacts, artifact analysis, report writing, and all of the other phases of good undersea exploration. Although MERC's initial focus would be the excavation and history of the *Whydah,* our plan was to move beyond this project to other wrecks on the Cape, and indeed around the world.

MERC would link with a local college so it could share facilities and be used easily by a student population, yet it would be supported by grants, tuition, summer courses, and other museums.

Ken and I worked hard on the concept of MERC. It was an idea that we could not afford to dwell on for very long. We were short-staffed at the museum, so Ken had to spend much of his time manning the cash register and giving tours of the exhibits. I had to attend to business, too. It was time to plan for a whole new season.

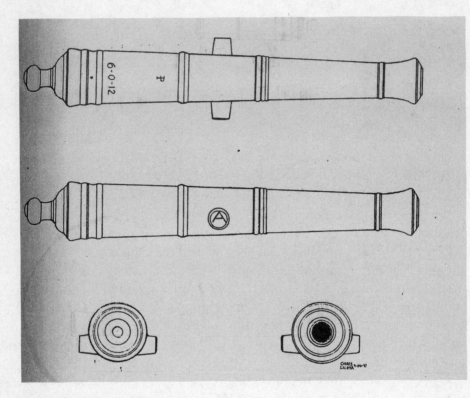

TYPICAL CANNON

Although muzzle-loading cannons were of varying lengths, they were categorized by the weight of the shot they fired. The twenty-seven cannons so far recovered from the wreck include three-, four-, and six-pound guns. The weight of the cannon shown here was marked by the gun founder. The  first number refers to "hundred-weight" (actually 112 pounds), the second refers to "quarters" (units of twenty-five pounds), and the last refers to individual pounds. Thus, when this gun was manufactured, it weighed [112 x 6]+12, or 784 pounds. It probably fired a three-pound shot.

27

A Near-Death Experience

Without fast action, the grounding of the *Vast Explorer* could have been the end of our search for more *Whydah* artifacts.

❋ There was almost no opportunity for a new season, or any future seasons, for that matter. Shortly after we closed the deal for the museum property at MacMillan Pier, a heavy storm tore the *Vast Explorer* from her mooring and cast her on top of the stony breakwater at the mouth of Provincetown Harbor. The high seas would have pulled her toward open water if a sharp rock on the jetty hadn't spiked through the hull, pinning the *Vast* on this rocky crag.

I was attending to some business in Orleans when I received a call from Stretch Grey, who was in Provincetown making sure his lobster boat was secured so it could ride out the storm. I could tell that something dire had happened by the tone in his voice.

"You had better get down to the pier quick," he said. "The *Vast* is stuck on the breakwater and she doesn't look so good."

Fear hit the pit of my stomach. I sped toward Provincetown, hoping the roads were clear of the usual police stakeout that awaits speeders just outside of Truro.

I wove through the narrow streets of Provincetown and gunned my car down the pier toward the site of our museum. A small crowd of spectators were braving the weather to offer commentary on the *Vast,* a boat that, in their view, would clearly be beaten to pieces by the wind and the waves if we didn't get her off soon. I ditched my car and joined them.

"Boats can't survive that," said one of the veteran fishermen, looking solemnly at my high and dry vessel.

"I've seen this happen before," said another fisherman. "Eventually the water starts to slam against it and breaks it to pieces."

"That's a dead boat," said another fisherman. "She's gonna struggle for a while, but she's dead."

The feelings I had at that point are hard to convey. I felt as though a woman I loved had been in a car accident and now the doctors in the emergency room were pronouncing her dead before my very eyes. Only she wasn't dead. The *Vast Explorer* was sitting on the rocks in front of us, but she hadn't been destroyed yet. For sure she is in critical condition, I thought, but she's not dead yet.

I took over.

John Beyer showed up and the two of us took a boat to the breakwater. It was low tide and the *Vast* was completely out of the water, groaning like a person in agony as her joints strained under the burden of her own weight. Boats are meant to be supported by the water, not a pile of sharp rocks. A lesser boat would have come unsprung at the joints in this situation. The *Vast* was made to last under the worst of conditions, which she certainly was in now.

The rock holding her in place had penetrated the hull, leaving a twelve-inch gash that opened into the engine room. Aside from that, there were no holes and no real signs of damage beyond deep gouges in the wooden hull from the scraping of the rocks.

With Beyer, local fisherman Tony Jacket, and Dave Dutra, a veteran fisherman, we began the retrieval of the *Vast.* The Coast Guard arrived with a powerful pump, which I lugged into the engine room of the *Vast* with the help of one of the petty officers. Meanwhile, Dutra and Jacket secured a line from the bow of the *Vast* to his fishing boat, the *Richard & Arnold.* Then we waited for high tide.

As the water rose, the waves came over the breakwater and into the pierced hull. We started the pump and the battle began. As the tide rose the trickle of water coming into the hull grew to a steady torrent that increased with each wave. Only the high-speed pump manned by the coast guardsman held back the sea.

For hours, we were wet and freezing, and frightened that the boat might roll off the breakwater and trap us beneath her. Finally, high tide came and a swell lifted the boat. When he saw the lift, Dutra engaged the powerful engines of his trawler and pulled until the line became taut. With the next swell, the *Vast* rose off the stony breakwater and slid back into the ocean where she was safe.

With the pump operating at full capacity and water pouring into the bilge, we towed the *Vast* to a local boatyard and hauled her out of the water for repairs. Hole aside, the only repair needed was to the shoe, a protective piece of steel laid over the length of the keel, which had been bent by the pressure of the rocks.

The boatyard owner's comment on all this was a testament to the workmanship of Harvey Gammage, the *Vast*'s designer. "Whoever built this boat knew what he was doing," he said. "She can take a beating."

The grounding of the *Vast* was an inspirational incident for me. Losing the *Vast Explorer,* after all, would have been like a farmer losing his tractor and having no machine with which to plow his field. Sometimes I look at her by the dock and think that she shouldn't be there, that those last few hours on the breakwater should have been the end of a great boat. Still, despite the fear that the incident can still generate, it was also a blessing. Had it not happened, I might not be digging on the site today.

Just before the dramatic rescue of the *Vast,* I was spent. Like a tired farmer who is no longer certain he wants to work the earth, I was no longer sure that I wanted to dig on the *Whydah* site. The work was extremely difficult and dangerous and in no way routine. There was no such thing as letting your guard down, even for a moment. Whenever any of us relaxed on the site, something slapped us in the face. A rogue wave would sweep over the gunwales, flattening someone; a piece of equipment would break at a critical time; or we would find we had wasted our time on a particular task, like digging all day to reach what we thought was a chest of gold, only to find it was a modern-day anchor. There was always something to keep us off balance and in harm's way.

Undersea exploration on a shoestring is difficult and often thankless. When you aren't begging for money, you are battling with the archaeology community. In addition to worrying about the next way you will be blindsided by these ivory-tower dwellers, you have to think about the law, safety on the site, where you are going to store the artifacts you bring up, how much diesel fuel you can afford, whether you will be able to pay for your own dinner after paying everyone else. . . . The list is endless, and when you are a one-horse operation with few employees, your head is constantly buzzing with responsibility. I didn't know if I wanted that responsibility anymore.

The final report prepared by archaeologist Christopher Hamilton for the *Whydah* Joint Venture had given me a perfect out, if I was looking for one. The report declared that very little other significant shipwreck material existed in the main body of the site. In essence, it said that we had found everything worthwhile there was to find, and the only thing left on the site was "modern jetsam and expended rockets and bullets from World War II." I knew this wasn't true. I was 95 percent certain that we had brought up only a fraction of the artifacts and treasure, that there was a lot more to be found if we explored other hot spots. But that 5 percent of uncertainty weighed on me. What if there really was nothing else to be found? What if all of the swivel guns and cannons and pieces of eight and God-knows-what-else really had washed away over the years? That doubt, in combination with my case of burnout, made me wonder if I wanted to continue working the *Whydah* site.

Seeing the *Vast* on the breakwater that day was a clarifying moment for me. I felt the sting of lost opportunity. If she sank, I knew that I would never know the full truth about the *Whydah*. On that day, I decided that the dig must go on.

For that to happen, I needed multitalented crew members. One of those, Chris Macort, came to me in a roundabout way. I had put out feelers for an experienced diver when a friend, John Baldwin, told me about a fellow they called "Clifford" who worked at the Ayers Pond Boat Yard in Orleans.

He was called "Clifford" because he knew everything about the *Whydah* project and because he loved to salvage-dive. He was even involved in a number of amateur archaeological projects of his own, including an ongoing dig of his grandmother's backyard that had yielded more than two hundred bottles from the Civil War era and artifacts from the Revolutionary War, including a primitively engraved powder horn.

I hired Chris sight unseen on his birthday, June 12, 1997. I offered him salary and a room at the pier house so he could roll out of bed in the morning and get right to work.

A major problem, of course, was that I had no spare rooms. Catherine Harker, the assistant site archaeologist, was staying in the big room overlooking the channel, and the other rooms were occupied by equipment and a constant stream of staff, investors, and visitors.

With no real room to offer Chris, I decided that his temporary quarters could be the second-floor equipment locker, which was really no more than

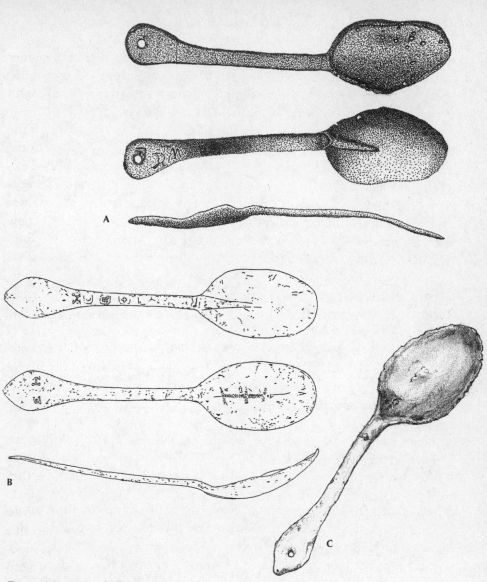

DAVID MERREDITH'S SPOON

Artifact A exhibits features of the "Round End" class of spoon manufactured after 1710 as well as of the "Puritan/Early Round End" made much earlier. On the back of the stem are the crudely etched initials D.M.—possibly those of a crewman named David Merredith. Note the hole bored in the stem, which could be used to hang the spoon.

The presence of an X quality mark on Artifact B means it was probably made in England after 1690. Being etched, the initials E.H. are probably those of the original owner. The unusual cross-hatched design on the inside of the spoon bowl, however, remains a mystery.

The wavy end of Artifact C indicates that it was probably made in England sometime after 1700. It too has a hole bored in its stem from which it could hang.

EXACTLY EQUAL

Pirates were insistent on equality. Even valuable gold jewelry was broken up into tiny fragments so that the pieces could be equally divided by weight.

These troy weights were used to measure small amounts of gold and other material such as medications. The smallest of the nested weights is appoximately 1.944 grams. Known as a drachm, it is one-sixteenth of a troy ounce. A number 4 on the outer cup indicates four troy ounces (twelve troy ounces make one pound).

By British law, all weights had to be marked with a G and a crown design, and were to be tested. In practice, however, they were seldom tested and were frequently off-measure. Foreign weights were also often used. In this instance, the entire set of weights is 9.5 grams less than its marked weight.

The maker's mark appears to be crossed tulips and rosebuds with the faintly impressed initials W.H.

Among the pirates who may have used these scales were Palgrave Williams, a former goldsmith, and Doctor [James?] Ferguson, ship's surgeon.

a large, glorified closet. I was concerned that this windowless and airless space might represent a deal breaker, but when I showed it to Chris he just tossed in his duffel bag and declared it home.

Later I discovered that Chris was no stranger to closet living. In an effort to make it as a rock musician, Chris had rented a closet—literally—in a New York City apartment on Twenty-third Street and Eighth Avenue. There he would retreat after a night of playing and singing in the clubs of the Lower East Side. With a head full of beer and a body coursing with adrenaline, he would set up his manual typewriter and write poetry until dawn. Then, when the secretaries he rented from got up and prepared for their day, he pushed the closet door shut and slept until sundown.

During this closet period, he secretly nurtured his love of diving and collected books on maritime history. He had developed those obsessions while being raised on the Cape and in Palm Beach, where his father, an Episcopal minister, had been sent to tend the flock at the Breakers Church.

Certified to dive at age twelve, Chris spent as much time as he could underwater, collecting objects from sunken ships and tropical fish, which he captured using a tubular syringe dubbed "the slurp gun." He had eight aquarium tanks in his room as a kid. Withdrawn around humans, he treated his fish like his best friends.

Chris hid this love of the sea from all of his friends in the rock and roll scene except Brendan Feeney, with whom he had played music since he was fourteen years old. Songs and music Brendan and Chris had written together were beginning to make a buzz in the record business. A Boston record producer had signed them to a deal, but died unexpectedly of a heart attack before the record could be produced.

The two musicians continued to perform and create. Other record companies were interested, and CNN had plans to follow Brian and Chris with a camera crew, producing a documentary about this coming new act headed for musical stardom. It would be one of those shows, as the producer described it, that would take the viewers from the hardscrabble world of the struggling musician to the glittery world of superstardom.

The problem with all of this was that Chris was no longer interested in the music scene. Somehow, as the music business came into focus for Chris, it became less appealing. As that happened, his love of the sea took center stage.

He began spending more and more time at his family home in Orleans, on the Cape. He would take the bus from New York City a couple of times a month, mystifying his music friends, who were all hard-core denizens of the Lower East Side. They couldn't understand the attraction of the Cape or the lure of the sea.

His secret obsession with the Cape filled his mind. He read about it, dreamed about it, even wrote poems to it. Finally, the Cape won.

"The only place I could really relax was at my grandmother's bay house," said Chris. "One day I just lay down on the grass and relaxed so much I didn't go back."

Now he was living in a closet again, but the world was opening up for him. He was starting over as an undersea explorer.

I put the refurbishing of the *Vast Explorer* in his able hands. This was no easy task. Years of not being used in expeditions had turned her into a sort of floating storage shed, filled with dive equipment, rope, paint guns, and other pieces of flotsam and jetsam from my life in undersea archaeology. The deck and superstructure had been poorly painted and were covered with bird dung from the hundreds of seagulls that had taken liberties with her over the years.

The *Vast,* back in shape after her near-death experience.

Chris spent weeks doing a face-lift on the *Vast,* removing all signs that the birds had been there and then all signs of the last paint job. He sanded the *Vast* and painted her classic white with red-and-black trim. Then he cleared her out and did the same belowdecks.

By the time we were ready to go back on site for the first time in seven years, the *Vast Explorer* looked as good as on the day we had found the *Whydah,* more than ten years earlier.

The 1997 season was a short and unproductive one. It wasn't that my expectations were high; they weren't. For one thing, I was rusty after not having dug on the site for so many years, but other things also conspired to keep this from being a fruitful season.

In some areas where a mag hit told us there was a large piece of metal, several feet of extra sand kept us from digging down to the hit. Even though we blew for long periods of time, we never made it down to the hard cobbled bottom where the artifacts lay. More than once, the weather worked against us, literally blowing us off the site. And, of course, the same dumb luck that helps you find things sometimes keeps you from finding things as well. So it was in 1997.

In the last few weeks of the season, we tallied up the artifacts we had found. It was one of our worst years ever. All told, we found only a few objects. So few were our finds that I was beginning to believe, as Hamilton's final report had stated, that the site had been emptied of artifacts and we had found everything there was to find.

The possibility that the *Whydah* site might be tapped out weighed heavily on my shoulders for the next eight months.

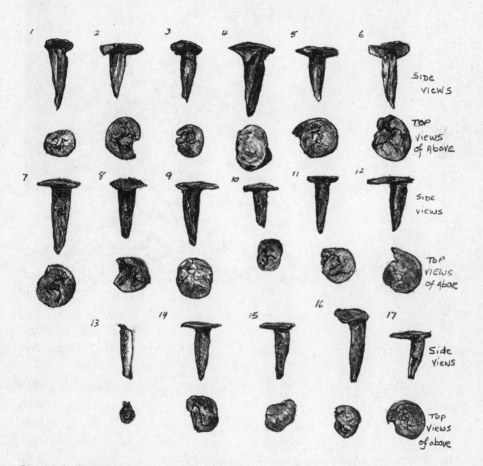

CAPTAIN'S CARPET TACKS

In keeping with a spirit of equality, pirates lived in common. If there wasn't a hammock available for each pirate on board, then everyone slept on the deck. There were no special quarters for anyone except the captain, and his cabin was usually quite spartan. Containing at least a pair of cannons, it was kept ready for action, free from such furniture as tables, chairs, and beds. Instead, it was strewn with rugs and carpets for comfort.

These pewter tacks were used for upholstery and may have fastened fine carpet in place on deck.

28

Jackpot

A pile of artifacts awaits us in a freshly blown pit.

✸ The galley was the favorite ship of pirates. Not only could the galley carry a large amount of cargo, it was lightweight and shallow drafted, which made it easy to operate in shoal water where a pursuing man-of-war would quickly run aground. Plus, its reduced superstructure gave it a low silhouette, making it hard to spot. That was an advantage whether a pirate captain was the pursued or the pursuer. Best of all was the galley's narrow beam, a feature making it the fastest vessel of its size.

At this precise moment in 1717, two galleys were matching speeds, and the *Sultana Galley* was having trouble catching the *Whydah*.

The crew of the *Sultana* had hoped that the captain of the other ship would not notice them on his tail, or would perhaps slow to see if the ship behind him was a vessel he wanted to convoy with. But the *Whydah* heeled over and sailed hard, and Bellamy and his crew had no choice but to sail hard, too. At times they may have reached speeds up to thirteen knots, extraordinarily fast for an eighteenth-century sailing ship.

With Williams behind him in the *Marianne,* Bellamy pursued the rapidly fading ship. At one point, Bellamy's pirates lost sight of the three-masted galley and nearly gave up the chase. Bellamy guessed the course and soon the furled sails were visible again above the horizon. As the day went on Bellamy closed the distance, which makes me think that the *Whydah* had substantially more weight in her holds than the *Sultana,* even though Bellamy's ships were thought to be full of booty and manned by more than 180 men. The next day, the *Sultana* pulled within cannon range of the *Whydah.*

"Load and fire," ordered Bellamy, and his men did just that, firing two cannon rounds across the bow of the *Whydah.*

This was a defining moment in the chase. The *Whydah* had eighteen guns, and with fifty able-bodied seamen, its crew could have put up a savage battle against the attacking pirates. There was a downside to such a fight, and the captain of this three-masted beauty obviously knew what it was. Pirates who took a ship unopposed were generous in their treatment of captives. If shots were fired, then there were no limits to the length pirates would go in order to teach their captives a lesson.

The captain of the *Whydah* knew not to fire a gun in self-defense. Lawrence Prince was no newcomer to the ways of pirates. He had seen many things in his thirty years at sea and no doubt knew that he was defenseless despite his armament. With a heavy heart, he lowered his sails and stood ready to receive the boarding party of pirates.

Prince had been a Royal Navy officer early in his career, then went on to become a trader on the west coast of Africa. For at least thirteen years, he had sailed cargo from London to Africa, where he traded goods to African kings for the slaves they captured. These slaves were generally kidnapped from tribes in the interior of Africa by slave-hunting parties organized by the kings. Captives would then be kept in camps referred to as "slave factories," where they were housed in warehouses known as "barracoons" or in underground dungeons known as "trunks" or "holes." They would be kept in these poorly ventilated facilities, forced to sit or stand in their own excrement until they were purchased by Europeans.

There were many areas of Africa known as slave-trading ports. The *Whydah* was named after one in an area now known as Benin.

Although the name means "Paradise Bird," the location was anything but paradise. The English factory at Whydah was on low marsh ground infested with swarms of mosquitos that transmitted malaria and yellow fever. The only advantage to its location was the industrious nature of the local kings, who would do anything for wealth, including selling captured members of other tribes to slave traders.

A description of one such king is found in *A New Account of Some Parts of Guinea and the Slave-Trade,* a 1734 autobiography of Captain William Snelgrave, a slave trader. At one point Snelgrave was granted an audience with a king, and he provides a rich picture of a potentate at his prime.

> His majesty was in a large court, sitting (contrary to the custom of the country) on a fine gilt chair. There were held over his head, by women, three large umbrellas, to shade him from the sun: And four other women stood behind the chair of state with Fufils on their shoulders. I observed, the women were finely dressed from the middle downward, (the custom of the country being not to cover the body upward, of either sex) moreover they had on their arms many large manelloes, or rings of gold of great value, and round their necks,

SHARP OFFENSE

When preparing to board, the first wave was armed with pistols, swords, axes, and cutlasses. Members of the second wave often carried "boarding pikes," which were eight-foot-long spears with double-edged blades about four inches long. Remnants of at least one such pike have been recovered from the *Whydah* site. Pikemen stood by on deck to either repel enemy boarders or to act as a second wave of boarders themselves. Boarding parties were usually led by the quartermaster or boatswain; it was the captain's duty to remain in overall command.

Boarders typically pelted the decks of a hostile ship with hand grenades before leaping over her side.

Flying through the air together with the grenades were lines attached to heavy grappling irons with sharpened points. Once such a grapnel had anchored itself, pirates could then haul on the lines to draw the two vessels closer together.

Sometimes netting was rigged along the sides of a ship to keep an enemy boarding party from getting aboard. As boarders tried to slash their way through the nets, their opponents jabbed at them with sixteen-foot repellers' pikes. Boarding nets and pikes usually only delayed the inevitable, however, as hand grenades scattered groups of pikemen, and boarding axes swiftly slashed through rope netting.

and in their hair, abundance of their country jewels, which are a sort of beads of diverse colours, brought from a far inland country, where they are dug out of the earth, and held in the same esteem with the negroes, as diamonds amongst the Europeans.

The King had a gown on, flowered with gold, which reached as low as his ankles; an European embroidered hat on his head, with sandals on his feet. We being brought within ten yards of the chair of state, were desired to stand still: the king then ordered the linguist to bid us welcome; on which we paid his Majesty the respect of our hats, bowing our heads at the same time very low, as the interpreter directed us. . . .

Then chairs being brought, we were desired to sit down, and the king drank our healths; and then liquor being brought us by his order, we drank [to] his Majesty.

This particular king paid his soldiers in cowries: twenty shillings' worth of these East Indies shells for the capture of a man and ten shillings' worth for each woman or child. Even though this was considered good pay, it still took several months for these raiding parties to capture potential slaves. A crew of a ship like the *Whydah* had to wait out this period to take on a full cargo of slaves. How long Prince and his crew had to wait on the coast of Africa to fill their holds is not known. My guess is that it took at least two months, since it would usually take that length of time for a captain to select as many prime slaves as Prince would have needed to fill his ship.

Built at or near London two years before its capture by Bellamy, the *Whydah* was a top-of-the-line slave ship, one that held at least six hundred captives in a supine position, shackled together on two levels, in an area approximately thirty by one hundred feet.

Prince purchased several hundred slaves with a cargo of cloth, utensils, liquor, firearms, gunpowder, and the cowrie shells that were used as currency on the African coast. There is no record of how much he paid for so many human lives, but records from the Royal African Company, a large slave-trading concern, show that forty slaves were sold to the company in 1731 for 337 trading guns, forty muskets, and 530 pounds of gunpowder. Once his transaction was complete, Prince sailed across the Atlantic to the West Indies, where he sold his human cargo to plantation owners.

If the weather was good or if the captain felt like it, the captives were brought upon deck for exercise during the lengthy trip to the plantations of the Western Hemisphere. As they danced in place, guards stood watch to prevent a mutiny. The guards were armed with shotguns loaded with lead shot the size of poppy seeds, which stung severely but did not break bones.

WEAPON FOR ALL OCCASIONS

Most muskets were black-powder longarms which fired a
.75-caliber ball weighing about an ounce. They were usually three and a half to four and a half feet long and weighed
eight or nine pounds. Most were flintlock-fired, but a few
long-range matchlock arquebuses were still in use in 1717.

Under ideal conditions flintlocks were reasonably accurate to about eighty yards,
but conditions were seldom ideal on a heaving and pitching ship's deck. Some
pirates were phenomenal marksmen, however, and some reckoned four good mus-
keteers to be worth more than a cannon in a sea fight. Although badly damaged by
the violence of the wreck, the weapon depicted here was a "fusil fin" ("fine musket") of French manufacture.

While the slaves were exercising, some of the crewmen would swab the
holds with water and vinegar as a crude disinfectant, opening the hatches
to air them out as much as possible.

If the weather was not good, or the captain was paranoid about having
so many unshackled captives on the deck of his ship, they remained shackled belowdecks, stewing in their own excrement as the ship pitched and
rolled in those hellish months of crossing the Atlantic known as the Middle Passage. Stench aside, these filthy holds hosted "bugs" from three conti-
nents—North America, Africa, and Europe—and were breeding grounds
for infectious disease. The death rate of slaves carried aboard Royal African
Company ships was about 15 percent between 1700 and 1725. Bad food
and water and seasickness contributed to the high mortality rate of slaves
crossing the ocean, as did depression. Many slaves starved themselves to
death, refusing to eat even if their lips were burned with hot pokers. Dead
slaves were thrown overboard or used as bait to catch sharks, which were
then fed to the slaves.

There are few known eyewitness accounts from any of the victims of the
Middle Passage. An account that comes close was written by a white rebel
convict who had been put on just such a boat for transport to the West
Indies, where he was to serve ten years of servitude. From him we get an
idea of what it felt like to be transported as a slave:

The master of the ship shut ninety nine of us under deck in a very small room where we could not lay ourselves down without lying on one another. The hatchway being guarded with a continual watch with blunderbusses and hangers, we were not suffered to go above deck for air or easement, but a vessel was set in the midst to receive the excrement, by which means the ship was soon infected with grievous and contagious diseases such as smallpox, fever, calenture, and the plague, with frightful blotches. Of each of these diseases several died, for we lost of our company twenty two men . . . in the night fearful cries and groaning of sick and distracted persons . . . added much to our trouble. Some days we had not enough in five men's mess to suffice one man for one meal . . . our water was exceeding corrupt and stinking, and also very scarce to be had.

There were no slaves on board when Bellamy's boarding party set foot on the wooden decks of the *Whydah*. Prince had already sold his cargo somewhere in the Caribbean basin and was now completing the homeward leg of his journey. When Bellamy's men searched belowdecks, they found the compartments stuffed with valuable cargo. Hundreds of elephant tusks were stacked like cordwood. Bags of lapis-blue indigo dye filled other areas of the hold, and slabs of quinine bark for medicine were fastened together like roof tiles. Other spaces were crammed with large sacks of sugar and casks of molasses.

To the displeasure of Captain Prince, Bellamy's men looked further, exclaiming joyfully as they found sacks of precious gold and silver. Veteran pirate Peter Hoof later testified, "The money taken in the Whido, which was reported to amount to 20,000 or 30,000 pounds [sterling] was counted over in the cabin, and put up in bags, fifty pounds [weight] to every man's share, there being 180 men on board." This seems reasonable, since by itself the amount garnered from the sale of six hundred souls into slavery could easily have topped £25,000. Also included were bags of gold dust and magnificient examples of Akan gold jewelry, much of which was eventually hacked apart by the pirates so it could be shared among them.

It isn't difficult to imagine how Bellamy and his crew felt. This was one of the biggest single hauls made in the decade by pirates in the Caribbean. It is even rumored that a small casket of East Indian jewels was aboard, its contents including a ruby the size of a hen's egg.

"Lads, we've gotten enough," Bellamy is said to have declared when he saw the precious cargo. "It's time to go home."

The pirates anchored the *Whydah* off Crooked Island and redistributed the booty. That was when Bellamy broke the bad news to Prince. In addi-

Hoisting one of the *Whydah*'s cannons onto the *Vast*.

tion to taking all of his cargo, Bellamy had also decided to take his ship. The inscription on the ship's bell told Bellamy that the *Whydah* was new, and Prince told him that it had made the triangular voyage only once from Africa to America and back to London. Bellamy knew that she had speed and maneuverability because he had chased her for three days. He could also see that she was heavily armed, with eighteen cannons that fired balls ranging from three to six pounds and a number of swivel cannons that could rake the decks of opposing ships.

The pirates transferred their booty from the *Sultana* to the *Whydah*. They brought over ten cannons they had taken from other ships and mounted them on the deck of the *Whydah*, giving her the firepower of a fifth-rate man-of-war. Into the holds they loaded another dozen cannons, along with a wide variety of booty. They also picked up as many as ten new pirates from Prince's crew, about a half dozen who joined voluntarily and three more who were forced because the pirates needed their special skills. This is where Davis, the forced carpenter from an earlier conquest, took the opportunity to petition Bellamy for release. Bellamy was willing to let the unhappy crew member leave with Prince, but the other pirates rejected the proposal. "No, damn him," one of the pirates shouted. "We would rather shoot him or whip him at the mast" than let him leave. He stayed.

The pirates held another vote to elect officers of their new ship. Bellamy was confirmed as the captain of the *Whydah*, while Williams continued as captain of the *Marianne*. Richard Nolan, veteran of the Hornigold gang, replaced John Fletcher as quartermaster of the Bellamy crew and John Lambert and Jeremiah Burke were elected sailing master and boatswain of the *Whydah*.

Prince and his remaining crew were given the *Sultana* and a small quantity of supplies with which to make it to the next port. As a parting gesture, Bellamy gave the angry slave-ship captain a donation of £20. Loaded to the gunwales with cargo and more than 180 men, Bellamy sailed his new ship southward to continue his plunder of the Caribbean Basin, where he planned to take a few more ships for good measure.

By now, this multinational crew of renegades were calling themselves "Robin Hood's men." And they were conducting themselves accordingly. Off Petit Goave near Haiti, they took the frigate *Tanner,* a Jamaican vessel chartered by French merchants to sail to Rochelle, France, with a cargo of sugar, indigo, and about 5,000 livres in French money. They helped themselves to the silver and pressed on.

The quartermaster counted the booty and found that each pirate had a share that exceeded a lifetime's earnings for an ordinary person of that day. Cape Cod legend has it that Bellamy was now ready to retire in style, returning to the Cape where his lover awaited him. I don't know if this is why the *Whydah*'s crew turned north for the coast of the colonies or if they planned to head for Maine to found a "pirate kingdom" as Captain Charles Johnson (or was it the sometimes inventive Daniel Defoe?) wrote in his nonfiction book on piracy. Whatever their reason, the pirate flotilla made for the Carolinas so it could skirt north along the coast.

Once again, Bellamy had luck on his side. All the British guard ships were out of commission or had not yet taken up station from their winter posts in the Caribbean, meaning that the coast was clear for the Bellamy flotilla. Once Bellamy and his men reached the North American coast, they were free to pillage at will.

The voyage northward from Haiti was uneventful, filled with the routine of sailing a ship and passing free time with games like checkers, backgammon, and a wide variety of card games. Some of the sailors were musicians who played drums or wind instruments like trumpet or flute, or who sang the bluesy songs about love and separation known as "sailor's laments."

Pirates also engaged in amateur theatrics, impromptu plays that portrayed the hypocrisy and corruption of British society. One such play, *The Royal Pirate,* was performed so well by some of the thespians on board that it was mistaken for real life and resulted in a fatality. The play, according to Captain Johnson's book on piracy, featured a mock pirate trial that had one of the actors being sentenced to death for the crime of piracy. Several of the actor's shipmates were sleeping off hangovers and had missed Act I. They emerged from belowdecks just in time to see the ship's company watching a trial that was condemning their friend to death. Not knowing this was a play, they listened in horror as the judge in the play stood over one of their mess mates and declared,

Know'st thou that Death attends thy mighty Crimes,
And thou shall'st hang to Morrow Morn betimes.

Hearing the death sentence, they vowed to save their friend from the gallows.

Slipping belowdecks, they returned with hand grenades and cutlasses. Before they could be subdued, they had killed a member of the audience, had injured the author of the play so severely that he lost his arm, and had broken the leg of their "condemned" friend with the blast of a hand grenade. The show closed after a run of one incomplete performance. The men who had launched the attack were not punished because they had reacted sincerely to help their comrade.

A few days later, 120 miles from South Carolina, the Bellamy flotilla spotted a sloop commanded by Captain Simon Beer. After plundering this man's ship, Bellamy offered to let him leave. Bellamy's crew saw things differently. What if he reports us to the authorities? they asked. The crew voted to sink his boat and keep him prisoner on Williams's boat, the *Marianne*.

Beer was shocked by what he saw, a ship run so democratically that members of her crew could vote to override the wishes of the captain. Courageously, given the position he was in, he prodded Bellamy with a question.

"Have you no control over your men? Or do they they control you?"

The question ignited Bellamy's deepest feelings in a heartfelt speech about who pirates were and what they stood for. Although I have recounted this incident once before in this book, it is worth repeating to help understand who Bellamy was.

Damn my Blood. I am sorry they won't let you have your sloop again, for I scorn to do any one a mischief when it is not for my advantage. Damn the sloop, we must sink her, and she might be of use to you. Though, damn you, you are a sneaking puppy and so are all those who will submit to be governed by laws which rich men have made for their own security, for the cowardly whelps have not the courage otherwise to defend what they get by their knavery, but damn ye altogether. Damn them for a pack of crafty rascals, and you who serve them, for a parcel of hen-hearted numbskulls. They villify us, the scoundrels do, when there is only this difference, they rob the poor under the cover of law, for sooth, and we plunder the rich under the protection of our own courage. Had you not better make one of us, than sneak after the asses of these villians for employment? . . .

I am a free Prince, and I have as much authority to make war on the whole world as he who has a hundred sail of ships at sea, and an army of 100,000 men in the Field, and this my conscience tells me.

But there is no arguing with such sniveling puppies who allow superiors to kick them about deck at pleasure, and pin their faith upon a pimp of a parson, a squab, who neither practices nor believes what he puts upon the chuckel-headed fools he preaches to.

Captain Beer and his crew were then transferred to the *Marianne* and his ship sunk. He was later released unharmed at Block Island when Williams stopped to visit his mother and sisters.

Soon after Beer's capture, ships in the Bellamy flotilla were separated by a storm so powerful that it sprang the *Whydah*'s mainmast and threatened to sink her. Captain Johnson wrote about the full fury of this storm and the damage it did to the *Whydah,* providing a colorful account of Bellamy facing down the elements of nature. Captain Johnson's account also refers to the damage caused by this storm, which may have affected the condition of the ship and been part of the reason she shipwrecked just two weeks later.

The storm encreased towards night, and not only put them all by sail, but obliged the Whidaw to bring her yards aport, and all they could do with tackles to the Goose Neck of the Tiller four Men in the Gun Room, and two at the Wheel, was to keep her Head to the Sea, for had she once broach'd to they must infallibly have founder'd. The Heavens, in the meanwhile were cover'd with Sheets of Lightning, which the Sea by the Agutation of the saline Particles seem'd to imitate; the darkness of the Night was such, as the Scriptures says, as might be felt; the terrible hollow roaring of the Winds, could be only equalled by the repeated, I may say incessant, Claps of Thunder, sufficient to strike a Dread of the supreme Being, who commands the Sea and the Winds, one would imagine, in every Heart, but among these Wretches, the Effect was different, for they endeavoured by their Blasphemies, Oaths, and horrid Imprecations, to drown the Oproar of jarring Elements. Bellamy swore he was sorry he could not run out his Guns to return the Salute, meaning the Thunder, that he fancy'd the Gods had got drunk over their Tipple [liquor], and were gone together by the ears: They continued scudding all that night under their bare Poles, the next Morning the Main-Mast being sprung in the Step they were forced to cut it away, and, at the same time the Mizen came by the Board. These Misfortunes made the Ship ring with Blasphemy, which was encreased, when by trying the Pumps, they found the Ship made a great Deal of Water; tho' by continually plying them, it kept it from gaining upon them: The Sloop as well as the Ship, was left to the Mercy of the Winds, tho' the former, not having a Tant-Mast did not lose it. The Wind shifting round the Compass, made so outrageous and short a Sea, that they had little Hopes of Safety; it broke upon the Poop, drove in the Tafrel, and wash'd the two Men away from the Wheel, who were saved in the Netting. The Wind after four days and three Nights abated of its Fury, and fixed in the North, North East Point, hourly decreasing, and the weather clearing up, so that they spoke to the Sloop, and resolv'd for the Coast of Carolina.

According to legal depositions that were taken later, the pirates had seen the storm coming and made contingency plans on where to meet if separated. After raiding off the capes of Virginia, they planned to cruise for ten days off Delaware Bay and then spend another ten days intercepting vessels leaving from Philadelphia and New York. Ultimately they were going to meet at a place called "Green Island," now known as Richmond Island, off Cape Elizabeth in Maine.

The crew of the *Whydah* continued to plunder.

April 7: The *Whydah* bore down on the merchant ship *Agnes* about fifteen miles off Cape Charles, Virginia, and forced her to surrender her cargo of rum, sugar, molasses, and European goods. Ship and crew were released.

April 7: The *Mary Anne,* a one-hundred-ton galley from Glasgow, Scotland, was taken. Cargo: unknown. Ship was taken as an auxiliary supply vessel and quartermaster Richard Nolan placed in charge.

April 7: The *Endeavor,* a pink out of Brighthelmstone, England, was captured. Cargo: Unknown. Ship and crew were released five days later.

Bellamy's movements for the next two weeks are not recorded. By Captain Johnson's account, the pirate fleet, including the *Marianne,* sailed past New York and Boston to the Machias River in Maine, where the crews built a fortification and careened their vessels to clean the barnacles off their hulls. With the hulls made sleek for added speed, they cruised off the coast of Newfoundland, where a number of unidentified merchant ships were robbed and sunk. Then, exhibiting great courage or madness, the Bellamy flotilla attacked a thirty-six-gun French warship in the mouth of the St. Lawrence River. Johnson writes that Bellamy and his crew suffered heavy casualties in the two-hour battle and barely escaped capture. After rendezvousing with Williams, the pirates then turned southward for Cape Cod, according to Johnson.

I don't think this account is true. Depositions taken from the survivors show the ship met its doom while in the course of its northbound journey from the Caribbean. Even if the pirates had gone to Maine and returned, it would not have been possible to have built fortifications and careened their ships in two weeks. I think it is important to mention Johnson's account of the supposed sojourn in Maine, because he wrote that, during this time, the notion of a pirate kingdom was presented to Bellamy and Williams by the same anonymous crew member who wrote *The Royal Pirate*. According to Johnson, this spunky sailor thought that his two captains should found a kingdom at the mouth of the river that "might subject the World, and extend its conquests beyond those of the Roman Empire."

> Increase your power and propagate the species, by taking into your protection the Indians of these parts, and the discontented and desperate people of the neighbouring English and French Colonies . . . superior force was always acknowledged a just title . . . when you have once declared your selves lawful monarchs, and that you have strength enough to defend your title, all the universities of the world will declare you have a Right Juro Divino; and the kings and princes of the earth will send their ambassadors to court your alliance.

The idea appealed to Bellamy and Williams, on paper at least. They thanked the author for his advice and promised him the job of "prime minister" or "quartermaster ashore" if the kingdom was ever founded. Then they ordered a "bowl of punch" for every man and drank to the notion of a pirate kingdom.

Had they been able to see just a few days into the future, they might have held a premature wake rather than drinking a jolly toast. Most of these pirates were headed toward a kingdom, to be sure, commonly known as "kingdom come."

29

Whydah's *End*

✳ For the last year, Black Sam Bellamy and his crew of pirates had cherry-picked the Caribbean Sea. Now, they continued to prey on ships as they rode the southwestern wind toward Cape Cod.

At nine in the morning on April 26, 1717, a Dublin merchant ship, the *Mary Anne,* came into view between Nantucket and George's Bank. Without hesitation, Bellamy brought his ship alongside and ordered the captain to strike his colors. The captain of the ship, Andrew Crumpstey, immediately did as told. Bellamy then ordered that the sails be "braced abox" to spill the wind from the cloth and stop the ship dead in the water.

When that was done, Bellamy put a rowboat over and sent seven armed pirates to man his new prize. In charge of the boarding party was Thomas Baker, the former tailor from Holland. His second in command was a tough-talking Jamaican named John Brown, who armed himself with pistols and a sword in order to make a strong first impression. Another tough was John Shuan, who went to the prize ship with no weapons whatsoever. Thomas South, a forced man from a ship taken earlier, was a timid member of this boarding party. He made it immediately clear to the captured sailors that he was not a pirate and had no desire to become one.

Captain Crumpstey and five of his seamen were taken at swordpoint to the *Whydah* with the ship's papers, leaving only three of his men on board to stand a futile watch over their cargo, which the boarding party was now in the joyous process of discovering.

The *Mary Anne*'s manifest revealed that she was laden with more than seven thousand gallons of Madeira wine, a revelation that must have inspired shouts of elation when Bellamy read the ship's papers out loud. The last twelve months had been amazingly profitable, with a ship being captured on the average of once every two weeks. And now this: a prize filled with fine wine! Nothing could be better at this point than liquid loot.

THE *MARY ANNE*

Bellamy sent more men to the *Mary Anne* with the goal of retrieving at least two barrels of wine for the thirsty crew of the *Whydah*. Instead, the boarding party returned with several bottles of wine from Captain Crumpstey's own stock. The barrels were blocked in the holds by large coils of the ship's rope, they explained, preventing the removal of the large casks from belowdecks. They would have to do with the bottles they had taken from the captain's cabin and break into the barrels later when they got to safe harbor.

As Crumpstey watched in anger, Bellamy ordered his prize crew on the *Mary Anne* to follow him on a north-by-northwest course toward Cape Cod.

Bellamy's decision to steer directly for the Cape is a mystery that can only be explained by the fact that he was planning to stop at one of the Cape towns, probably Provincetown. There is little question in my mind that Bellamy planned to accomplish two tasks with one stop: picking up Maria Hallett in Eastham and selling smuggled goods at the Great Island Tavern. If Bellamy didn't have such a plan, and he was planning to proceed directly to Maine, the knowledgeable captain would have steered a northern course— perhaps even northeast—until his flotilla was clear of the treacherous waters of the Cape.

But he did not do that, and the ship made the fatal turn for shore.

On this day, the *Whydah* must have been a comical sight, made so by the almost improbable success of the pirates who now sailed her. There were at least 150 men sailing on the *Whydah,* and it is a safe bet that most of them were above deck, since the lower decks were jammed with booty. In a space that was only thirty feet wide and one hundred feet long, the ethnic mix on the sagging deck of the pirate flagship must have resembled a bus stop at the United Nations. Virtually every race in the Western Hemisphere was represented, a true Rainbow Coalition, some of whose members could not understand one another's native tongues.

They all communicated clearly about two things, though: freedom and booty. They must have been a happy crew on this April day, knowing that they were masters of a ship filled with cargo that would make them all rich men. Elephant tusks, sugar, molasses, rum, cloth, quinine bark, indigo, and tons of dry goods could easily be sold in the colonies. Then there was the precious metal, 180 sacks of coin, each sack weighing fifty pounds. It is no wonder that the ship sat low in the water, wallowing under the weight of its own wealth.

LAST PRIZES

Two of the *Whydah*'s consorts on the day of the wreck were the *Mary Anne* and the *Fisher*.

The *Fisher* was a small sloop, with a cargo of deer hides and tobacco, that had been taken by Bellamy that morning. The *Mary Anne* had been captured earlier. She was a galley-built snow of about a hundred tons. A snow was a two-masted square-rigger with a trysail on a pole mounted in a socket just aft of the mainmast.

It wouldn't take much in the way of bad weather to cause trouble for such a heavily laden ship. Right now, the weather was fine. The wind was still coming from the southwest and off the land, carrying with it the smell of spring's earth in bloom. Months at sea had left the crew craving the feel of firmness under their feet. The heavenly smell of the wind that pushed their ship conjured dreams of the bounty that Mother Earth held for them. In a few more hours, they would touch that earth again.

"Fog ahead," came the shout of a lookout.

Ahead, near what is now Chatham, a bank of gray clouds could be seen rolling across the water. This was not a good sign. The fog not only limited visibility, it also indicated that the warm air that had been pushing them had wedged into a bank of cold air, possibly signifying a worsening of the weather.

"Lay to," shouted Bellamy, an order for the seamen to loosen the sails to let the wind out. Without a local pilot to guide the way, it was dangerous to proceed in such a fog. Bellamy decided to stay dead in the water until the weather announced its intentions.

Within half an hour, a small sloop emerged from the fog. As the boat approached, the *Whydah* crew could see that her name was the *Fisher* and that she was slowing down at the sight of the former slave ship.

"Do you know these waters?" shouted Bellamy.

"We do," replied Robert Ingols, who told Bellamy that he was a coastal trader who had plied these waters many times.

"Then we need you," shouted Bellamy, and sent a four-man crew to capture the *Fisher.*

It was Bellamy's plan to use Ingols and his mate as pilots to navigate these treacherous waters. At about 5 P.M., the situation worsened. Quartermaster Nolan, who was now in charge of the *Mary Anne,* came under the stern of the *Whydah* to report that land had been sighted through the growing mist. Bellamy immediately ordered a northerly course to skirt the land rather than a northeastern course to get away from it, another sign that he intended to stop in Provincetown and was underestimating the potential force of what now appeared to be a gathering storm.

Fog increased as evening came, and Bellamy ordered all three ships to hang lanterns from the yardarms to avoid losing each other in the growing darkness. The *Mary Anne* took the lead, followed by the *Whydah* and then the tiny *Fisher.* The *Mary Anne* soon fell out of formation and began to lag behind.

"Make haste," shouted Bellamy to the crew of the *Mary Anne.*

"Aye, Captain," shouted John Brown, a little too enthusiastically. "I will carry the sail until she carries her masts away."

Brown's problem was that he was raving drunk, as were all of the pirates on board the wine ship. They had been liberally sampling the ship's cargo and were threatening the crewmen of the *Mary Anne* as they gulped down the smooth Madeira wine.

At one point, running low on wine, Van Vorst the pirate told one of the crewmen that he would "break his neck" if he could not find more alcohol. The same crewman, Alexander Mackconachy, was then threatened by John Brown, who, according to later legal depositions, growled that "for a small matter he would shoot Mackconachy through the head as soon as he would a dog and that he should never tell his story" to anyone if he was allowed to survive by the pirates.

There was a growing question as to whether any of them would survive. The weather was getting worse and the *Mary Anne* was taking in so much water through its leaky hull that all hands were forced to pump hard. "Damn this vessel. We wish we had never seen her," declared one of the pirates.

It was becoming obvious that this was no ordinary fog. An arctic storm from Canada was driving into the warm air that had swept up the coast from the Caribbean. The last gasp of a frigid New England winter, the cold front was about to combine with the warm front in one of the worst storms ever to hit the Cape. Technically known as an occluded front, the warm and moist tropical air is driven for miles upward where it cools and falls at a very high speed, producing high winds, heavy rain, and severe lightning.

The cyclone that devastated the sailing vessels in the December 1998 Sydney-to-Hobart race is a prime example of what high winds and heavy seas can do to even the most sophisticated of ships.

Despite adequate warning from the Australian weather service that a storm was brewing, 115 boats set out on the 725-mile race through the Bass Strait, a dangerous stretch of water referred to by veteran sailors as "Hell on High Water." This analogy became a reality when the winds climbed to nearly ninety miles per hour and the waves swelled to as high as thirty-five feet.

By the end of the race, more than half of the boats that started were either abandoned or forced to seek shelter. Two of the boats rolled completely over twice, spun by the powerful and relentless wind. Masts were snapped off, sails ripped, and the danger of being blown off the boat so great that one sailor declared afterwards, "If you fall off the boat, you die."

In the end, six did die, including three men whose life raft was shredded by the wind and an Olympic-class sailor who was washed from his boat into the sea.

The sailors in that race were given twenty-four hours' notice by the Bureau of Meteorology that a storm was coming. Despite the warning and the area's reputation for deadly storms, the sailors opted to venture forth anyway.

The shores of the Cape are witness to hundreds of ships wrecked after they chose to chance a storm that became more powerful than expected. Henry David Thoreau wrote that so many vessels wrecked off Barnstable in the early nineteenth century that "the inhabitants hear the crash of vessels going to pieces as they sit round their hearths, and they commonly date from some memorable shipwreck."

Exposure to the dangers of the ocean gives one a different perspective on its beauty. A sailor who views the North Atlantic knows that every gorgeous day is backed up by at least four days in which the water is treacherous and potentially deadly.

"The stranger and the inhabitant view the shore with very different eyes," wrote Thoreau. "The former may have come to see and admire the ocean in a storm; but the later looks on it as the scene where his nearest relatives were wrecked."

Had Bellamy known that a powerful storm was coming, he might have taken the chance and continued his journey. He was anxious to get to his destination. Given that it was later April and past the storm season, Bellamy may have gambled that a storm would not build to such a deadly intensity. After all, the wind was warm and the smell of spring was in the air.

As the wind shifted, the smell of the air changed. The sweet odor of loamy earth was replaced by the fish scent of salt spray. Then came the nerve-wracking swells and the whitecaps, as the North Atlantic surged with the wind.

Many of the old salts on the crew began to sweat, despite the cold. They knew that strong winds from the east were dangerous near the Cape, and that skeletons of ships that had tried to make it and failed lined the shoreline. If the wind had started shifting a few hours earlier they would never have attempted the Cape. Now they were trapped and could only make the best of it.

An added horror was the rising darkness. They were surrounded by the ghostly sounds of the rising wind and a swirling stew of fog and rain that was thickening by the minute and driving them toward that dreaded hook of land.

Following the *Mary Anne* blindly was the *Fisher,* whose crew had also lost sight of the *Whydah.* Although the sailors on each ship did not see the breakers until they were in them, they at least had the presence of mind to drop anchor, which kept them from hitting the shore with hull-crushing force. The first to run aground was the *Mary Anne*. Her drunken and exhausted crew had lost sight of the *Whydah* and drifted toward shore. Thomas Baker, still sober enough to think about survival, grabbed an axe and chopped down the foremast and mizzenmast to keep the ship from tipping over when she hit the shore. Both ships rode out the storm with relatively little damage.

The crew of the *Mary Anne* was so downcast and frightened by the storm that they cowered in the holds throughout the night, forcing crewman Thomas Fitzgerald to read by candlelight from the Church of England's *Book of Common Prayer,* which calls on the reader to repent, "for the Kingdom of heaven is at hand."

Still, the men of the *Mary Anne* survived. In the morning, the pirates drank more wine, ate sweetmeats (sugared fruits) they found in a chest, and told the ship's legitimate crewmen that they were leaving for Rhode Island. Within a few hours, however, they were all captured by the local deputy sheriff at the Eastham Tavern, where they had stopped to have a drink before the long walk to the end of the Cape. They were jailed in Eastham while the sheriff awaited orders from the colonial governor in Boston.

The *Whydah* was not as lucky as its two consorts. Bellamy continued to battle the storm northward, largely because he had no choice. Galleys handle poorly in high winds, and the rising gale coming from the northeast made it virtually impossible for the ship to tack out to sea. His only realistic strategy was to try to head north and hope the storm would diminish in strength.

The strong winds from the sea made a northerly course impossible. With every lunge forward, the *Whydah* would lurch toward the west, pushed by winds that may have exceeded seventy miles per hour. The pirates tried every trick in the sailor's book to make headway, but by eleven-thirty, their doom was sealed.

"Breakers! Breakers!" shouted a lookout at the rail who could hear, but not see, the crashing waves.

In a split second, the deck became an anthill of chaos. The helmsman was joined by another crewman, because to steer in a storm like this would require more strength than one man has. Together, they pulled on the wheel hard and tried to change the ship's direction. Sailors climbed the foremast and struggled to trim the sails while deckhands grabbed loose ropes and secured them to stays, since a rope swinging in a gale is a deadly weapon.

For a few moments, they thought their hard work had turned them out to sea. Then, through the howl of the storm, someone heard the waves slapping on the shoreline and the cry of "Breakers! Breakers!" went up again. Frenzy and fear became the order of the day. With a deep knowledge of the sea and the will to survive, the pirates began to act on their own, as they had in so many other desperate situations, deeply frightened but steadfastly professional.

"Drop the main anchor," shouted Bellamy. The pirates knew that this desperate measure, called "club-hauling," was meant to turn the ship around so she could face the waves and avoid being capsized.

The *Whydah* began a slow turn toward the wind, taking thousands of tons of water over the gunwales as she was swept by forty-foot waves. Many of the 148 men on board must have been swept over the side at this point. The ones who weren't had probably taken refuge in the holds or were clinging desperately to the rigging, where the wind was colder than the forty-degree water.

Still the ship turned. As she did, there must have been hope among those on board that they could face into the storm all night long and somehow survive until morning. Then came the fateful bump that meant the stern had run aground and the ship could turn no more. More water swept the deck, filling the holds and slowly rolling the ship. Within fifteen minutes of striking land, the mainmast was snapped off and floated free. Then, with nothing left to keep her upright, the ship began to roll upside down. Pirates were crushed as cannons and goods stored below came crashing through the decks. Those who could, swam, but in water so cold, there were few who could make it the five hundred feet to shore. The ones who did froze to death trying to climb the steep sand cliffs of Eastham.

In a moment, 144 pirates were dead or missing. Only two from the *Whydah* were thought to have survived that night.

It was here, virtually at Maria Hallett's doorstep, that the *Whydah* crashed that perilous night. What did she see? If she was there, as all the legends say she was, she arose that morning to a scene of incredible carnage. Perhaps she stood on the cliffs and looked down at the dozens of sailors who had been swept ashore and were now floating like rag dolls in the frothy, storm-churned surf. In front of her the *Whydah* would have been upside down, its oak hull protruding from the ocean like a turtle's shell.

Perhaps, not knowing this was Bellamy's ship, she climbed down the sand cliff and stripped clothing and pieces of jewelry from the dead sailors, as so many of the townspeople did.

She probably would not have recognized her dead lover, given the fact that traumatic wounds from the wreck and the hours of being worked over by the ocean's wave action had left the pirates swollen and mutilated.

Later in the day, after the survivors' stories were told, Maria Hallett would have discovered that her lover had died at her doorstep. Perhaps she went down to the beach to search for the body of Bellamy. If she did, she walked for miles, combing through the bodies and rubble that had washed down the shoreline from the wreck site.

Perhaps she found his body and mourned her horrible fate, the loss of a triumphant husband preceded by the death of his infant son. Some say she did and went mad, spending days sewing apple blossoms from the apple tree where she met young Bellamy on a hyacinth-blue dress. According to the legend, she put the dress on, slit her own throat, and jumped off the edge of the sand cliffs. Thankful Knowles, daughter of the man who discovered Maria's dead baby in his barn, was said to have found Maria stiff at the bottom of the cliff, her eyes shining, a gash across her white throat, and a knife stained red in her hand.

Another legend has it that she rescued one of the pirates, an Indian named John Julian—who actually did disappear mysteriously after the wreck—and tried unsuccessfully to nurse him back to health. Out of gratitude, he told her where treasure was buried just before he died. From that day forward, Maria Hallett had money enough for a fine house, servants, and beautiful clothing that was "as lovely and strange in design as the robes of a princess." She never went anywhere, the legend says, except on nightly walks along the cliffs, where she watched and waited for something from the sea.

More sinister legends put her in league with the devil, living in the belly of a "whistling whale" that would capsize whaleboats for recreation, crushing their wooden hulls. In the winter, Maria and the devil would play cards in the belly of the whale, "dicing" for the souls of dead sailors who were sitting nervously in the whale's front parlor awaiting their fate.

Game after game, Maria defeated the devil until he finally choked her to death out of anger. Many years later, say the myth makers, whalers killed a whale that contained a pair of red lacquer shoes in its belly. This, they declared, had been Maria's "whistling whale."

So the legends go.

The fact is that no one really knows what happened to Maria Hallett after the *Whydah* crash. Still, that didn't keep the irrepressible Ken Kinkor from looking for her. The *Whydah* historian spent days searching tombstones, death notices, and other forms of public record for anything that might have indicated the who, what, when, and where of Bellamy's lost girlfriend.

In the public records of Barnstable County, Ken found the last will and testament of a Mary Hallett, prepared on April 19, 1734. He has never been sure whether this will is that of the Maria Hallett of legend, and indeed she would have been only about forty years old at the time of her death if it was her. An item she did *not* leave behind is the reason Ken has given this particular document close scrutiny.

A spinster, Mary Hallett divided half of her estate among two of her siblings and their respective children. To her sister Hope, she left the other half of her estate, two silver spoons, two gold rings, and her "Wearing Appearell." The one item she took with her was a string of precious gold beads, last seen, most likely, worn close to her heart as the casket lid was closed.

There is nothing in her last will and testament that tells where those beads came from.

30

The Ghosts of 1717

On the first day of the new season, Chris Macort, Stretch, and myself all have our ears tuned to an engine malfunction that will send us back to the dock.

❋ Nineteen-ninety-eight would be our first full season in eight years. The ownership problems, coupled with financial and legal hassles, had kept me away from the wreck site for nearly a decade. I hoped this year we would find more of what we were looking for. The season began with the usual mixed messages from Bellamy and the pirates.

In May, I flew over the *Whydah* site in an airplane. I wanted to take some photos so we could see if there was more sand on the site than in months past. The pilot made several expert passes over Marconi Beach so I could get the photos I needed. After about an hour, we turned for the Province-town airport. Since it was a windy day, the pilot took extra care to line up on the runway so we wouldn't be blown off. Maybe it was the wind that broke the pilot's concentration or maybe it was the pirates playing their game, but somehow she forgot to put the landing wheels down. "Oh my

God!" she said as the plane's metal bottom touched the tarmac and began to spray sparks.

As soon as the airplane stopped skidding, the pilot, a veteran of the Marine Corps, got out, lay on the tarmac next to the totaled airplane, and cried.

I realized how lucky I had been despite the wheels-up landing. When I described the accident later to Bob Lazier, an excellent pilot in his own right, he said that a slight tipping of the wings on impact could have caused the airplane to cartwheel. "If that happens, you would have been slammed down on your head," he said. "Someone was definitely on your side."

Maybe, but someone was against me, too.

What would happen next? I wondered.

On June 18, I got my answer. At 5 A.M. we shoved off in the *Vast Explorer* for the first day of the '98 season. Many of the usual crew members were working other jobs, leaving us greatly undermanned. Wes Spiegel, who along with his brother Jeff had dived with us on the *Maritime Explorer,* was working a wreck in Virginia that I and one of the *Whydah* investors had found. He would not be available for the entire season, which was a blow given his tremendous diving talents. Another was in Peru looking for several Spanish ships that had sunk in 125 feet of water. He had hoped to be back in time for the first trip to the site, but was forced to stay longer when they found the ships in very dark and muddy water.

Even Charlie Burnham, the ever-present computer genius who had operated our electronics equipment since the beginning, was on an assignment he couldn't refuse. A company called R.M.S. Titanic, Inc., wanted him to be involved in a project to film the *Titanic* from stem to stern. As the *Whydah*'s '98 season was getting under way, Charlie was making plans to take nine dangerous dives in a French deep-exploration vessel that would give us the only truly complete view of the great luxury liner in her watery grave more than two miles below the ocean.

R.M.S. Titanic, Inc., eventually raised a twenty-ton section of the rusting hull for "Raising the Titanic," aired live on *Dateline NBC*. This program was assembled amid sharp criticism from a number of archaeologists opposed to any kind of excavation for profit. An international group of marine museums even went so far as to take an official stand against the excavation of the *Titanic,* saying they would not allow the display of any artifacts if they were offered a chance to do so. This didn't appear to bother the president of R.M.S. Titanic, Inc., who circumvented museums entirely by renting convention centers in major cities to display his five thousand artifacts.

On one hand, I felt proud at having inspired a whole new generation of explorers. I had given search fever to many people who were now fielding and manning their own expeditions. On the other hand, I didn't like being short on crew on my first day at work.

Still, I was thankful for the fine crew I did have. In addition to Chris and Catherine, Stretch Grey was back aboard as captain, giving the *Vast* an air of calm and good humor. After selling motorcycles in Wellfleet, he was ready for more of the adventurous life. Also joining us were my co-author, Paul Perry, and his fourteen-year-old son, Ben. They helped crew the boat.

Undermanned but ready for the hand we would be dealt by the new season, we took to sea.

From the moment we left Provincetown Harbor, things didn't seem right. One of the diesel engines began to malfunction, nearly forcing us back to shore. Rather than abort the trip, Stretch and I worked on it for a while and got it back into operation.

As we rounded Race Point and headed south toward the wreck site, a thick fog began to settle over the water. "It's that fog machine again," said Stretch, who will jokingly tell newcomers on the boat that foreign operatives run a secret fog-generating machine in Chatham for the purpose of slowing down the fishing fleet.

The fog worsened, and soon became so thick that visibility was reduced to less than a hundred yards. Stretch slowed the boat and we continued to motor toward the site.

Once we arrived, we ran into other problems. Our new Global Positioning Satellite (GPS) equipment was not working properly and we were unable to plot accurately the coordinates for the artifacts on our site map. Without exact positioning information, there would be little reason to put the mailboxes down and blow any holes through the sand. Without those coordinates, trying to find artifacts was like trying to hit the bull's-eye of a dart board while blindfolded.

Disappointed, we ate a quick lunch and decided to return to Provincetown. The fog was extremely thick and the sunlight that did shine through created phantom shapes that for frightening moments looked like boats on a collision course. Adrift in this vapor of uncertainty, we decided to try the GPS again to chart our course home.

Stretch and Catherine were punching in coordinates and taking their bearings from the GPS. The two of them became so engrossed in navigating with the new equipment that they failed to notice that it had told them to steer toward shore.

The first inkling that anything was wrong came from Ben. He was standing on the bow, straining to see through the fog, when he caught a glimpse

Bearing down on the shore, we could hear a child on the beach shout: "Hey, Mommy, look at that big boat!"

of the shoreline dead ahead. For a long moment he couldn't believe his eyes. Then he erupted.

"Stretch! Stretch! Shore's dead ahead!"

Stretch exploded into action. He spun the wheel hard left with one hand while reversing the left engine with the other. The hull hit the bottom hard, and for a sickening moment the boat stopped dead. A wall of green water rose behind her and over the stern, slapping Chris to the deck and washing through the engine room.

I ran to the bow and, with Paul's help, cut a line securing the anchor so we could throw it overboard and kedge off. If we were going to run aground, I wanted an anchor over the side to turn the bow into the waves and keep us from being swamped.

Before we could get the anchor over the side, the *Vast* seemed to rise up and turn. As anxious seconds passed, the *Vast* heaved sideways and headed into deep water. At our closest point to shore, we could see a stunned mother and child watching the *Vast* bear down on them from the breakers. We could even hear the boy shout with innocent enthusiasm, "Hey, Mommy, look at that big boat!"

In a moment it was over. We were back in deep water and cloaked in a fog that made the events of just a few seconds ago seem like a bad dream. There was silence for a few moments and then fear took over as we dissected the events that had led to this near-wreck.

This event served to remind us of the dangers that are ever-present in these waters. A momentary lapse of concentration can sometimes spell disaster. They also gave us a small taste of what that fateful night must have been like for Bellamy and his crew, when they tried desperately to turn the *Whydah* around and head for the safety of deeper water.

When I look back on this event, I am sure it was just a small reminder from the pirates of what their final minutes were like on that night when they heard the breakers that sealed their fate. Without powerful engines, fast reaction time, and a large helping of luck, we would have ended up on the same beach as Bellamy and his crew.

On the way back to port, we were reliving the day's events in the wheelhouse when I noticed an enormous fin dead ahead. "Shark!" I shouted and all of us raced for the bow to see what kind of behemoth was under that fin. Suddenly, like a torpedo, the shark sped for the boat, coming toward us at a fast clip. A few feet from the bow it veered out to sea, never to be seen again.

The shark was enormous and caused a stir among the crew.

"It was a great white!" someone declared.

"Not a chance," said Stretch. "It was a big basking shark."

I never did get a fix on the type of shark it was, but I do think that it was an exclamation point from the pirates, a warning that they would always be with us in one way or another.

I wish I could say that the season shifted into high gear after that, but that was not to be the case. Our second voyage to the site was aborted when the turbocharger on one of our diesel engines blew a bearing and began spewing oil into the bilge. We limped back to port on one engine and maneuvered carefully to our dock site next to the museum. Stretch had telephoned Buddy Johnson from the boat when the engine blew, and he was waiting for us when we tied to the dock. Buddy is a self-taught mechanic who lives on a boat all summer with his wife, Pam. I have never had an engine breakdown that Buddy couldn't fix, and many other people in Provincetown harbor would say the same thing.

In addition to being a mechanical savior, Buddy is a bit of a philosopher. He listened to Stretch angrily recount the straining sound of the engine as it gave out and then broke into a sly grin through the ample beard he was rubbing.

"There must be some real interesting stuff where you are going to dig," he declared. "Because those pirates are making it hard for you to get out to the site."

The scowl on Stretch's face melted. Now an outsider, someone not on the *Whydah* expedition, had broached the possibility of supernatural intervention. Stretch began to relax and accept the possibility that we were being toyed with by the ghosts of 1717. We all did. It became clear that we were on the trail of something big and we would find it eventually, when the pirates thought we had earned it.

Two days later Buddy had the boat repaired, and we were back at sea. This time we made it to the site and anchored up. The big bow anchor held our face to the light southerly wind while the two lighter stern anchors were clipped to their cables so the boat could be maneuvered over the GPS coordinates with the hydraulic winches. Dropping the mailboxes, Chris suited up and dove into the water to insert cotter pins that would keep the digging devices in place and stable. Then Stretch started the engines and with all the power the *Vast* had, we dug the first hole of the season.

It turned out to be the last, for that day at least. Chris went down into the pit and found one small concretion. After looking at the map on Catherine's computer screen, we decided to move the boat several yards to the northwest and dig another pit.

Pulling the handle that would spin the hydraulic winch, Stretch heard a hissing sound and saw hydraulic fluid spraying from a hose in the back of the boat.

"Amazing," he said. "We're out of business again!"

This time no one became upset or depressed about the breakdown. We struggled to unhook from the anchors, a much more difficult task without functioning hydraulic winches, and headed back to port.

Rather than being upset at the day's events, we were oddly elated. It was as though we were being allowed to take one small step at a time, with each step putting us a tiny bit closer to our goal.

As we motored into harbor, we could see Buddy standing on the dock, his hands on his hips and a grin flashing through his beard. After helping us tie up, Buddy jumped on board to measure the hydraulic hose so he could buy a replacement.

"You must be sitting over the rubies," he said before ducking his head into the compartment where the guts of the hydraulic system were housed. "You'll be hitting big stuff next time."

"I'm gonna make sure we do," said Chris, jumping off the boat and heading down the dock toward town. "I think I've figured out what the pirates want."

Chris had had an experience that afternoon he felt had put him in close contact with the spirits of 1717. He told us about it on the way back to port, shortly after it happened.

He had been on the *Crumpstey*, hooking the buoys onto the anchors, when the handheld radio we used to communicate with each other began to crackle. Chris thought we were calling him, so he held it up to his ear to listen. At first he heard the unmistakable sound of props making their *thump-thump-thump* sound underwater. Along with the sound of props he could hear a stream of static that contained a voice. Not quite able to hear, he turned up the volume. Slowly the static disappeared and he could hear clearly the voice, making a demand in a flat and nasal intonation.

"We want your boat . . . We want your boat . . ."

The voice then faded away into the static, followed by the fading away of the prop sound.

The experience left Chris stunned. I chalked it up to newcomer fever. He felt sure the pirates had communicated with him over the radio. He wondered what their message meant. "We want your boat . . . We want your boat . . ."

We had been monitoring the same channel and had heard nothing, which puzzled us even more.

What was going on in Chris's mind I didn't know. As soon as the boat was tied up, he was up the gangplank and headed for town. When I asked him where he was going, he said, "I have to get something," and left it at that. Although I don't ordinarily accept such a cryptic answer from a member of my crew, I decided to let it go at that. As he strode off like a man on a mission, I just figured I would know soon enough what that mission was.

31

First Blood, Again

Chris and I giving something back to the pirates.

✳ A week of storms and wind kept us in port, followed by a two-day window of opportunity that brought us all together on July 7 so we could head back to the site. Shortly after 5 A.M., we backed the *Vast Explorer* away from the dock and headed past Long Point lighthouse before turning east for the North Atlantic.

It was another of those mornings on which the fog was thick and dangerous. I posted two crewmen on the bow to keep a watch for fishing boats and stood in the wheelhouse with Stretch so we could both monitor the radar screen as it scanned the waters around us. Ordinarily, one pair of trained eyes on the radar would be all the guidance we would need. Since the last three times we had been out did not qualify as being ordinary, I decided to take all precautions that I could. No one resisted the extra caution, I might add. We were all wary of the next trick from Bellamy and his crew.

In another part of the wheelhouse, Catherine checked the GPS coordinates on her laptop computer. It was an arduous process, but much easier with the GPS system than it had been in the old days, when we'd needed a survey crew on shore to tell us if we were magging in straight lines. Then, the process had been considerably more hit-and-miss in determining the exact location of the boat over a suspected artifact. Thanks to the Trimble GPS, which relies on government satellites that give exact positions within a few inches, the process of undersea aechaeology is much easier and requires far less manpower. What used to take as many as six people can now be accomplished with one trained person and a sky full of satellites.

Our week in port had resulted in an interesting find on our computerized treasure map. By comparing site maps from past digs, Catherine had discovered that the area we were going to dig in was virgin territory. Over the years we had dug all around it, but had never blown a hole within this area. Our mag readings for this area showed some heavy hits, registering as high as three hundred gammas. A hit that big in a site like this usually meant cannons or something equally large. I tried not to get too excited by this kind of information, but it was difficult. From past experience, I knew it could be something that had nothing at all to do with the *Whydah,* possibly even a Buick, as Stretch suggested. Still, I was elated at the prospect of a spectacular find. That is what being an optimist is all about.

As we rounded Race Point and turned south toward Wellfleet, the fog lifted. The ocean turned lapis blue with the brightening sun, and the dunes on the shoreline went from dull khaki to a honey-mustard yellow.

Ever the tuna fisherman, Stretch scanned the horizon for the telltale signs of his favorite fish. In the distance he could see the water roiling from a group of tuna as they fed anxiously on a school of bluefish. The sight of the game fish was hard for Stretch to resist. A good tuna could sell for as much as $35 per pound and could weigh more than a thousand pounds. It could also put up a delicious fight. A true fisherman, declared Stretch, thought of fishing before he thought of food, sex, or even life itself.

"What the hell are you talking about?" I asked Stretch as he rambled on philosophically.

As the tuna disappeared in the distance, he told me a story that clarified the meaning of fishing to a fisherman. I include it here because it is a metaphor for the way I feel about undersea exploration:

"A charter boat operator named Ralph Gray used to operate out of Provincetown, right down MacMillan Wharf from the pirate museum," began Stretch.

One day, a man from South Carolina chartered the boat to do some tuna fishing. He showed up at the dock smoking a cigarette and looking dangerously overweight, but was filled with enthusiasm at the thought of fighting a game tuna. He had not caught a tuna for several years, he told Ralph, and hoped that this would be his lucky day.

The man waved good-bye to his wife, who said she would be back at 6 P.M. to pick him up.

As Ralph's boat neared Stellwagen Bank, about ten miles out to sea, the man hooked a tuna. It was a big one that Ralph envied. He slowed the boat and then stopped it so the drag would wear out the tuna. Then he watched as the man began the fatal struggle.

It didn't take long for Ralph to become concerned about the fisherman he had on board. The man was red-faced and straining like a plow horse as he pulled and reeled, trying to break the tuna's strength.

"Want me to fight him for a while?" asked the concerned Ralph.

The man just shook his head no, too tired to speak.

Ralph went back to tend to the wheel and never actually saw the man die. When he turned around, the man was crumpled in his chair, held in only by his straps. The straps also held the fishing pole with the tuna still straining on the end.

Ralph slid his hand down the side of the man's neck and could find no pulse. He thought about cutting the fish loose, but only for a moment. The thought of losing such a fine fish *and* a paying customer all in one day was too much to bear. Instead, Ralph unstrapped the man from the chair and laid him respectfully on the deck. Then he sat down in the chair and landed the fish himself.

When he got back to Provincetown, people lined the dock to see the unusual spectacle of a tuna laid out full length in a charter boat next to a customer. Ralph cringed when a fellow charter boat owner asked him if he was going to try and sell both of the "dead animals" in his boat to the fish market.

This had already been a trying day, but Ralph expected the worst of it would be facing the man's wife. In fact, that wasn't the case. When the woman saw what had happened from up on the pier, she ran down the gangplank and pushed through the attendants from emergency medical services. She stood over her husband for a moment and turned her attentions to Ralph.

"It's okay," she said to him, a sympathetic smile curving her lips. "He thought about fishing all of the time. At least he died doing what he liked the most."

Like the driven fishermen in search of game, I am compelled to search for shipwrecks.

We arrived at the site and anchored near one of the GPS coordinates. As Catherine shouted out coordinates, Stretch adjusted the length of the anchor cables with the hydraulic winches and fine-tuned our position. Within thirty minutes of tying up, we were over one of the most promising mag readings, a large hit that had all the earmarks of a cannon.

We dropped the mailboxes with a thunderous splash and Chris dove in to secure them in place with cotter pins and a ratcheting device called a "come-along." Then, with Chris safely out of the water, Stretch put the engines on high throttle and the prop wash was directed straight down to dig a pit in the sandy bottom.

The powerful stream of water causes the yellowish sand to roil to the surface, where the tide carries it away from the boat. A pilot once told me that from the air it looks as though we are plying through very shallow water and kicking up sand the way a car would kick up dust on a dirt road. From the boat, though, the sand that streams out behind us looks like a golden road leading to a treasure.

The sand comes up in a golden pudding until the prop wash finally digs through the sand and makes a pit that hits the bottom. Then there is a change in color from golden to dull red as clay is dislodged from the Ice Age streambeds that formed the Cape. When the surface of the ocean turns slightly red, we call it "first blood." On this, the first digging day of the new season, it took us an hour to see red.

"Look at that color," said Stretch, admiring his handiwork from the stern of the boat. "I've popped Bellamy's heart! All I want, boys, is to find Bellamy's bony hand clutching one of those rubies. Find that, Chris, and you've got the ultimate artifact!"

Chris smiled and nodded. He was dressed in a wet suit and was about to put on his fins when he suddenly remembered something. He ran back into the engine room and came out with a brown paper bag that had taken on the shape of a healthy-sized bottle inside.

"I figured out what that radio message was all about," he said, pulling out a bottle of Captain Morgan rum. "The pirates are going to give us something on this trip, but they want something in return. I am going to give them rum."

We gathered around as Chris twisted the top off and unceremoniously poured the pirates' favorite drink into their watery grave. Leaving a small amount in the bottle, we all joined the pirates in a drink and then got on with the day's work.

Whatever Chris paid for that rum, it was well worth the price. July 7, 1998, was the beginning of one of the best seasons we have ever had. The first hole rendered two pieces of eight and signs of gold dust, which had settled in the cracks and between the rocks that make up the clay subsurface.

Chris reclaimed some of this gold by sucking it up with the turkey baster and squeezing it into a sandwich bag. Then he came up with his pocket-sized finds and we repositioned the boat to dig again. Catherine said that a very large hit had been made about sixty feet to the south by the magnetometer. Following that lead, Stretch let out the stern anchor cables, pulled in the bow cable, and positioned us directly over the GPS coordinates indicated on Catherine's laptop.

The process of blowing a hole started all over again. Stretch put the engines at full speed ahead and the prop wash began to kick up the sand underneath us. First came the golden road of sand that was carried away by the running tide. Then came the faint red of the clay bottom, rising and drifting away with the gold.

"Now we're ripping his heart out," said Stretch, showing his pleasure at the fact that we had reached bottom. "Methinks the treasure lay in the red clay."

With the engines shut off, Chris donned his face mask and fins and went down to examine the spot that had registered so hot with the magnetometer. Attached to us by an air hose and a two-way radio, Chris could give us an eyewitness account of what was happening below the surface.

"I'm at the top of the pit," he said, stopping at the top of the cone-shaped hole that had been dug by the prop wash. He gave his depth, tested his breathing equipment, and then went to the bottom of the pit.

"Unbelievable!" he shouted excitedly. "I have a grinding stone! It is about two and a half feet across and a foot wide. The center hole is cut square and there is a groove around the circumference."

A find like this is made more amazing by the fact that a grinding stone contains no metal and does not register on a magnetometer. It was pure happenstance to find an object like this, and it told me that we were in an area of the site that was so rich with artifacts that we would find many that were unexpected.

Chris continued to search the bottom of the pit and found the source of the mag's hit, a three-and-a-half-foot-long cannon that was covered in concretion. Armament of this size was a swivel cannon, a small antipersonnel weapon, usually mounted on the quarter rail in the aft of the ship. This was a very exciting find. Although we knew from historical research that this ship had swivel cannons, we had never found one until now. If this truly was

THE POPULAR SWIVEL GUN

Swivel guns were small muzzle-loading cannons about three feet long which fired a one- or two-pound roundshot, or, more commonly, the equivalent in musket balls or buckshot. Mounted on pivots along the sides of a ship or in the ship's rigging, they could be aimed in any direction and were very popular with pirates as close-range antipersonnel weapons. Pirate vessels similar to the *Whydah* in size are known to have carried as many as two dozen of these weapons.

Pedreroes were a specialized type of swivel gun fitted with breech chambers that allowed for a higher rate of fire. A concretion recovered during the 1998 field season appears to be very similar to the the overall size and shape of a *pedreroe*.

a swivel cannon, and not an odd piece of iron, we were over the aft portion of the ship, where we had never been before.

"If that's a swivel cannon then it's a whole new world down there," said Stretch, who knew that the aft portion of the ship was likely to house the bulk of the treasure. "Keep looking!" he shouted to Chris over the radio. "The riches with the cannons are buried in the sand!"

Chris continued to find more and more objects. In addition to several coins and an ever-present stream of gold dust, he found a cannonball with coins concreted to it and a curved piece of metal that resembled the flukes of a small anchor.

I put on my dry suit and joined Chris on the bottom. Visibility was limited by a growth of mung weed, an algae that blooms in the waters of Cape Cod in the warmer months of summer. We joked of our dives as being "among the mung," but the effect of this insidious weed was no laughing matter. When it was in full force, as it was today, the mung limited our visibility to just several inches. To see something that registered on our metal detectors, we had to feel around in the cobble or turn upside down and put our faces extremely close to the hot spot. By working that way, we each found several coins and small concretions in that hole and the other holes that we dug that day.

Our plan was to spend the night on the site and work the area again the next day and even the next if possible. After several hours on the water, the wind shifted and the swells started battering us. We considered riding out the turbulence, but the marine weather report said that winds from the southeast would continue and possibly worsen. We had to break anchor and go home.

During the next few days, as we worked on the boat and waited out the weather, members of the *National Geographic* television and magazine staffs began arriving. Explorer's Hall, the *Geographic* museum, was planning an exhibit of artifacts from the *Whydah,* and both the magazine and the television program were taking advantage of this upcoming exhibit to do stories on the expedition. Among the group who came to record the next few days of working on the site were Donovan Webster, a writer who had just finished spending several months in the Sahara Desert, and Brian Skerry, a photographer who had dived a dozen times on the *Andrea Doria,* a cruise ship that sank off Nantucket Island in 1956 after colliding in a fog with a Swedish ship.

Skerry is a quiet, bookish photographer whose intellectual looks give no hint of the adventures that he has seen. In addition to the dangerous dives to the *Andrea Doria,* a deep wreck that claimed three lives the summer he photographed our work on the *Whydah,* Skerry had dived on sunken German U-boats and been face-to-face with great white sharks.

On the day he showed up to begin his assignment, he showed me a jaw-shaped bruise on his tricep that was from being "nipped" by a blue shark off the coast of Rhode Island only two days before. "The bite didn't break the skin because I pushed my arm into the shark's mouth instead of pulling away," declared Skerry. "I think that triggered its gag reflex."

One day we were trading stories on the dock when Skerry told of events on some of the early expeditions to the *Andrea Doria* that left some of the divers wondering about the supernatural nature of shipwrecks. Some of the divers waiting to dive on the *Doria* in the morning heard strange voices through the hull of the boat. The first photographic expedition to dive on the ship reported that the lines they fastened to the ill-fated cruise liner kept coming undone, although they were attached with iron O-rings, not tied by hand.

"No one could ever explain it," said Skerry. "They eventually got all the pictures they needed, but someone made it hard for them."

I knew exactly what he was talking about. I told him about the last few weeks and the strange events that had surrounded this season's excavation.

"I think the pirates want me to be here," I said, confident that I was not insane or irrational for believing that the spirits of dead buccaneers looked over the wreck of their ship. "They have always tweaked me because taking another man's booty isn't supposed to be easy."

There was general agreement that this was true. A sunken ship belongs mostly to the crew that went down with her. You might file a claim and have the permission of every court in the land to have your way with what is on that wreck, but eventually you have to contend with the real owners.

32

Willful, Wicked, Felonious

✳ On October 18, 1717, seven of the nine captured survivors of the *Why-dah* disaster and the crash of the *Mary Anne* stood at the bar of a Boston courtroom, on trial before a judiciary court of the admiralty for the felonious crimes of piracy and robbery. Davis was tried separately and Julian was never tried and was possibly sold into slavery. They had been in jail for nearly seven months now, and were wearing the same clothing they had on when the sea regurgitated them onto the shore. The darkness of the Boston jail combined with a diet of bread and water had left them looking like emaciated moles. Suddenly being thrown into the public limelight had unnerved them so much that they stood fidgeting nervously.

In front of them sat the thirteen men who would decide their fate, a specially appointed commission to "try, hear and adjudge" cases of piracy, robbery, and felony committed on the high seas. They were an illustrious group of high officials that included Samuel Shute, "Captain general, Governor and Commander in Chief of this Province, and Vice Admiral, & President"; William Dummer, lieutenant governor of the province; three members of His Majesty's Council for the province; a judge of the Vice Admiralty; a captain of a man-of-war; and John Jekyll, "Collector of the Plantation Duties."

When it was time for the indictment against the pirates to be read, the sheriff of Suffolk County had the prisoners stand. With rapt attention they listened as Mr. Smith, his majesty's advocate, read the lengthy and flowery indictment. The spelling is as it was in the original document.

Albeit the Crimes of Piracy and Robbery are most Odious and Detestable, being Repugnant to the Laws of Almighty God, Destructive of Government, and Directly Tending to Subvert and Extinguish the Natural and Civil Rights of Mankind, and therefore are strictly Prohibited and Proviced against by divers Express Laws, Statutes and Ordinances of our Sovereign Lord the King, and more particularly by an Act of Parliament, Made in the Eleventh and Twelfth Years of the Reign of King William the Third, Entitled, An Act for the more Effectual Suppression of Piracy; Whereby it is Enacted and Ordained, "That such Persons, as shall be attainted & found Guilty of Piracy, Robbery & Felony committed in, or upon the Sea, or in any Haven, River, Creek or place where the Admiral or Admirals have Power, Authority or Jurisdiction, by their own Confessions, or their Refusing to Plead, or upon the Oath of Witnesses by Process founded on the Authority of His Majesty's Commission or Commissions by the said Act directed and appointed, shall be Executed and put to Death and also to suffer Loss of Lands, Goods and Chattles. . . ."

Nevertheless so it is, that the said Simon Van Vorst, John Brown, Thomas South, Thomas Baker, Hendrick Quintor, Peter Cornelius Hoof and John Shuan, To the high displeasure of Almighty God, in open Violation of the Rights of Nations and Mankind, and in Contempt and Defyance of His Majesty's good and wholesome Laws aforesaid, Wilfully, Wickedly, and Feloniously, all and each of them, being Principal Actors and Contrivers, Associates, Confederates, and Accomplices, Did, Perpetrated and Committed on the high Sea sundry Facts of Piracy and Robbery, Distinctly Specified and Expressed, and Qualified with respect to time and place, and manner, when, and where, and in which the said facts were so done, perpetrated and committed by all and each of them. . . .

One by one, the charges against the seven were read:

1. "On or about the Twentieth & Sixth day of April . . . in Hostile manner with Force & Arms, Piratically & Felonionously, did surprise, Assault, Invade and Enter on the High Sea, between St. Georges Bank and Nantucket Shoalls, a free Trading Vessel or Pink, called the Anne of Dublin . . ."

2. The defendants "having in manner aforesaid, entred the said Vessel or Pink, did at the same time and place, aforesaid, Piratically and Feloniously seize and imprison Andrew Crumpstey Master thereof, and him the said Crumpstey did force & constrain with five of his Crew to leave and abandon the [Mary Anne] and to go on board a Ship named the Whido," which "imployed" the defendants and others "in continued acts of Piracy & Robbery on this, and other Coasts of America."

3. The defendants "Piratically and Feloniously Imbezil, Spoil and Rob the Cargoe . . . consisting chiefly of Wines, and also the Goods & Wearing Apparel of the said Master and his Crew."

4. The defendants "over powered and subdued the said Master and his Crew, and made themselves Masters of the said Vessel . . . then and there Piratically and Feloniously Steer and Direct their Course after the above-named Piratical Ship, the Whido, intending to joyn and accompany the same" with the intent to "oppress the innocent and cover the Sea with Depredations and Robberies."

The king's advocate declared all the defendants "principal Actors and Contrivers" in the crime of piracy, which, if found guilty, should punish them all with "the pain of Death" as an "example and Terror to all others."

The order to stand was given to the prisoners and they were told to plead: guilty or not guilty.

Six of the seven pleaded "not guilty." The seventh, John Shuan, told the court that he was a Frenchman and able to understand very little English. Peter Lucy, a French-speaking merchant, was sworn in and read the indictment to Shuan. The Frenchman then raised his hand at the bar and joined his fellow defendants in a plea of not guilty.

The prisoners were given one day to prepare for their trial and an attorney named in the court record as "Mr. Auchmuty" to help them with their defense.

The spectators in the Boston Courthouse were packed and standing that Tuesday morning, October 22, 1717, as the thirteen special commissioners of the king took their place on the bench before the seven accused felons whose lives they held in their hands.

Court was called into session by the bailiff and the alleged pirates were asked by one of the judges if there was any objection to their trial proceeding immediately. When no objections were offered, the indictment was read again and the accused were asked if they had any objections or additions to the charges against them.

The defense attorney interjected at this point, asking if Thomas Davis, another of the accused pirates who was awaiting indictment in jail, could be allowed to give evidence for the defendants. His request was denied on the grounds that Davis was accused of the same crimes as the defendants and his guilt or innocence had not yet been determined by a court of law.

Bringing in Davis as his key witness apparently represented Auchmuty's only hope in defending at least some of his clients. It was probably his hope that Davis would declare that some of the defendants were forced men, as he was. But with his only legal gambit up in smoke, the defense attorney resigned his legal duties and became a spectator in the trial of his defendants.

The accused pirates were now alone to swim in a sea of deadly legal problems. And it didn't take long for the sharks to circle.

The court record reveals the eloquence with which Mr. Smith, the king's advocate general, slipped the noose around the necks of six of the defendants. Against the skills of this well-trained prosecutor, the pirates stood no chance.

To a hushed courtroom, Smith defined a pirate as "an enemy of mankind," a thief and robber who can "claim the Protection of no Prince, the privilege of no Country, the benefit of no Law; He is denied common humanity, and the very rights of Nature, with whom no Faith, Promise nor Oath is to be observed, nor is he to be otherwise dealt with, than a wild & Savage Beast, which every man may lawfully destroy."

Making points with his analogy to natural law, the prosecutor declared that "all persons by the right they have to preserve Mankind in general may and ought to draw the Sword against Robbers, with who Man can have no Society nor Security. Every one, that findeth me, shall slay me, is the voice of Nature. . . ."

Piracy, declared the prosecutor, is a "complication of Treason, Oppression, Murder, Assassination, Robbery and Theft," all of which are worse when "perpetrated on the High Sea" because they are done in "remote and Solitary Places, where the weak and Defenceless can expect no Assistance or Relief; and where these ravenous Beasts of Prey may ravage undisturb'd, harden'd in the Wickedness with hopes of Impunity, and of being Concealed for ever from the Eyes and Hands of avenging Justice . . . by the law of GOD, Theft in the Field was more grievously Punished, than Theft in a House."

With rapier eloquence, he offered two other reasons why piracy was the ultimate crime.

"Another Aggravation of this Crime is, That the unhappy Persons on whom it is acted, are the most Innocent in themselves, and the most useful and Beneficial to the Publick.

"The third Circumstance, which blackens exceedingly and augments a Pirates Guilt, is the Danger, wherewith every State or Government is threaten'd from the Combinations, Conspiracies and Confederacies of Profligates and Desperate Wretches united by no other tie than a mutual consent to extinguish first Humanity in themselves, and to Prey promiscuously on all others. Hannibal's Victorious Army was never more terrible to Rome, than that of Spartacus, who in three set Battles shook the power of that Mighty Empire, slew their Consuls, and cut down the flower of Italy."

One by one, the witnesses for the king were brought in to court to provide damning evidence against the defendants. All of the witnesses were victims of the defendants, whose criminal pasts must have presented a frightening sight at this point in their losing battle with the state.

Thomas Fitzgerald was first to take the stand. He had been first mate under Captain Andrew Crumpstey on the *Mary Anne* when she was overtaken and captured by the *Whydah*. He testified that all the seven prisoners now at the bar had boarded his ship armed with "musquets, pistols and Cutlasses," except Thomas South and John Shuan. South, he said, declared his intention to escape from the pirate ship as soon as the opportunity presented itself.

Meanwhile, other pirates from the *Whydah* rowed to the *Mary Anne* when they discovered that the smaller ship was carrying wine.

They carried a load of wine back to the *Whydah* and most of the clothing belonging to the *Mary Anne*'s crew.

Next on the stand was James Dunavan, a crewman aboard the *Mary Anne* and brother-in-law to Captain Crumpstey. He testified that the prisoners at the bar "drank plentifully of the wines on Board," but that Thomas South was "civil and peaceable."

He further testified that John Brown threatened to shoot the ship's cook because he failed to steer the correct course. A few drinks later, Brown became even more surly, declaring that he would shoot him like a dog to make sure that he would not live to tell his story.

Alexander Mackconachy, the cook of the *Mary Anne,* testified that all the pirates who boarded his ship were armed except for Thomas South and John Shuan. All of them, said the cook, "made all imaginable speed in order to escape from the hands of Justice" when the ship ran aground.

Despite their desire to get away from the law, Mackconachy did point out that Thomas Baker took the time to cut down the foremast and mizzenmast of the *Mary Anne* to reduce the chances of the ship's capsizing on the shore.

After testimony was taken from the crewmen of the pirates' most recent conquest, victims from other ships taken as prizes by the crew of the *Whydah* were called to the stand.

Thomas Checkley, a seaman aboard the frigate *Tanner,* said that John Shuan willfully joined the pirates when they captured his ship.

"They pretended to be Robin Hood's men," said Checkley, who recalled that Bellamy promised to "take no body against their wills." As a point of fact, there were several men under Bellamy who were forced to serve because they possessed special skills that were needed to keep the *Whydah* in good repair.

Moses Norman took the stand. He claimed to have seen Thomas Baker with "the pirates belonging to Capt. Bellamy" when Norman was held pris-

oner on an island for seventeen days along with the rest of his ship's company in June of 1716.

Finally, John Cole testified that he had seen the accused pirates shortly
after the shipwreck, when they stayed briefly at his house and "look'd very
much dejected and cast down." Although he invited them to stay and refresh
themselves, they refused. Instead, they asked for directions to Rhode Island
and made "great haste" from his house. Later, on April 27, the same men
who now sat before him at the bar were arrested at Eastham Tavern, where
they confessed to the arresting sheriff that they were members of Captain
Sam Bellamy's crew.

Court was adjourned until three in the afternoon to give the accused
pirates time to prepare their defense. I don't know what went on as they
gathered together to consider their fates, but I do know that their options
for alibi were very slim. All of them had been seen in the company of Bellamy's pirates, so they couldn't claim that they weren't there. Their roles in
the taking of the *Mary Anne* were now a matter of record, so they couldn't
claim that they didn't do it. And, for the most part, they all seemed to be
willing participants in the taking of a ship on the high seas.

They must have considered all of these points as they pondered their
defense. By the end of their preparation time, they all agreed to the only
defense that could possibly save their lives: they had been forced to become
pirates.

One by one they took the stand to declare that they were forced men.
Thomas South said that he was taken by Bellamy from a ship out of Bristol, England. When he protested, Bellamy threatened to put him on a desert
island where there was no food or water to support him. Thomas Baker
declared that he and Simon Van Vorst were taken from a captured vessel, and
when they attempted to escape at Spanish Town on the island of Virgin
Gorda, Bellamy told the island's governor that he would "burn & destroy
the Town" if his escaping crew members were not brought to him.

Hendrick Quintor asserted that he was taken by Bellamy, but that Bellamy promised to set him free when they arrived in Caracas, Venezuela.
Quintor was transferred to a French ship that was going to take him to the
South American coast, but the captain died and Bellamy "unavoidably
forced" him to stay with his crew. Peter Cornelius Hoof was taken from a
captured ship, he insisted, and forced to serve Bellamy, who "Swore they
would kill him unless he would joyn with them in their Unlawful Designs."

The story from John Shuan was slightly different. Through his interpreter,
the Frenchman claimed that he was sick when taken aboard the pirate vessel and was advised by the doctor of the *Whydah* to stay until his cure. By

boarding the *Mary Anne,* Shuan hoped that he could make an escape because "he had a better way of getting his living than by Pirating."

The court record shows favoritism to the state. There are few direct quotes attributed to the accused pirates; most of what they say is paraphrased. On the other hand, the prosecutor is quoted directly throughout the court record, perhaps because of his eloquence but most likely because the pirates had no chance to win acquittal. The effort had probably not been made to quote them accurately.

It was clear that the state did not care whether the defendants had been forced to serve as pirates or not. In his closing argument, prosecutor Smith moved for the death penalty with every eloquent word he delivered. It must have been obvious to the defendants that they were headed for the gallows.

"Their pretence of being forced out of the respective Ships and Vessels, they belonged to . . . if it was true, can never excuse their Guilt," insisted Smith. "Since no case of Necessity can justify a direct violation of the Divine and Moral Law, and give one the liberty of Sinning."

Even boarding the *Mary Anne* unarmed, as Shuan and South had done, did not make them less criminal in the eyes of the state, said Smith.

"Suppose one or two Ruffians having no Arms meet a Man in the Highway, and instead of threatnings and force, give him good Words, and at the same time put their hands in his Pockets and rob him of his Money, Are they not to be accounted Robbers because they did not draw a Sword or Pistol? The guilt is incurred by possessing the Innocent Persons mind with such just apprehensions and dread of extream danger, as to determine him to avoid a greater evil by exposing himself to a less one, that is to save his life by delivering up his goods."

South's inoffensive behavior, declared Smith, did not reduce "the pressure of his guilt" in the eyes of the law. "He might not have seemed so active as the rest, yet his presence on board the Pink involved him in the same crime."

Overall, the state didn't buy the notion that the defendants had been forced into service. Although evidence revealed that some of the sailors were forced to serve by Bellamy for their special skills, the state seemed to rely upon testimony from witnesses indicating that Bellamy had stated his opposition to pressing people into service. Although a pirate may repent to "save his soul," that repentance cannot protect him from the punishment due his crime, "It being a Maxim both in Law and Morality, That an involuntary act taking its rise from an act that is voluntary, is likewise accounted voluntary."

In short, the pirates were guilty and should be sentenced to death. "That to shew the least Pity in matters of this kind, where the Proofs are so full

REVEREND COTTON MATHER,
PASTOR OF THE SECOND (NORTH)
CHURCH, BOSTON, 1685–1728

and Pregnant, and not the least presumption in favour of the Prisoners, would be the greatest cruelty."

Six of the seven were found guilty that day and sentenced to death by hanging. Only Thomas South escaped the noose, because the court felt that he had been "taken from on board of a Jamaica Vessel and compelled utterly against his Will to joyn with the Pirates."

When South heard his sentence, he fell to his knees and thanked the court, weeping and promising "amendment of life."

The six found guilty were returned to the Boston jail after hearing their death sentence read aloud. "That you shall go hence to the Place from whence you came, and from thence you shall be carryed to the Place of Execution, and there you and each of you, shall be hanged up by the Neck until you & each of you are Dead; And the Lord have Mercy on your Souls."

Until the last seconds of their lives, the *Whydah* six had a "divinely inspired" companion, Cotton Mather.

Mather was a well-known fire-and-brimstone preacher. The son of Increase Mather, a noted Salem witch-trial judge and respected president of Harvard University, Cotton Mather believed that the world was populated by spirits and devils that were mostly unseen but always present. These spirits constantly fought for the souls of mortals in an unrelenting battle between good and evil. Sometimes the evil spirits won, as in the case of the pirates, but Cotton Mather intended to devote a good portion of his time to rescuing their souls in their final days.

Some who study history have regarded Mather as a televangelist without the television, and there are certainly aspects of his life that make him appear as little more than a spiritual huckster. But to dismiss him this way would oversimplify the man. A graduate of Harvard at the age of sixteen, Mather published nearly five hundred books and pamphlets and was recognized for his scientific writing by the Royal Society when he became its first American member.

Mather worked hard at the job of saving the souls of his flock, of which he now considered the *Whydah* six to be members. For the many months that the pirates awaited execution, Mather could be seen walking piously to the Boston jail, his dark clothing sharply contrasting with the long gray hair he parted in the middle so that it billowed out on either side of his head.

Several times each week he ministered to the condemned, advising them that the only way to be saved would be to die with a clean heart and rely upon God's mercy.

"My friend, this is the very first thing that I am to advise you," he told Baker as the frightened renegade neared his final hours. "There is a pardon to be had! The blessed God has made this gracious proclamation; that His name is, A God Gracious and Merciful, forgiving iniquity, and transgression and sin. He is a GOD ready to pardon. You have not sinned beyond the bounds of a mercy that has no bounds."

The conversations that Mather had with the condemned pirates were dutifully recounted in the dramatic sermons he delivered to his parishioners at the Second Church of Boston, where he shared the pulpit with his father. They were also dutifully recorded in a pamphlet he wrote called *The End of Piracy*, in which he recalled the story of "the Whido" and the "Marvellous Deliverance" of the shipwreck in which "these Monsters" perished. He wrote of the final minutes of the pirates' lives, as they were taken from the miserable confines of the Boston jail on that gray November day in 1718 and rowed to the gallows that had been erected in Charlestown, across the harbor.

"Your determined hour is now arrived," Mather declared to the pirates. "You cry in the destruction which God this afternoon brings upon you. I am come to help you what I can, that your cry may turn to some good account."

Mather was then treated to a torrent of confession as the pirates lingered on the pathway to their death. They in turn received an outpouring of advice on redemption and repentance. One such example of the many exchanges recorded in this pamphlet is this between Mather and Baker.:

MATHER: I'll mention to you a sweet word of your Great Saviour; a word worth a thousand worlds! Have you not a mighty load lying on you?

BAKER: Oh! A load, a load, that is too heavy for me.

MATHER: Now hear the word of your Saviour: Come to me, all ye that labour, and are heavy laden and I will give you rest. Answer to it; but first look to him for help to find the answer; Our Saviour, I come unto thee.

BAKER: O Almighty God, look upon me.

MATHER: I perceive you are in a very great agony. But, the Strait Gate must be entered with such an agony.

Mather exchanged redemption for repentance, moving solemnly from one pirate to the next as they took the last walk together. At the foot of the gallows, Mather was stopped as guards took the *Whydah* six up the steps and looped a noose around each of their necks. He described the scene before him:

On the scaffold, as the last minute came on, several of the malefactors discovered a great consternation.

Baker and Hoof appeared very distinguishily penitent.

But Brown, behaved himself at such a rate, as one would hardly imagine that any compos mentis, could have done so. He broke out into furious expression, which had in them too much of the language he had been used unto. Then he fell to reading of prayers, not very pertinently chosen. At length he made a short speech, which every body trembled at; advising sailors to beware of all wicked living, such as his own had been; especially to beware of falling into the hands of the pirates: But if they did and were forced to join with them, then to have a care whom they kept and whom they let go and what countries they came into.

In such amazing terms did he make his exit! With such madness, to go to the dead!

The rest said little, only Van Voorst, having (with Baker) sang a Dutch Psalm, exhorted young persons to lead a life of religion, and keep the sabbath, and carry it well to their parents.

Behold, reader, the end of Piracy!

33

Aesop's Tables

A night at Aesop's Tables, where the ghost incident took place.

✻ I have learned to expect the unexpected, but I still find it hard to deal with the unexplained. Things that go bump in the night are bothersome to me, not because they are frightening, but because I don't know how they happen or why.

As you know by now, strange things happened on the *Whydah* expedition. And they continue to happen. They were as much a part of the experience as the pieces of eight, the waves that cover them, and the wind that whips the water into a frenzy.

One of them occurred on the night before we went to the wreck site with the *National Geographic* magazine and video crew. We had dinner at Aesop's Tables, a colonial-era building on Main Street in Wellfleet that had been converted into a restaurant. Built in the eighteenth century from ship's timbers, the restaurant is a sprawling, sagging structure with a sloping front yard, a candlelit dining room, and a steep, narrow staircase leading to a bar in the attic with exposed rough-cut beams and overstuffed couches and chairs that engulf you with comfort.

Bellamy certainly passed this place a number of times as he scouted Wellfleet when first arriving at the Cape. Maria Hallett probably visited whoever lived here in those days, given that Wellfleet was a small, tight-knit community.

It was here at Aesop's Tables, after we left the restaurant, that another in a string of unexplained events took place. The manager of the restaurant told us this story and showed us the credit card receipt as proof. Here is what happened:

Shortly after we left, a man who was eating dinner alone at the far end of the bar went into the rest room. In a moment he came out white and shaking, "wearing the pallor of death," as an Irish relative used to say.

"I need to get out of here right away," he said, handing his credit card to the waitress with trembling hands.

"What's wrong?" asked the waitress.

"You might think I'm going crazy here, but I just saw a ghost in your bathroom."

The apparition he described was a lovely young woman with flaxen hair and an ability to make the room exceedingly cold in July.

The man signed his credit card slip and made a hasty retreat from the restaurant. After he left, the waitress told the manager what he had said and the manager immediately went into the bathroom to see what he could see. He saw nothing. When he came out, he asked what the man's name was. The waitress thumbed through the receipts.

"Here it is," she said. "His name is Bellamy."

I have no idea why this happened or what it means, if anything. I just know that it took place and needs to be reported here, because it seemed to be beyond coincidence.

34

"We've Got Wood!"

The sighting of the hull was accompanied by a flurry of activity as we suited up to dive. From left: Paul Perry, Bob Cembrola, Dave Labrecque kneeling, Stretch, Chris Macort, Ben Perry, and me.

✻ On July 19, 1998, we discovered the hull of the *Whydah*. In all the years I had been digging on this site, discovering the actual vessel that held Bellamy and his crew ranks as the most exciting of all finds, even more so than the discovery of the ship's bell or the finding of the first bar of gold. This was, after all, the ship itself, a significant piece of the vessel that allowed the world of Bellamy and his pirates to exist.

That we found such a perishable artifact at all shows that destiny, and perhaps even the pirates, were on our side. Not to mention, of course, hard work and a tremendous amount of luck.

The story of finding the hull began on July 17. We were searching for the type of metal artifacts, including cannons and rigging, that we had been finding all summer.

Since the season began, we had been working an artifact field that was rich in metallic hits, the kind that register solidly on the magnetometer. It was an area we had considered excavating several years earlier, but at the last minute we had decided to move the boat closer to shore.

Now, probably nine years later, we decided to take another look. With us were photographers and a writer from *National Geographic,* who had shown up a few days earlier and were ready for action after waiting a couple of days in Provincetown for good weather.

We reached the site and anchored over some of the more prominent hits. We blew holes to see what kind of artifacts were in them. With the first hole, we found concreted artifacts. It seemed as though we couldn't miss, moving from coordinate to coordinate on the laptop treasure map as we found objects ranging from swivel guns to coins and spoons. Before long, the deck was filled with artifacts that hadn't been touched since that horrible night 281 years before.

The crew was ecstatic. We had closed the site nine years earlier because our partners declared that there were no more artifacts to be found. Now, despite a "final report" that declared the wreck site barren, we were finding a rich stream of artifacts, and interesting ones at that. One object, for example, looked like a heavily concreted crown, the kind that a king might wear. We still have no idea what this odd object is because it may take several years for it to deconcrete. In the weeks to come, we would find hun-

Next to the hull I found a spoon from the *Whydah*'s mess.

dreds of coins in this area. At one point, I was picking coins from the sand like seashells with the help of a metal detector with a probe end. Another find was a brass wax seal with the bust of what was probably Alexander the Great, most likely used as a mark on documents by a pirate who could not sign his name. Another unique find was brass hypodermic syringes, primitive instruments probably used to treat gonorrhea and syphilis.

Despite the incredible luck we were having and would have in the weeks to come, the *National Geographic* photographers were having some of the worst conditions possible. Not only was the water cloudy from the sand being churned up by wave action, but an unusually high influx of mung weed had reduced visibility to less than two feet. Even when the tide current was running, the mung settled into the holes we had dug like confetti in a ticker tape parade.

ROYAL SEAL

Recovered in 1998, this brass object is still undergoing study. Although its post is of unusual design, it is most likely a wax seal. The bust is Greco-Roman in style and appears to represent a hero of that age such as Alexander the Great or Julius Caesar of Rome.

SAFE SEX!

One of the occupational hazards for sailors of this period was venereal disease. Various mercury salts would provide a clear passage for the elimination of the contagious factor element responsible for the malady. Some mercurial

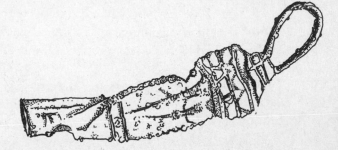

compounds, such as calomel, were taken orally over prolonged periods. Others, such mercuric chloride (aka "corrosive sublimate"), were made into unguents which would be applied directly to the afflicted body part by injection.

This may have been one of the functions of the badly battered brass syringe recovered during the 1998 season.

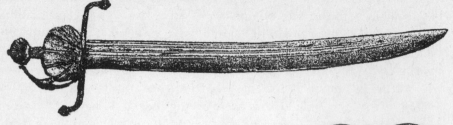

SAVAGE SWORDS

Several types of blades were used in hand-to-hand combat. Rapiers and "small swords" had long thin blades designed to slide between an opponent's ribs to puncture the lungs or heart. They were lightweight weapons that demanded a great deal of skill and agility. A cutlass, on the other hand, was shorter, thicker, and wider. Similar to a machete, it was well suited for lopping off assorted portions of an opponent's anatomy. Cutlasses required far more strength than rapiers, but far less expertise. Rapiers were therefore considered "upper-class" weapons, and were much more finely made than cutlasses.

This silver, clamshell design knuckle guard is from just such a rapier. Its loops would come in quite handy in extracting the blade from the chest of an opponent.

Being relatively thin, the blades of all edged weapons from the *Whydah* site have eroded away during their time underwater.

Repeatedly during the first two days, the photographers came to the surface frustrated by the acute lack of visibility. Especially frustrating was the effort required just to get into the water. Not only did they have to suit up like the rest of us, they also had to contend with awkward and heavy collections of camera equipment that dangled with so many arms and lights that they looked like tiny sea monsters. Despite all of their effort, they were getting nothing.

"It has to get a whole lot better than this," said Brian Skerry, the *Geographic* photographer, after a particularly frustrating effort.

"It doesn't get much better than this," I said, pointing to the pile of artifacts we now had soaking in tubs of seawater for the trip to the lab.

Still, I knew what he meant. The visibility down below was so bad I found myself working with my eyes closed to avoid the fluttering distraction of the mung.

The crew started to make jokes about being "among the mung," in the grips of a "mungster," but eventually the high-spirited photographers stopped laughing. They wanted at least a moment of clarity to get their underwater pictures and they weren't getting it.

There was nothing we could do but keep digging, so dig we did. For two days we blew one hole after the other, working from sunrise to sunset, loading the decks with concretions that emitted the sickening metallic smell of iron, clay, and two hundred years of seawater. By 1:30 P.M. on the second day, Catherine's notes indicated that we had dug thirteen holes in which we had found a total of thirty-seven artifacts, including two swivel cannons, a grinding stone, and several coins. With every hole we dug, we also found streaks of gold dust that had been captured in the cracks of the clay bottom underneath the sand.

Another crewman's notes declared that we had also found "a lot of exhaustion, hard work, satisfaction, and friendship."

By the evening of the second day, there were stacks of concreted artifacts. Everyone on the boat was happy except the photographers. The weather radio said that rough seas would be coming, probably within the next day, which would drive us from the site. That meant time was running out, and they still hadn't found their shots.

That night the photographers asked if we could spend the morning of our last day focusing on what they needed. Brian Skerry wanted some pictures of me in the bottom of a pit, looking for coins. Joe Kaminsky needed some pictures of us working on the bottom, and if possible, hoisting a large object like a cannon from the ocean floor to the *Vast Explorer*.

Marine archaeologist Bob Cembrola on one of his dives to identify the hull as that of an eighteenth-century ship.

"That's all easy to do," I said. "But if the water is cloudy, then it might be another bad day for you."

Stretch and I held a brief conference and decided that the clearest part of the morning would be between eight and eleven o'clock. A strong north-running tide would be in effect then, and the current would carry the sand particles and mung weed out of the pit.

"That's as good as it'll get this time of year," declared Stretch. "It's a catch-22. The mung makes it hard to see, and the only time the mung isn't here is in the winter, when it's too cold and rough to dive."

That night, we received another visit from the pirates. At about 2 A.M., a loud crash and a horrible scream awoke Brian Skerry, Chris, and Jeff Leemon, the television sound man. Brian and Chris, who were sleeping down below in the galley, jumped out of their bunks immediately and turned on their flashlights. Thinking that someone had fallen overboard, they immediately began a head count of all eleven people on board. Together they counted the four others in the room with them and then they ran topside to count everyone else.

Back by the concretions they were greeted by Leemon, who was conducting his own head count. Everyone was on board.

"Maybe a boat collided with our whaler," surmised Chris.

All three fixed their lights on the *Crumpstey,* which was anchored about twenty feet from the *Vast Explorer.* They could see nothing except the little boat heaving in the swells. There was no sign of wreckage and, of course, there were no people.

"What *was* that?" asked Skerry. They stood together at the railing and compared notes. They agreed that they had all heard something—a crashing sound followed by a bloodcurdling scream. They just couldn't tell what it was or where it had come from. By now, Chris was of the belief that it wasn't the pirates at all who were involved in supernatural play, but Captain Crumpstey, who had lost his ship, the *Mary Anne,* when the pirates decided they wanted the seven thousand gallons of wine she was carrying.

Chris believed this story so much that he took a bottle of Madeira wine out of his backpack, the kind being carried by the *Mary Anne* when she was taken by the *Whydah* pirates, and poured it into the water as his second votive offering of the season.

"I think they want us to find something big," Chris said prophetically. "But they still want something in return."

When I heard them tell the story the next morning, I was reminded of *Palatine,* a poem by John Greenleaf Whittier that memorialized the ghosts and ghostly quality of a ship that was wrecked in these waters. Although written about an accident that took place more than twenty years after the wreck of Bellamy's flotilla, it conveys the supernatural resonance of ships— and people—who go down before their time.

> Down swooped the wreckers, like birds of prey,
> Tearing the heart of the ship away, And the dead had never a word to say.
> And then, with ghastly shimmer and shine,
> Over the rocks and the seething brine
> They burned the wreck of the "Palatine."
> In their cruel hearts, as they homeward sped, "The sea and the rocks are
> dumb," they said:
> "There'll be no reckoning with the dead."
> But the years went round, and when once more
> Along their foam-white curves of shore
> They heard the line-storm rave and roar,
> Behold! again with shimmer and shine,
> Over the rocks and the seething brine,
> The flaming wreck of the "Palatine"!

After breakfast, we moved the *Vast Explorer* into position and blew a hole. A small hit had been registered by the magnetometer in this area, but when Chris went down, he found nothing.

As the photographers waited anxiously on deck, we moved the *Vast* again and blew another hole. Once again, Chris went down and we all lent an ear to the communication system that turned each dive into a radio program.

"I'm at thirty-two feet," said Chris. There was a long pause and some stumbling with words before he spoke clearly. "I've got wood! I've got wood here!"

It took a few moments for Chris to calm down. When he did, the image that emerged was of a long, curving section of the ship with some of the decking still intact. The decking was double-planked, like a well-made ceiling. A portion of the bulkhead was lined with a well-manufactured piece of sheet metal, a detail of construction that was a mystery to us. Why would a portion of a room be lined with metal?

The youngest crew member, Ben Perry, answered that question. He had been reading a book on ship architecture and noticed that the gunpowder room on many sailing vessels was often lined with lead or other types of metal to keep the room dry and prevent dangerous sparking. The portion of the ship we had found was probably the powder room, which was near the captain's quarters.

"It's Bellamy's cabin!" shouted Stretch.

I now began to put it all together in my head. Many of the artifacts we had found—the swivel cannons, the coins, and the trail of gold dust that we had been following just as Hansel and Gretel followed the bread crumbs—were leading to the aft portion of the ship.

Catherine and I looked at our laptop treasure map and realized that we were only six feet from the first hole we had dug that season. We had hit all around it, and now, setting up for a photo shoot, we had landed right in the middle of it.

We were excited but restrained, knowing that such a find would be unimaginably fortuitous, yet highly unlikely. After all, we were dealing with wood from a shipwreck nearly three hundred years old. Was it possible that such a large piece of the hull could have survived intact and underwater? Was this really the hull of an eighteenth-century ship, or some ship that had crashed over the *Whydah* many years later?

The person with the answer to our question was standing on shore.

While the *Geographic* team went overboard to get their photos, I noticed a man with a mirror flashing us from the beach. I thought that maybe it was Todd Murphy, or one of the other old crew members, come out to work for the day. When I looked through the binoculars, I could see that the man in the wet suit was Bob Cembrola, a marine archaeologist who had worked with us in the past and now taught at the Naval War College in Rhode Island.

I swam to the *Crumpstey* and took the boat into shore to meet him. By the time we got back to the *Vast,* he was fully briefed on what we had found. Within five minutes, he had a tank on and was in the water.

Before I could suit up to get in, he came back up carrying a fist-sized piece of wood with an iron nail sticking out of it like a stem from an apple. I knew we had the *Whydah*. There were also handmade screws of a type I had never seen before. Everything looked well preserved.

"It's the sand," said Bob. "It's been covered with sand most of the years since it sank and the sand keeps it from deteriorating."

Once again we were blessed by our major barrier, the ravenous sand. Without it everything would have deteriorated or been swept away. With it, wooden hulls were preserved and even gold dust was kept in place. We just had to contend with its seemingly eternal grip on objects, and be thankful that it wasn't harder to get through than it was.

I put on a tank and Cembrola and I joined the other divers. Stretch had fixed up the engines and blown a little more to clear the area, so by the time we arrived on the bottom about twenty feet of the structure was exposed.

Staff archaeologist Catherine Harker makes sure that the newly raised artifacts are put into tubs and covered with seawater.

Rising out of the sand, wooden timbers reached toward the surface. Smaller beams at right angles from the structure showed us where the deck had been. On the inside of the structure, planks that were four inches wide and two inches thick created a bulkhead that was covered with a sheet of lead about four feet long and two feet wide.

Visibility was good and I drew back for a moment to take in the whole scene. Although I had been elated on the surface, seeing the structure gave me a solemn feeling, the kind that Howard Carter must felt when he discovered the doorway to King Tut's tomb. *This was a ship full of people sailing to safe harbor to share their bounty,* I thought, looking at the wooden structure that had been preserved in brine for twenty-eight decades. *This was where the most successful pirates of their time spent their fatal moments. This was their tomb.*

Chris later said that a calmness and goodness filled him up as he pondered the meaning of the find. I agree with that assessment, and have to say that I had a solid feeling after seeing the sunken structure, almost as though I had opened the door into a long-lost cathedral.

With my metal detector I began to explore the sandy floor at the bottom of the hull. The instrument chirped and I dug into the sand to pull out a spoon. It was like the others we had found on the site and dubbed "the *Whydah* silver set." Chris had found a spoon earlier and we both agreed that

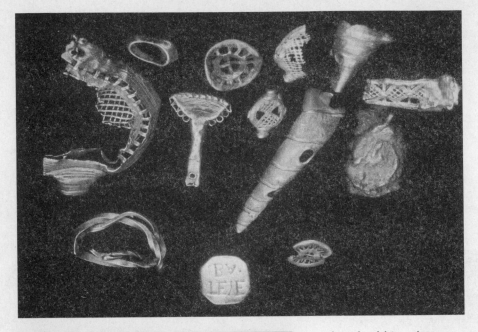

A cache of gold jewelery.

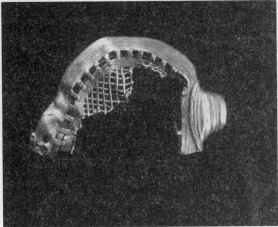

it left us with an oddly satisfied feeling to know that we were probably in the galley, holding important personal tools of the pirates' everyday life.

Gradually, the tide stopped running and the mung and sand began to settle over the hull, erasing our excellent visibility. It was as though the pirates had given us a glimpse of the ship we had looked for for so long and were now putting it back where it belonged. I looked at the hull one more time, wondering at the world of discovery that might lie underneath it. Were there coins, cannons, and gold bars under that waterlogged wood? Were there more bones concreted to iron objects? Maybe, I thought as I drifted slowly toward the surface, I would find out some other season. I turned my attention upward, feeling elated yet melancholy as I swam toward the boat above.

On the *Vast Explorer* there was jubilation as everyone realized the importance of finding so rare an object. As we broke anchor and made for port, we began to ponder how the hull could be brought to the surface and preserved so others could see it. Stretch, whose mind is most active on such matters, offered a bizzare suggestion: Have an oil company erect a platform over it, clear the sand away, and put it on a platform that they pull up with a bunch of cranes.

Whatever the final solution, it will take the type of money an oil company can muster to retrieve such a huge and ancient piece of the ship and restore the water-soaked wood.

Even if we never bring this portion of the *Whydah* to the surface, there is deep satisfaction in discovering it. "Finding this piece of the *Whydah* is something like finding the cover to a rare book," I said to Stretch on our way back to port.

"Yeah," he said, a grin of satisfaction on his big face. "Now we just have to find all the missing pages between that cover to make the story complete."

Postscript

Some of the season's take includes this pile of coins and a grinding wheel used by the *Whydah* pirates to sharpen weapons.

✳ As fall approached, the days shortened and the ocean became less and less amiable. Still, we continued to dig on the site as much as weather would permit, and the effort was worth it. We found more artifacts of the pirate's life, including cannons and smaller weapons, and another grinding stone on which the pirates would sharpen their knives and swords. We continued to find coins and gold nuggets and even more gold dust, which has somehow remained on site for nearly three centuries, trapped between the Cape's rocky bottom and the sand that covers it.

We also had the opportunity to further examine the hull and to scout the area around it with metal detectors. The area was rich with "hits," indicating that there are a number of objects to be found underneath and around the remnants of the hull. I dug into one spot and found more than one hundred coins and several cannonballs. Whether they are a sign that the mother lode is close I do not know. I only know that every time the meter on the metal detector jumps, it takes my heart with it. I love the search for treasure as much as I love finding it.

By early October, it became clear that another season of artifact hunting had ended. We were sailing back to Provincetown when the seas became so rough that none of us could stay on our feet without holding onto the railing. When the bow began dipping beneath the waves, we all retreated to the wheelhouse and opened the door just in time to see Stretch lose his footing during a heavy swell and fly across the cabin. The ocean had gotten the best of Stretch, which meant it was an ocean to be feared.

"I think the season's over," said Stretch, quickly getting up and regaining control of the wheel.

And it was. We considered going out a few times after that, but the shifting winds kept us moored to the dock. Finally, on a gray day when the wind shifted so much that the flag on the museum waved from all points on the compass in a two-hour period, I declared the season over. After that, the only thing left to do was secure the gear, cleaning and stowing it so it would be ready for the next year.

The new season left me more convinced than ever that we have found only a small percentage of all the booty that is down there. The metal detector hits that we did not have time to explore indicate that a wealth of nautical artifacts and treasures wait to be discovered underneath the thick layer of sand that has been both our help and hindrance.

To think that we have found only a small portion of the *Whydah* treasure gives me pause. The two hundred thousand artifacts we have already found have caused a bursting at the seams of our conservation lab. Yet how can we stop? There are thousands of precious coins littering the ocean floor, and in their midst are more relics of the pirate life, some of which I never imagined existed. The syringes that we found, for example, were objects we never suspected were part of the pirate's medical kit. In an age of primitive medicine, they represent a high degree of medical sophistication that we would not have thought existed. And the wax seals, those metal icons used to compress the sealing wax on letters sent to loved ones at home, reveal touchingly human sentiments, feelings of love, hope, and desire that might not be expected of brutish pirates. In that sense, their primal value is immeasurable to someone attempting to understand the emotional life of one of history's least understood subcultures.

Understanding history is what the *Whydah* expedition is all about, and why we have spent so much time, effort, and money on the preservation and display of the artifacts we have retrieved. I am proud to say that I have

Pieces of eight
found in 1988.

not sold a single object from the *Whydah*. It is my belief that the entire collection must be kept together so it can be studied and understood, not just
by professional historians and academic archaeologists, but by everyday people, too.

One of my greatest joys is watching the expressions of people as they tour
the *Whydah* museum that we have assembled in Provincetown. There, both
stories—Black Sam Bellamy's and mine—are expressed in words, pictures,
and artifacts. His life is told from his beginnings as a pirate and his love for
Maria Hallett through his death on the shores of Cape Cod in the storm
that took down the most richly packed treasure ship of its time. My story
is told from my childhood fascination with Bellamy through my relentless
search for the *Whydah* and all of her treasures.

Unlike Bellamy's, there is, as of yet, no end to my story. Even though I have searched for sunken ships all over the world, I am always drawn back to the *Whydah*. I continue to search for everything that will tell me the whole story of Bellamy, his youthful lover Maria, and the men who followed him to their deaths.

In reality, I don't know that I will ever find all those missing pages. I do know that those pages and the clues to what are on them can be found beneath the cobalt blue of the Cape's sandy shore. I will go back again and again, in hope that I find them all.

The flag painted on the wheelhouse of the *Vast Explorer* is a reminder that the *Whydah* expedition will continue for many more exciting years.

Acknowledgments

✻ In July 1997, the noted maritime writer James Nelson sailed down to Cape Cod from his home in Harpswell, Maine, to see the artifacts from the *Whydah*. While he was at the museum, he happened to meet Barry Clifford. The two hit it off immediately and talked for hours about nautical life in the eighteenth century.

As the author of a nautical fiction series, The Revolution at Sea Saga, Nelson felt that the efforts of Clifford and those who have worked with him throughout the years deserved a book.

Nelson made this recommendation to Nat Sobel, his literary agent, who took to the idea immediately. He flew to Provincetown and spent several days at the pirate museum, listening to expedition stories, examining artifacts, and even visiting the wreck site on the *Vast Explorer*. Eventually, Nat contacted one of the many nonfiction writers he represents, me, and insisted that I travel to the Cape myself to see if the *Whydah* expedition was something that I could envision as a book.

The rest, as they say, is history. I am grateful to James Nelson for kindly bringing this terrific story to the attention of Nat Sobel, and to Nat for thinking of me as the person who could bring this story to life. Nat and I have been friends and associates for twenty years now, proof to me that friendship and business mix very well. From the very beginning, Diane Reverand, publisher of Cliff Street Books, HarperCollins, has been an enthusiastic supporter of this project. We have produced eight books together on a variety of topics. With this book, as with all of the others, she has provided kind and patient guidance, helping me express myself in the clearest ways possible. She has an eclectic sort of genius that makes her uniquely suited to the book business and a passion for what she does that makes her a joy to work with.

Without the work of historian Ken Kinkor, this book would not have contained the rich historic detail that it does. Ken is a meticulous researcher who leaves no stone unturned in his search for details of the past. I have come to call him "the human Internet," because there seems to be no answer that he can't download from that World Wide Web of knowledge inside his skull. In other ways, the same can be said for Stretch Gray, who seemed able to remember events of ten years ago like they happened yesterday.

His telling of stories is so animated that it was a struggle to present them in writing as well as he told them orally. Other great stories about excavation of the *Whydah* came from Bob Lazier, Chris Macort, Catherine Harker, Todd Murphy, Charlie Burnham, Bob Cembrola, Wes Spiegel, Dave Dutra, Buddy and Pam Johnson, Alan Tufankjian, Paul Gasek, and a host of other people who live on the Cape and volunteered stories and impressions that contributed to the reconstruction of this story.

Ultimately, my thanks go out to Barry Clifford. Having a writer research your story is not easy nor is it always pleasant. Writers are like psychic parasites in that they have a constant need to drain you of memory and impressions about the events of your life, many of which you might not want to recall in vivid detail. Barry was always accepting of the fact that I had to ask questions until there were no more answers. He has a tenacity and focus that are rare in any profession. Without those qualities, the *Whydah* would still only be a folktale and not living history for all to enjoy.

—PAUL PERRY
www.authorsnetwork.com

For more information on *Whydah* expeditions, contact
www.whydah.com.

Photograph and Illustration Credits

Frontispiece: Steve Pope; 1: *Whydah* Joint Venture, Inc.; 3: Barry Clifford Collection; 14: Barry Clifford Collection; 18: Barry Clifford Collection (top), John Beyer (bottom); 22: Clifford Family; 26: Paul Perry; 31: Paul Perry; 32: *Whydah* Joint Venture, Inc.; 35: *Whydah* Joint Venture, Inc.; 41: *Boston Herald;* 51: William Curtsinger; 52: Barry Clifford Collection; 64: Barry Clifford; 66: Scott Magoun; 80: Chris Macort; 83: Ron Fowler; 84: Barry Clifford. 91: William Burgis; 93: Barry Clifford; 95: Bill Dibble; 99: *Whydah* Joint Venture, Inc.; 100: *Whydah* Joint Venture, Inc.; 103: Paul Perry; 106: Barry Clifford; 108: Barry Clifford; 110: Bill Dibble; 115: Bill Dibble; 117: Bill Dibble; 119: *Whydah* Joint Venture, Inc.; 123: Bill Dibble; 124: Bill Dibble; 126: Barry Clifford; 129: Howard Pyle; 134: Bill Dibble; 137: *Whydah* Joint Venture, Inc.; 142: Bill Dibble; 145: *Whydah* Joint Venture, Inc.; 146: *Whydah* Joint Venture, Inc.; 148: William Curtsinger (top), Brian Skerry (bottom); 149: Barry Clifford; 150: William Curtsinger; 151: William Curtsinger; 152: *Whydah* Joint Venture, Inc.; 155: Bill Dibble; 159: Chris Macort; 160: *Whydah* Joint Venture, Inc.; 161: Scott Magoun; 163: Barry Clifford; 167: Engraving from *General History of the Most Famous Highwaymen, Murderers, Pyrates* by Captain Charles Johnson, London, 1734; 168: William Burgis; 170: Engraving from *General History of the Most Famous Highwaymen, Murderers, Pyrates* by Captain Charles Johnson, London, 1734; 171: William Curtsinger; 173: Barry Clifford; 174: William Curtsinger (photo), *Whydah* Joint Venture, Inc. (illustrations); 176: *Whydah* Joint Venture, Inc.; 177: *Whydah* Joint Venture, Inc.; 178: *Whydah* Joint Venture, Inc.; 179: *Whydah* Joint Venture, Inc.; 180: Brian Smith; 181: *Whydah* Joint Venture, Inc.; 182: Bill Dibble; 186: *Whydah* Joint Venture, Inc.; 187: Barry Clifford Collection; 189: *Whydah* Joint Venture, Inc.; 190: Barry Clifford Collection; 191: Barry Clifford; 192: *Whydah* Joint Venture, Inc.; 193: Barry Clifford; 194: *Whydah* Joint Venture, Inc.; 200: Barry Clifford; 201: Roger Prueitt; 204: Barry Clifford Collection; 206: Dr. Martha Ehrlich and Geoff Gordon; 207: Dr. Martha Ehrlich and Geoff Gordon; 209: Roger Prueitt; 213: *Whydah* Joint Venture, Inc.; 221: Roger Prueitt; 222: *Whydah* Joint Venture, Inc.; 223: *Whydah* Joint Venture, Inc.; 227: Steve Pope; 229: Barry Clifford; 233: Roger Prueitt; 235: Paul Perry; 236: *Whydah* Joint Venture, Inc.; 237: Property of John Beyer; 241: Roger Prueitt; 242: *Whydah* Joint Venture, Inc.; 244: Barry Clifford; 245: *Whydah* Joint Venture, Inc.; 246: Brian Skerry; 248: *Whydah* Joint Venture, Inc.; 250: *Whydah* Joint Venture, Inc. 252: Barry Clifford Collection; 259: Steve Pope; 260: Steve Pope; 268: Paul Perry; 271: Barry Clifford; 275: Paul Perry; 280: *Whydah* Joint Venture, Inc.; 290: Peter Pelham; 293: Paul Perry; 295: Margot Nicol–Hathaway; 296: Margot Nicol–Hathaway; 297: Chris Macort; 298: *Whydah* Joint Venture, Inc.; 299: Margot Nicol–Hathaway; 303: Margot Nicol–Hathaway; 304: William Curtsinger; 306: Margot Nicol–Hathaway; 308: Brian Skerry; 309: Margot Nicol–Hathaway.